First World War
and Army of Occupation
War Diary
France, Belgium and Germany

29 DIVISION
Divisional Troops
17 Brigade Royal Field Artillery
1 March 1916 - 28 February 1919

WO95/2291/3

The Naval & Military Press Ltd
www.nmarchive.com
Published in association with The National Archives

Published by

The Naval & Military Press Ltd

Unit 10 Ridgewood Industrial Park,

Uckfield, East Sussex,

TN22 5QE England

Tel: +44 (0) 1825 749494

www.naval-military-press.com

www.nmarchive.com

This diary has been reprinted in facsimile from the original. Any imperfections are inevitably reproduced and the quality may fall short of modern type and cartographic standards.

Contents

Document type	Place/Title	Date From	Date To
Heading	WO95/2291/3		
Heading	29th Division Divl Artillery 17th Brigade R.F.A. Mar 1916-Feb 1919		
Heading	29th Division 17th Brigade R.F.A. Ammunition Column March 1916		
Heading	17 Bde R.F.A. Aim Col Vol II BEF From MEF		
War Diary	Camp Sum 3	01/03/1916	08/03/1916
War Diary	Alexandria	09/03/1916	14/03/1916
War Diary	At Sea Marseilles	15/03/1916	17/03/1916
War Diary	Train Port Remy	18/03/1916	19/03/1916
War Diary	Longueil	20/03/1916	31/03/1916
Heading	17th Bde Ammn Col R.F.A. App I		
Heading	29th Division Arrived Marseilles From Egypt 16.3.16 17th Brigade R.F.A. March 1916		
Heading	17 Bde R.F.A. Vol I BEF From M.E.F		
War Diary	Suez	01/03/1916	09/03/1916
War Diary	Alexandria H.T "Kingstonian"	09/03/1916	09/03/1916
War Diary	H.T Kingstonian	10/03/1916	31/03/1916
Heading	29th Division Ammunition Column 17th Brigade R.F.A. April 1916		
Heading	17 Bde R.F.A. Am Col Vol III		
War Diary	Domart	01/04/1916	05/04/1916
War Diary	Acheaux	06/04/1916	06/04/1916
War Diary	Domart	07/04/1916	08/04/1916
War Diary	Amplier	09/04/1916	30/04/1916
Heading	29th Division 17th Brigade R.F.A. May 1916		
War Diary	Englebelmer	01/05/1916	31/05/1916
Heading	29th Division 17th Brigade R.F.A. June 1916 Appendices Attached:- Ammunition Expenditure. Roll Of Officers Casualties Postings Situation Map 1.7.16		
War Diary	Englebelmer	01/06/1916	22/06/1916
War Diary	Mesnil Valley	23/06/1916	30/06/1916
Miscellaneous			
War Diary	Mesnil Valley	24/06/1916	30/06/1916
Miscellaneous	Appendix III		
Miscellaneous	Appendix III (II) Officers Postings		
Map	Appendix IV		
Heading	29th Division 17th Brigade R.F.A. July 1916		
War Diary	Mesnil Valley	01/07/1916	07/07/1916
War Diary	Engelbelmer	07/07/1916	13/07/1916
War Diary	Between Engelbelmer and Forceville	13/07/1916	26/07/1916
War Diary	Engelbelmer	27/07/1916	31/07/1916
Miscellaneous	Appendix I	30/06/1916	30/06/1916
Miscellaneous	Appendix II. Casualties during month of July		
Heading	29th Division 17th Brigade R.F.A. August 1916		
War Diary	Englebelmer	01/08/1916	31/08/1916
Miscellaneous	Appendix II		
Miscellaneous	Wire Cutting August 7th		
Miscellaneous	Wire Cutting August 8th		
Miscellaneous	Wire Cutting August 9th		

Miscellaneous	29th DA		
Miscellaneous	29 DA Inf. Report 8th-9th August Appendix III		
Miscellaneous	Intelligence Report 9th To 10th		
Miscellaneous	29DA Intelligence 10th 11th		
Miscellaneous	29DA Intelligence Report-11th to 12th		
Miscellaneous	29DA/Intelligence Report 12th-13th		
Miscellaneous	Intelligence Report 13/8/16-14/8/16		
Miscellaneous			
Miscellaneous	29 D.A Intelligence 14th 15th AKA		
Miscellaneous	29DA/Intelligence 15th To 16th		
Miscellaneous	Intelligence Report 17th		
Miscellaneous	29DA/18		
Miscellaneous	29DA/18th Intelligence 18th		
Miscellaneous	Concentration given at 2305 in "B' 2 Units		
Miscellaneous	29DA/Casualty 2 Return 18th To 19th		
Miscellaneous	29DA/20th Intelligence 0700-19th To 0700 20th AAA		
Miscellaneous	29 DA/20th Casualty Report 20th August		
Miscellaneous	29DA/20th Intelligence 0700-1900		
Miscellaneous	29DA/21 AAA Supplementary Intelligence 1900 204		
Miscellaneous	Report 21/8/16	21/08/1916	21/08/1916
Miscellaneous	29DA/		
Miscellaneous	29DA/22		
Miscellaneous	Intelligence 0700 22nd-0700 23rd AAA		
Miscellaneous	29DA/ Casualty Report AAA		
Miscellaneous	Intelligence 0700 23rd To 0700 24th AAA		
Miscellaneous	29DA/Intelligence 0700 24th-0200 25th A&A		
Miscellaneous	29DA/Intelligence 0700 25th-0200 25th A&A		
Miscellaneous	29DA/Intelligence 0700 25th-0200 26th A&A		
Miscellaneous	29DA/casualties A & A		
Miscellaneous	29DA Intelligence 0700 26th To 0700 27th A&A		
Miscellaneous	29DA Intelligence 0700 27th To 0700 28th A&A		
Miscellaneous	29DA Intelligence 0700 28th To 0700 29th A&A		
Miscellaneous	29DA Intelligence 0700 29th To 0700 30th A&A		
Miscellaneous	29DA Intelligence 0700 30th To 0700 31st A&A		
War Diary	29DA Intelligence 0700 31st To 0700 1st A&A		
Heading	29th Division 17th Brigade R.F.A. September 1916		
Heading	War Diary of 17th Bde R.F.A. 1st To 30th Sept 1916 Volume No 18		
War Diary	Englebelmer	01/09/1916	06/09/1916
War Diary	Authieule	07/09/1916	11/09/1916
War Diary	Poperinghe	12/09/1916	20/09/1916
War Diary	Houtkerque	21/09/1916	30/09/1916
Heading	29th Division 17th Brigade R.F.A. October 1916		
Heading	War Diary of 17th Bde. R.F.A. From 1st-Oct 16 To 31st Oct 16 Vol No 19		
War Diary	Houtkerque	01/10/1916	09/10/1916
War Diary	Herzeele	10/10/1916	10/10/1916
War Diary	Daour	11/10/1916	31/10/1916
Heading	29th Division 17th Brigade R.F.A. November 1916		
Heading	War Diary of 17th Bde. R.F.A. From 1st-Nov 16 To 30th Nov 16 Volume No 20		
War Diary	Longueval	01/11/1916	30/11/1916
Heading	29th Division 17th Brigade R.F.A. December 1916		
Heading	War Diary of 17th Brigade. R.F.A. From 1st-December 1916 To 31st December 1916 Volume No 21		
War Diary	Meaulte	01/12/1917	31/12/1917

Miscellaneous			
Heading	29th Div War Diaries 17th Brigade R.F.A. Jany-December 1917		
Heading	War Diary 17th Brigade RFA From 1st January 1917 To 31st January 1917		
Heading	War Diary of 17th Brigade R.F.A. From 1st January 1917 To 31st January 1917 Vol No 22		
War Diary	Leuze Wood	01/01/1917	17/01/1917
War Diary	Leuze	17/01/1917	18/01/1917
War Diary	Leuze Wood	19/01/1917	31/01/1917
Heading	29 Div War Diary Of 17th Brigade RFA From 1st February 1917 To 28th February 1917 Vol No 23		
Miscellaneous	17th Brigade R.F.A.		
War Diary	Leuze Wood T.20.D.40	01/02/1917	28/02/1917
Heading	War Diary March 1917 17th Brigade RFA Vol 24		
War Diary	H Q Lellgroup Centrearduery T.20.D.4.0	01/03/1917	05/03/1917
War Diary	T.20.D.40 Lenzewood	06/03/1917	10/03/1917
War Diary	Leuze Wood	10/03/1917	19/03/1917
War Diary	HQ Carnoy	20/03/1917	20/03/1917
War Diary	HQ Morlancourt	21/03/1917	23/03/1917
War Diary	H Q Franvillers	23/03/1917	23/03/1917
War Diary	H.Q. Plesselles	24/03/1917	25/03/1917
War Diary	HQ Bealcourt	26/03/1917	27/03/1917
War Diary	H Q Honval	27/03/1917	28/03/1917
War Diary	H Q Arras	29/03/1917	30/03/1917
War Diary	Arras	30/03/1917	31/03/1917
Heading	17 Bde R F A Vol 14 April 17		
Miscellaneous	On His Majesty's Service. D.A.G. G.H.Q 3rd Echelon		
Heading	War Diary 17th Brigade RFA April 1-30 1917 Vol 25		
War Diary	H Q 4 Rue St Barbe Arras	01/04/1917	03/04/1917
War Diary	H Q Formber St Jauveur Arras	03/04/1917	08/04/1917
War Diary	H Q Arras	09/04/1917	09/04/1917
War Diary	H Q N3a45 E. Atilloy	10/04/1917	16/04/1917
War Diary	Maison Rouge	17/04/1917	18/04/1917
War Diary	H Q Near Maison Rouge E Yarras N3a45	19/04/1917	19/04/1917
War Diary	H Q Near Maison Rouge Arras N3a45	20/04/1917	22/04/1917
War Diary	Maison Rouge	23/04/1917	23/04/1917
War Diary	H Q At La Fosses Farm Au Cambrai Rd	23/04/1917	30/04/1917
War Diary	In Anus	30/04/1917	30/04/1917
Heading	War Diary 17th Brigade RFA May 1-31 1917 Vol 26		
War Diary	H Q Cave Las Fosses Farm N-Arras N. Green	01/05/1917	01/05/1917
War Diary	H Q In Cane S. Q Road	01/05/1917	01/05/1917
War Diary	Cave S. Q Road	01/05/1917	06/05/1917
War Diary	H.Q.	07/05/1917	10/05/1917
War Diary	H.Q. N11a05	06/05/1917	19/05/1917
War Diary	H.Q N.11.a 20.90	20/05/1917	23/05/1917
War Diary	H Q Cave N.11.a 20.40	24/05/1917	31/05/1917
Heading	War Diary 17th Brigade R F A 1 June 1917-30 June 1917 Volume 27		
War Diary	H G Fosse Farm Cambrai Road Near Monchy	01/06/1917	05/06/1917
War Diary	H Q Bon De Boeufs N.2.a.4.6	06/06/1917	16/06/1917
War Diary	H Q Sumon Sumpits E Q Boeufs	17/06/1917	20/06/1917
War Diary	H Q Agny	20/06/1917	23/06/1917
War Diary	H Q Montenes Corps	24/06/1917	30/06/1917
Heading	Guemappe 3/6/17		
Miscellaneous	Barrage Map		

Map	Barrage Map		
Heading	Guemappe 3/6/17		
Heading	17th Brigade R F A War Diary 1-31 October 1917 Vol No 31		
War Diary	Chasseur Farm	01/10/1917	05/10/1917
War Diary	Wood House	06/10/1917	14/10/1917
War Diary	Pilckem	15/10/1917	16/10/1917
War Diary	Languemarck	17/10/1917	19/10/1917
War Diary	Cannes Farm	20/10/1917	23/10/1917
War Diary	Proven	24/10/1917	25/10/1917
War Diary	Authieule	26/10/1917	31/10/1917
Miscellaneous	Casualties For Month Of October 1917	31/10/1917	31/10/1917
Miscellaneous	Casualties For Month Of October 17 Brigade R F A Head Qrs	31/10/1917	31/10/1917
Heading	War Diary 17th Brigade R F A From 1st November 1917 To 30th November 1917 Vol No 32		
War Diary	Authieule	01/11/1917	13/11/1917
War Diary	Mannancourt	14/11/1917	19/11/1917
War Diary	Gouzeaucourt	19/11/1917	20/11/1917
War Diary	Marcoigne	20/11/1917	30/11/1917
Heading	War Diary of 17th Brigade R F A From 1st December 1917 To 31st December 1917 Vol No 33		
War Diary	Leacamp	01/12/1917	01/12/1917
War Diary	Ribecourt	02/12/1917	31/12/1917
Heading	War Diary of 17th Brigade R F A From 1-1-18 To 31-1-18 Vol No 34		
War Diary	Maresquel	01/01/1918	08/01/1918
War Diary	M.E.C.K	09/01/1918	13/01/1918
War Diary	Poperinghe	14/01/1918	20/01/1918
War Diary	Field	21/01/1918	31/01/1918
Heading	War Diary of 17th Brigade RFA From 1-2-18 To 28-2-18 Vol No 35		
War Diary	Field	01/02/1918	06/02/1918
Heading	War Diary of 17th Brigade R F A From 1st March 1918 To 31st March 1918 Vol 25		
War Diary	Peselhoek	01/03/1918	07/03/1918
War Diary	Field	08/03/1918	31/03/1918
Heading	29th Divisional Artillery 17th Brigade R.F.A. April 1918		
Heading	17 Bde R G Vol 37 War Diary For 17 Brigade R F A From 1st April 1918-30th April 1918		
War Diary	Field	01/04/1918	21/04/1918
War Diary	Ypres Field	21/04/1918	27/04/1918
War Diary	Field Goldfish Chataum	28/04/1918	30/04/1918
Heading	War Diary 17 Brigade R F A 1-31 May 1918 Vol 38		
War Diary	Field	06/05/1918	13/05/1918
War Diary	Peselhoek	14/05/1918	30/05/1918
Heading	17 Brigade R.F.A. June 1918		
War Diary	Field	01/06/1918	28/06/1918
Heading	War Diary of 17th Brigade R.F.A. From 1st July 1918 To 31st July 1918 Volume XXXIX		
Miscellaneous			
War Diary	Field	12/07/1918	31/07/1918
Heading	War Diary of 17th Brigade Royal Field Artillery. From 1st August 1918 To 31st August 1918. (Volume XXXXI)		

War Diary	Goldfish Field	01/08/1918	05/08/1918
War Diary	Field	06/08/1918	26/08/1918
War Diary	Field Laid In Beaulie Farm A Failure Army C.M.G.	27/08/1918	30/08/1918
War Diary	Field	30/08/1918	31/08/1918
War Diary	Field	01/08/1918	31/08/1918
Heading	17 Brigade R.F.A. 29 Div War Diary For September 1918		
War Diary		01/09/1918	04/09/1918
War Diary	In The Field	05/09/1918	26/09/1918
War Diary	Field	01/10/1918	27/10/1918
War Diary	Reubhoek	27/10/1918	27/10/1918
War Diary	Ypres	28/10/1918	30/10/1918
War Diary	Field	27/10/1918	31/10/1918
Heading	War Diary of 17th Brigade Royal Field Artillery. From 1st November 1918 To 30th November 1918 Volume XLIV		
War Diary	Field	01/11/1918	30/11/1918
Heading	War Diary 17th Brigade R.F.A. Volume 46 December 1918		
War Diary	Germany	01/12/1918	31/12/1918
Heading	War Diary of 17th Brigade Royal Field Artillery January 1919 Volume XLVI		
War Diary	Berg Gladbach	01/01/1919	31/01/1919
Heading	War Diary of 17th Brigade Royal Field Artillery February 1919 Volume XLVII		
War Diary	Berg Gladbach Germany	01/02/1919	28/02/1919

29TH DIVISION
DIVL ARTILLERY

17TH BRIGADE R.F.A.

MAR 1916 - FEB 1919

29th Division

<u>17th BRIGADE R. F. A.</u>

<u>AMMUNITION COLUMN</u>

<u>MARCH 1 9 1 6</u>

79

17 Bde R F A
Am Col

Vol II BEF
from MEF

Army Form C. 2118.

Instructions regarding War Diaries and Intelligence Summaries are contained in F. S. Regs., Part II. and the Staff Manual respectively. Title pages will be prepared in manuscript.

March 1916

WAR DIARY
or
INTELLIGENCE SUMMARY.

(Erase heading not required.)

17th Bde RFA
Ammn Column

Place	Date	Hour	Summary of Events and Information	Remarks and references to Appendices
Camp Suez	March 1916 1st		~~Nil~~ 12 Wagons 18pr Amn from Ordnance	[illegible]
	2nd		57 Mules from Inf. Bde	[illegible]
"	3rd		Nil	[illegible]
"	4th		2 Grs from Hospl, 1 Gr & 1 S.S. from Detention	[illegible]
"	5th		25 other ranks proceeded to Alex, advance party. 12 mules from Div train	[illegible]
"	6th		1 Gr to Hospl. 1 Dr to Bde H.Q. 2/Lieut. R. WILLIAMS to 3rd Echelon 29 other ranks joined from Base depot.	[illegible]
"	7th		2/Lieut DALE and 2/Lt C.S MORGAN joined as supernumerarys. 2/Lt R.N DALE ~~posted~~ transferred to 147 Bde	[illegible]
"	8th		2 Mules from D.T. 1 Cpl from Hospl Column entrained for Alexandria, strength 4 officers, 95 O.R. 101 Animals & 12 Wagons Ammn 18pr	[illegible]
Alexandria	9		Arrived at Alex & embarked on S.S Kingstonian. Rec 21 Horses.	App I
"	10	1100	Sailed from Alex	[illegible]
	11th to 13th		At Sea	[illegible]
"	14th	0400	Passed Malta	[illegible]

Instructions regarding War Diaries and Intelligence Summaries are contained in F. S. Regs., Part II. and the Staff Manual respectively. Title pages will be prepared in manuscript.

2nd Sheet

Army Form C. 2118.

WAR DIARY
or
INTELLIGENCE SUMMARY.
(Erase heading not required.)

Place	Date	Hour	Summary of Events and Information	Remarks and references to Appendices
	March 1916			
At Sea	15th		1 Br to 26th Battery, 1 Br from 26th Battery	JM
Marseilles	16th	1800	Arrived Marseilles commenced disembarkation	JM
"	17th	0900	Disembarkation completed, Column with exception of 12 Ammn Wagons entrained for PONT-REMY	JM
Train	18th		On Train	JM
Pont Remy	19th	0800	Arrived PONT-REMY, disentrained. 1 Br 2 Gr attached to A.S.C	JM
Longuet	20th	0900	Amn Wagons arrived and Column proceeded to Billets at LONGUET. 23 other ranks advance party rejoined. 1 Dr to Hospl.	JM
"	21st		12 other ranks, 24 horses, 4 Amn Wagons joined from 370th Battery, to complete Column to 4 Battery Estab. Column completed to Estab. with animals and vehicles.	JM
"	22nd		Home leave started, one man to go daily.	JM
"	23rd	-	1 Mule died. Major J. HAGAN & 1 O.R on leave to England	JM
"	24		Nil	JM
"	25		1 Wheeler Sergt 1 Dr to Hospl.	JM
"	26		Nil	JM

Instructions regarding War Diaries and Intelligence Summaries are contained in F. S. Regs., Part II. and the Staff Manual respectively. Title pages will be prepared in manuscript.

3rd Shut

WAR DIARY
or
INTELLIGENCE SUMMARY.
(Erase heading not required.)

Army Form C. 2118.

Place	Date	Hour	Summary of Events and Information	Remarks and references to Appendices
	March			
Longuel	27th		40 surplus animals left for Advance Remount Depot. 1 Dr from Hospl	M
"	28th		1 Dr to Hospl	M
"	29th & 30		Nil	M
"	31st	0900	The Column marched from Longuel to DOMART.	M

J A S Hagan Major
Comg 17th B.A.C

1577 Wt. W10791/1773 500,000 1/15 D. D. & L. A.D.S.S./Forms/C. 2118.

14th Bde. Ammn. Col. R.F.A. App I

Rank & Name		Total other Ranks	Remarks.
Major	Hagan J.		Embarked with 14th F.A. Bde. Ammn. Col. on S.S. Kingstonian 9th March 1916
Lieut.	King A. J.	95	
"	Rewtress A. W.		
"	Morgan W. S.		
		Animals 95 Mules 31 Horses Vehicles Wagons 18 pr - 12.	

S.S. Kingstonian
15th March 1916

Jas Hagan Major R.F.A.
Comdg. 14th F.A. Bde. Am. Col.

29th Division

Arrived MARSEILLES from EGYPT 16.3.16.

17th BRIGADE

R. F. A.

MARCH 1916

1

29

17 Bde R. F. A

Vol I B E F

from M.E.F

(1)

Instructions regarding War Diaries and Intelligence Summaries are contained in F. S. Regs., Part II. and the Staff Manual respectively. Title pages will be prepared in manuscript.

WAR DIARY

or

~~INTELLIGENCE SUMMARY.~~ (?)

(Erase heading not required.)

Army Form C. 2118.

Place	Date	Hour	Summary of Events and Information	Remarks and references to Appendices
			Diary of 17th F.A. Brigade, 29th Divisional Artillery,	
			MARCH 1916	
SUEZ	1st		The Brigade was completed as follows on the last day of February, in vehicles.	
			Each battery:- 4 guns 8 wagons [Horses & mules were drawn from 29th Divl Train.]	
			Brigade Ammunition Column. 12 wagons	
			Total :- 12 guns. 36 wagons.	
	4th		2/Lieutenant H.R. Remington, 26th Battery, left for embarkation at ALEXANDRIA, with 63 Drivers, to draw cooks wagons, G.S. Wagons, and limbered G.S. for the Brigade in France.	
			Colonel Monkhouse & Major Williams returned from leave to ENGLAND.	
	5th		2/Lieutenant R.W. Williams, 17th Bde A.C. supernumerary, left the Brigade & reported to	3rd Echelon.
	7th		2/Lieut. J.H.B. Fairley, 26th Battery, was admitted to hospital with jaundice.	
	8th		The Brigade entrained for ALEXANDRIA in three trains.	
			First Train left SUEZ 1920. 8th, arrived ALEX. 0700. 9th. } Headquarters. 26th Battery. Part of 13th Battery.	also some S.W.Bs
			Second Train left SUEZ 2210 8th, arrived ALEX. 1200 9th } 92nd Battery. Part of 13th Battery. Part of COLUMN.	also some S.W.Bs

(2)

Instructions regarding War Diaries and Intelligence Summaries are contained in F. S. Regs., Part II. and the Staff Manual respectively. Title pages will be prepared in manuscript.

WAR DIARY
or
~~INTELLIGENCE SUMMARY.~~ KJL
(Erase heading not required.)

Army Form C. 2118.

Place	Date	Hour	Summary of Events and Information	Remarks and references to Appendices
	9th		Third Train. Left SUEZ 0100 9th, arr. ALEXANDRIA 1600 9th } Brigade Ammunition Column. Part of 13th Battery. | also some of 15th HA Bde.	
ALEXANDRIA H.T. "KINGSTONIAN".			The Brigade embarked on H.T "Kingstonian" (Leyland Line). The following were on board:-	

		Officers.	Other ranks.	Horses.	Mules.	Guns.	Wagons.	Telephone Cart.
1. 17th F. A. Brigade.	Headquarters.	5	32	26	4	-	-	1
	26th Battery.	3	113	79	59	4	8	
	92nd Battery.	4	119	81	57	4	8	
	13th Battery.	4	125	77	61	4	8	
	17th B.A.C.	4	95	31	95	-	12	
		20	484	284	176	12	36	1
2. part of 15th H. A. Brigade.	'B' Battery	3	102	-	-	-	-	
	'L' Battery	4	132	67	60	4	8	
	15th B.A.C.	2	77	-	-	-	-	
3. part of 2nd Battalion South Wales Borderers.		7	275	2	-	-	-	
4. Infantry Grooms of various units of 29th Division		~~[illegible]~~	31	31	-	-	-	
		36	1101	394	336	16	44	1

Sheet I

Instructions regarding War Diaries and Intelligence Summaries are contained in F. S. Regs., Part II. and the Staff Manual respectively. Title pages will be prepared in manuscript.

WAR DIARY
or
~~INTELLIGENCE SUMMARY.~~
(Erase heading not required.)

MARCH

APPENDIX I

Army Form C. 2118.

Place	Date	Hour	Summary of Events and Information	Remarks and references to Appendices
			LIST of OFFICERS who embarked with the Brigade for service in FRANCE.	

Headquarters

Lt Colonel	W.P. Monkhouse	C.M.G. M.V.O.	Commanding.
Lieut.	A.G. Leadbetter	R.F.A.	Adjutant
2/Lieut	T.C. Ratsey	R.F.A.	Colonel's Orderly Officer
Captain	F. Harris	R.A.M.C.	Medical Officer
Captain	Magill	A.V.C.	Veterinary Officer

26th Battery

Captain D. Daly R.F.A.
* 2/Lieut H.R. Remington R.F.A. (S.R.)
2/Lieut. R. Chalkley R.F.A. (T.)
† 2/Lieut J.H.B. Fairley R.F.A. (S.R.)

92nd Battery

Major R.C. Williams R.F.A.
Lieut. F.E. Mocatta R.F.A. (S.R.)
Lieut. R. Marx R.F.A.
2/Lieut M. Clift R.F.A. (S.R.)

13th Battery

Captain R.S. Leach R.F.A.
2/Lieut D.M. Ely R.F.A. (S.R.)
2/Lieut W. Dalziel R.F.A. (T.)
2/Lieut F. Eggleton R.F.A. (T.)

17th Bde. Amm. Column

Major J. Hagan R.F.A.
2/Lieut A.J. King R.F.A.
2/Lieut A.W. Pentreath R.F.A. (T.)
2/Lieut C.S. Morgan R.F.A.
† Captain T.E. Hutchinson R.F.A. (T.)

* went on with advance party.
† left in hospital at SUEZ

1577 Wt. W10791/1773 500,000 1/15 D. D. & L. A.D.S.S./Forms/C. 2118.

Sheet II

Instructions regarding War Diaries and Intelligence Summaries are contained in F. S. Regs., Part II. and the Staff Manual respectively. Title pages will be prepared in manuscript.

WAR DIARY
or
~~INTELLIGENCE SUMMARY.~~
(*Erase heading not required.*)

March
Appendix. I.

Army Form C. 2118.

Place	Date	Hour	Summary of Events and Information	Remarks and references to Appendices
			OFFICERS. – Changes in March.	
			Lieut. H.T. Clare R.F.A. 13th Battery RFA. posted to 'Y' Battery R.H.A 6-3-16	
			2/Lieut. R.M. Dale R.F.A.(T.) attached to 92nd Battery transfered to 147th Brigade R.F.A 7-3-16	
			2/Lieut R.W. Williams 17th B.A.C. left Brigade to 3rd Echelon ALEXANDRIA 5-3-16	
			2/Lieut J.H.B. Fairley 26th Battery to hospital jaundice 7-3-16	
			2/Lieut. C.S.S Morgan from Camp Quartermaster 29th D.A. posted to 17th B.A.C.	

Instructions regarding War Diaries and Intelligence Summaries are contained in F. S. Regs., Part II. and the Staff Manual respectively. Title pages will be prepared in manuscript.

(3)

WAR DIARY
or
~~INTELLIGENCE~~ SUMMARY.
(Erase heading not required.)

NE84

Army Form C. 2118.

Place	Date	Hour	Summary of Events and Information	Remarks and references to Appendices
H.T. KINGSTONIAN				
	10th		Sailed from ALEXANDRIA (10 am.)	
	14th		passed MALTA in early morning - did not stop.	
	16th		arrived MARSEILLES.	
	17th		disembarked Marseilles. Brigade left in 3 trains 0900. 1400. 1900.	
	19th		arrived PONT REMY near ABBEVILLE.	
			Brigade in billets in LONG. Advance party drew horses and watercarts limbers carts, GS wagons and AA carts.	
			370th Battery RFA (New Army) Brigaded with us. The Brigade is now on Four Battery Basis - New Army War Establishments.	
			The weather was very cold - some snow and a lot of rain. Horses (most of which had rugs) stood it well.	
			Leave for 8 days to England was started. 4 officers and about 18 men got away on leave.	
	27th		Brigade Marching Order Parade. First time the Brigade has	

Instructions regarding War Diaries and Intelligence Summaries are contained in F. S. Regs., Part II. and the Staff Manual respectively. Title pages will be prepared in manuscript.

WAR DIARY
or
INTELLIGENCE SUMMARY.
(Erase heading not required.)

Army Form C. 2118.

Place	Date	Hour	Summary of Events and Information	Remarks and references to Appendices
			turned out as a Brigade since re-equipping. There has been plenty to do – clipping & shoeing – sorting harness and drawing ammunition.	
	31st		The Brigade rendez-vous'd at 0930 at LONG and marched to DOMART – 8 miles. At DOMART the 4 brigades of 29th Div! Artillery were concentrated.	
			A few officers and men were given 8 days leave to ENGLAND.	
			This diary completed by me –	
			R.G. Leadbetter Lt RFA Adjutant 17th. Brigade R.F.A. for Lt Colonel RFA Commanding 17th F.A. Bde.	
			DOMART – 1st April	

1577 Wt. W10791/1773 500,000 1/15 D. D. & L. A.D.S.S./Forms/C. 2118.

29th Division.

AMMUNITION COLUMN

17th BRIGADE R. F. A.

APRIL 1 9 1 6

29

17 Bde R F A
Am Col

Vol III

Instructions regarding War Diaries and Intelligence Summaries are contained in F. S. Regs., Part II. and the Staff Manual respectively. Title pages will be prepared in manuscript.

1st Sheet

Army Form C. 2118.

WAR DIARY
or
INTELLIGENCE SUMMARY.
(Erase heading not required.)

Place	Date	Hour	Summary of Events and Information	Remarks and references to Appendices
	April			
DOMART	1st		1 Dr from Hospl.	JM
"	2nd		19 Drivers from Base.	JM
"	3rd		nil	JM
"	4th		2/LIET. KING & 2 O.R left for ACHEAUX.	JM
"	5th		Left Section proceeded by Route March to ACHEAUX. strength 1 off. 41 O.R 52 Horses 17 Mules, 7 G.S Wagons 5 L.G.S Wagons 1 Water Cart. 2 O.R to 370 Batt.	JM
ACHEAUX	6th		Right & Centre Sec. marched to ACHEAUX, strength 1 off 90-O R. 43 Horses. 83 Mules 16 Amm Wagons 18pr, 2 G.S Wagons, 1 Mess Cart. Major J HACAN &	JM
"			1 O.R rejoined from Leave	JM
DOMART	7th		Right & Centre Sec returned to DOMART.	JM
"	8th		7-O.R. to course Trench Motar at VALHEUREAUX	JM
AMPLIER	9th		Right & Centre Sec proceeded by Route March to AMPLIER. strength 2 off.	JM
"	"		83-O R. ~~43~~ Horses 83 Mules 16 Amm Wagons 18pr. 2 G.S Wagons 1 Mess Cart.	
"	"		2 Mules died	
"	10th		2/Lieut ~~B~~ PEWTRESS & 13-O.R. to ACHEAUX for digging emplacements	JM
"	11th & 12th		nil.	JM

1577 Wt. W10791/1773 500,000 1/15 D. D. & L. A.D.S.S./Forms/C. 2118.

Army Form C. 2118.

Instructions regarding War Diaries and Intelligence Summaries are contained in F. S. Regs., Part II. and the Staff Manual respectively. Title pages will be prepared in manuscript.

2nd sheet

WAR DIARY
or
INTELLIGENCE SUMMARY.

(Erase heading not required.)

17th Bde RFA
Ammn Column

Place	Date	Hour	Summary of Events and Information	Remarks and references to Appendices
	April			
Ampleir	13th		1 Dr to Hospl	[initials]
"	14th		1 Sergt rejoined from ACHIEUX	[initials]
"	15th		1 Dr to Hospl	[initials]
"	16th		1 Dr from Hospl	[initials]
"	17th		Nil	[initials]
"	18th		1 Horse died.	[initials]
"	19. 20. 21st		Nil	[initials]
"	22nd		~~X~~ 2 O.R to 26 Battery. 1 O.R to 13 Battery, 1 O.R from ~~X~~ 370 Battery. 1 Horse died 2nd Lt PEWTRESS & 1-O.R rejoined from digging party.	[initials]
"	23rd 24th, 25th		Nil	[initials]
"	26th		Explosion in S.A.A Sec. at ACHEUX. 2/Lt. MORGAN, and 2-O.R wounded. Dr J. N. Smith killed.	[initials]
"	27 & 28		Nil	[initials]
"	29th		2/Lt. PEWTRESS & 1-O.R to ACHEUX	[initials]
"	30		~~1 O.R to 17 B.A HQ~~ Nil.	[initials]

[signature] Major
Comdg 17 B.A.C

29th Division.

17th BRIGADE

R. F. A.

M A Y 1916

29

17 Bde R.F.A.

Army Form C. 2118.

Instructions regarding War Diaries and Intelligence Summaries are contained in F. S. Regs., Part II. and the Staff Manual respectively. Title pages will be prepared in manuscript.

WAR DIARY

or

~~INTELLIGENCE SUMMARY.~~

(Erase heading not required.)

Vol 4

Place	Date	Hour	Summary of Events and Information	Remarks and references to Appendices
			17th Brigade R.F.A. WAR DIARY for May 1916	
Englebelmer	1/5/16		During the night the enemy opened heavy fire on Mary Redan. Under cover of this about 50 of the enemy attacked our trenches at Q17a 40/00. The O/C of that sector sent up the S.O.S. Signal i.e. 5 red rockets. The enemy were repulsed. Our trenches were slightly damaged, & working parties were cut (enemy). Observation (hostile) balloons up every day.	
"	2/5/16.		A quiet day. Retaliation seems to silence hostile fire if prompt. A.A. machine gun reported at Q12c 85.80. Capt. Daly to leave	
"	3/5/16		A slightly more active day. Enemy were registering between Q10-R&10-1. Hostile aircraft were more active than usual.	
"	5/5/16.		The enemy to-day were active with 10×15 cm. howitzers. This was accompanied 77 m guns on our front line. Damage was negligible, one or two casualties. Machine gun fire was busy during the bombardment.	
	6/5/16.		Enemy still fairly active. Some activity behind the German lines	

Instructions regarding War Diaries and Intelligence Summaries are contained in F. S. Regs., Part II. and the Staff Manual respectively. Title pages will be prepared in manuscript.

WAR DIARY
or
INTELLIGENCE SUMMARY.
(Erase heading not required.)

Army Form C. 2118.

Place	Date	Hour	Summary of Events and Information	Remarks and references to Appendices
Englebelmer	8/5/16		During the night at 11-30 the enemy opened a heavy fire on our front line and also the batteries, with 10cm & 15cm & 77mm & minenwerfer fire. At 11-45 our bombardment in connection with the 31st Division raid commenced. One of our trench mortars was knocked out & there were about 17 casualties in all along our sector. Gas shells were used by the enemy but without much effect. The bulk of the hostile fire was directed against the Mary Redan. It would almost appear that the enemy contemplated a raid on our trenches. They were very likely prevented from doing this by our bombardment	
"	9/5/16.		A very quiet day, no attempt by enemy to repair damage done by our bombardment.	
	10/5/16		A singularly quiet day all along the line. Capt Leach went on leave (8 days).	

1577 Wt. W10791/1773 500,000 1/15 D. D. & L. A.D.S.S./Forms/C. 2118.

Instructions regarding War Diaries and Intelligence Summaries are contained in F. S. Regs., Part II. and the Staff Manual respectively. Title pages will be prepared in manuscript.

WAR DIARY
or
INTELLIGENCE SUMMARY.
(Erase heading not required.)

Army Form C. 2118.

Place	Date	Hour	Summary of Events and Information	Remarks and references to Appendices
Englebelmer	11/5/16		Quiet day on our own sector. Fairly heavy artillery fire on our right. Hostile aeroplane dropped a bomb between Knightsbridge Barracks & Regent Street.	
"	12/5/16		Quiet. The fire of the following three trench mortar batteries particularly noticed. 4.5 Cm" at R7 B 61.50. 5.9 Cm" at R8 B 95.50. 77 mm at Q6 B 49.27. The 5.9" may be at R14 B 19.08 (Reported by Heavies).	
"	13/5/16.		More active than during the past few days. Constitution Hill, Mary Redan & our wire were all registered by the enemy. 4.5" & 5.9" were active firing on Peronne Farm & near 28th Battery. Some active behind German lines. Lt Platt in charge	
"	14th		Very quiet day indeed. No observation balloons up during day. Lt King in charge	
"	15th		Very quiet on the whole. 15 cm more active than previously	
	17th		At 0030 the enemy opened a heavy fire on the front & support	

Instructions regarding War Diaries and Intelligence Summaries are contained in F. S. Regs., Part II. and the Staff Manual respectively. Title pages will be prepared in manuscript.

WAR DIARY
or
INTELLIGENCE SUMMARY.
(Erase heading not required.)

Army Form C. 2118.

Place	Date	Hour	Summary of Events and Information	Remarks and references to Appendices
Englebelmer	16/5/16		trenches on the left of our sector & also on the Mary Redan. The O/c K.O.S.B. asked for fire from 26th F.O.O. This battery had already opened fire in response to red rocket signals seen by their sentry. We were informed by the left group that an attack was reported at Q10 Bays 6-7. The 13th Bty immediately opened fire on their barrage lines & the guns of 10th & 92nd Batteries were switched on to this target. F.O.Os reported slackening of enemy fire & orders were immediately given to batteries to stop. It afterwards became known that the enemy did not leave their trenches. Heavy fire continued on our left till 0200. We had few casualties. Considerable movement behind German lines.	
"	17/5/16.		Quiet. Mailly-Maillet, 26th Bty, Auchonvillers & Mesnil were shelled by 10 & 15 cm howitzers. Hostile aeroplanes were more active	

1577 Wt. W10791/1773 500,000 1/15 D. D. & L. A.D.S.S./Forms/C. 2118.

Instructions regarding War Diaries and Intelligence Summaries are contained in F. S. Regs., Part II. and the Staff Manual respectively. Title pages will be prepared in manuscript.

WAR DIARY
or
INTELLIGENCE SUMMARY.
(Erase heading not required.)

Army Form C. 2118.

Place	Date	Hour	Summary of Events and Information	Remarks and references to Appendices
Engelbelmer	18/5/16		Misty morning. Very quiet day. Enemy heavy guns shelled Auchonvillers & Mailly-Maillet. 2Lt. Eggleston went on eight days leave.	
"	19/5/16		Another quiet day in our sector. Some activity in the Thiepval Sector. A very ordinary day.	
"	20/5/16		Normal day. Hostile 15 cm. guns mostly confined their attentions to the 28th Battery. Hostile battery presumed to be at R.14.b. 2010 & strongly [illegible] in. Our 6" hows. retaliated, also our 8" but not to any extent. Hostile fire very accurate no casualties. 60 shell fell round the battery, as retaliation practically all the guns in the group were directed for a short period about 2100 & at intervals on enemy positions likely to be occupied by transport – e.g. Beaucourt Station, Station Road, Shaft of quarry near Cemetery at Beaumont Hamel, wagon road to Beaumont etc. Retaliation would seem to be effective as the enemy again retaliated on Auchonvillers & 26th Bty. with Howitzers.	

Army Form C. 2118.

Instructions regarding War Diaries and Intelligence Summaries are contained in F. S. Regs., Part II. and the Staff Manual respectively. Title pages will be prepared in manuscript.

WAR DIARY
or
INTELLIGENCE SUMMARY.
(Erase heading not required.)

Place	Date	Hour	Summary of Events and Information	Remarks and references to Appendices
Englebelmer	21/5/16.		15 cm. Howitzers again shelled the 26th Battery. British aircraft more active. Hostile trains & traffic normal.	
"	22/5/16		Extremely quiet day. Aircraft active on both sides.	
"	23/5/16.		The 15 cm Battery a gun was again active. 16th H.A.G. reported location as being R9B46.29. Train heard leaving Beaucourt Station at 22.25. During operations at night op our left the following signals were noticed.	
			Previous cessation of fire — Flares 1 green 1 red lasting each 1 min. intervals 1 min.	
			At 2235 Two red rockets no change in fire.	
			" 2240 One green rocket followed by a lull in M.G. & rifle fire.	
			" 2255 One red " apparently for operations to cease.	
			Lt Col. Monkhouse went on leave. Lt Col Smith temporarily Commanded the Group	
	24/5/16		Very quiet. 15 cm gun fired occasionally. The supposed position at R9B 80.75 must be very near the spot.	
	25/5/16.		Hostile artillery more active. Mining reported at Q10d 70/70.	

Army Form C. 2118.

WAR DIARY
or
INTELLIGENCE SUMMARY.
(Erase heading not required.)

Instructions regarding War Diaries and Intelligence Summaries are contained in F. S. Regs., Part II. and the Staff Manual respectively. Title pages will be prepared in manuscript.

Place	Date	Hour	Summary of Events and Information	Remarks and references to Appendices
Englebelmer	26/5/15.		Hostile Howitzers active. Heavy registering on Communication trenches & supports in the vicinity of Limerick Junction. A great many shell were blind. Activity behind German line	
"	27/5/15		Quiet normal day. Trains normal. Still a great deal of activity behind German lines.	
	28/5/15		Considerable activity still behind German lines. At 1300 a very large vehicle, accompanied by mounted & dismounted men & wagons, was seen about 4-4½ miles distant going towards a large wood.	
	29/5/15		Enemy Howitzers much more active. Even Acheux was shelled by a 6" gun. It is supposed that this is the gun that was seen going towards a wood yesterday. This shelling of Acheux continues for some days. 60 rounds fired 1st day.	
	30/5/15.		1030 heavy guns were observed firing from a wood 7° left of IRLES church spire (as seen from Limerick Junction) & about 3½ miles from it. The smoke of four rounds	

1577 Wt. W10791/1773 500,000 1/15 D. D. & L. A.D.S.S./Forms/C. 2118.

Army Form C. 2118.

Instructions regarding War Diaries and Intelligence Summaries are contained in F. S. Regs., Part II. and the Staff Manual respectively. Title pages will be prepared in manuscript.

WAR DIARY
or
INTELLIGENCE SUMMARY.
(Erase heading not required.)

Place	Date	Hour	Summary of Events and Information	Remarks and references to Appendices
Zillebeke	30/5/15		was distinctly seen. These sounds were reported to be falling in Ambusia. Traffic on the station road to Beaucourt was greater.	
"	31/5/15		At Q10B90/70 party at work evidently on the mining operations mentioned before. This work is supposed to be in progress under our own lines & is said to pass under Q10 bay 4. This work was reported in Corps Summary as far back as one month ago	
on 13th of the month			The B.A.C. left us & became No. 2 Section D.A.C. The 370th Bty also left & its place taken by 1317 (old 460th Bty). Lt Col Monkhouse returned from leave & reassumed command of the Right Group.	
			This Diary compiled by 2/Lt Ratsey	
			W. P. Monkhouse Lt-Col. R.F.A. Commanding 17th Brigade, R.F.A.	

1577 Wt. W10791/1773 500,000 1/15 D. D. & L. A.D.S.S./Forms/C. 2118.

29th Division.

17th BRIGADE

R. F. A.

J U N E 1916

Appendices attached:-

Ammunition expenditure.
Roll of Officers.
Casualties.
Postings
Situation Map 1.7.16.

Instructions regarding War Diaries and Intelligence Summaries are contained in F. S. Regs., Part II. and the Staff Manual respectively. Title Pages will be prepared in manuscript.

17 Bde R F A
(1)
Vol 5

Army Form C. 2118

29

WAR DIARY
or
~~INTELLIGENCE SUMMARY~~
(Erase heading not required.)

Place	Date	Hour	Summary of Events and Information	Remarks and references to Appendices
			17th Brigade R.F.A. 29th Divisional Artillery – for June 1916	
ENGELBELMER June 1916	1st, 2nd, 3rd, 4th, 5th, 6th, 7th, 8th		The fire reports during this period are not available. Occasionally the Germans shelled a little, and in order to prevent indiscriminate retaliation – a system of Retaliation on definite areas was fixed on, fire only being given at the request of O.C. Battalion. The system would have worked well as it concentrated the fire of 2 18 pdr batteries and 1 (4.5) How Battery, but the time taken for the approval of O.C. Battalion (since H.Q. Battalion is ~~usually about~~ in one sector 800 yds from Coy Commander) made the retaliation so late as to be of little use.	
	8th	1520	13th Battery fired 12 rounds on smoke issuing from Q11 c 05/85	
		2?1600	26th – 16 } 92nd – 12 } Retaliation Area 2a.	

1875 Wt. W593/826 1,000,000 4/15 J.B.C. & A. A.D.S.S./Forms/C. 2118.

Instructions regarding War Diaries and Intelligence Summaries are contained in F. S. Regs., Part II. and the Staff Manual respectively. Title Pages will be prepared in manuscript.

Army Form C. 2118

WAR DIARY
or
~~INTELLIGENCE SUMMARY~~
(Erase heading not required.)

(2)

Place	Date	Hour	Summary of Events and Information	Remarks and references to Appendices
ENGLEBELMER	June 9th		Normal train activity.	
		1415	26th Battery fired 4 on left barrage	
		1335-1700	460th Battery fired 40 rounds, mostly at minenwerfer – Q17a 90/90 ×	× Ref. France 57 D(SE) BEAUMONT 1/10,000.
		1915	92nd Battery fired 18 on Q17a 90/90 in conjunction with Heavy Battery.	
	10th	1215	26th Bty fired 19 on passage lines.	
		1315-1830	460th Bty fired 24 rounds on minenwerfer and in retaliation.	
	11th	2400	92nd – 111 } 460th – 10 } Barrage lines. Mary Redan was heavily shelled by enemy – with minenwerfer as well as guns & howitzers. No attack was made – but the bombardment was probably a feint to help the raid which the Germans carried out successfully at same time in the THIEPVAL AREA.	
	12th	0940	92nd Battery – 17 rds Q11c 60/10 at request of Infantry. Observation difficult owing to rain.	
	13th	1000-1600	26th Bty – 16 rds, 92nd Bty – 20 rds, 13th Bty – 16 rds } – Retaliation Area 4B. Weather bad – rain. 460th Bty 40 rds at 2200 on minenwerfer. During the night 92nd Battery moved to new position in MESNIL VALLEY.	
	14th	0705	13th Bty – 16 – Retaliation Area (3B)	

1875 Wt. W593/826 1,000,000 4/15 J.B.C. & A. A.D.S.S./Forms/C. 2118.

Instructions regarding War Diaries and Intelligence Summaries are contained in F. S. Regs., Part II. and the Staff Manual respectively. Title Pages will be prepared in manuscript.

WAR DIARY
or
INTELLIGENCE SUMMARY
(Erase heading not required.)

Army Form C. 2118

(3)

Place	Date	Hour	Summary of Events and Information	Remarks and references to Appendices
ENGELBELMER	14th	1305	13th Battery fired 16 rds. Retaliation [illegible]	
			During night 13th Battery moved up to new position in MESNIL VALLEY.	
	15th	1700	13th Battery fired 29 rds – registration.	
	16th		During night 15th–16th 26th Battery moved into new position.	
		1115	92nd Battery expended 54 rds registration.	
			The work on O.P.s was now pushed on with all possible speed – to be ready by 19th.	
	17th	1030	26th Battery fired 22 rds on [illegible] line, 25 – Puisieux trench } registration.	
			92nd Battery fired 42 rds – Puisieux trench; 13th Battery – 24 – Puisieux trench } & other registrations.	
			460th Battery – 35 – Aeroplane registration. During this time – i.e. several days – 460th Battery was taken out of the line – in order to turn all available men into making & finishing cable trenches.	
		1400–1800	26 Battery 55 rds., 92 – 115 rds., 13 – 106 rds., 460 – 87 rds. } Registration of Targets.	

1875 Wt. W593/826 1,000,000 4/15 J.B.C. & A. A.D.S.S./Forms/C. 2118.

Instructions regarding War Diaries and Intelligence Summaries are contained in F. S. Regs., Part II. and the Staff Manual respectively. Title Pages will be prepared in manuscript.

WAR DIARY
or
~~INTELLIGENCE~~ SUMMARY
(Erase heading not required.)

Army Form C. 2118

(4)

Place	Date	Hour	Summary of Events and Information	Remarks and references to Appendices
ENGLEBELMER	18th	1630	26th Battery fired 48 rds. STATION ALLEY – nightwire target.	
		1740 – 1840	68 shrapnel, 20 HE fired by 92nd Battery – registrations.	
	19th	1600	13th Battery fired 16 rounds – Retaliation Area 3A.	
		1830	26th Battery fired 20 rounds. Registration	
	20th	0900 – 1200	92nd Battery fired 50 A, 20 AX } Registrations of 1st & 2nd lines & Cemetery Road. + shrapnel HE & HE.	
			48 AX, 18 AX } Beaucourt Chateau trench in registration also O.P in Beaucourt trench.	
		1150 – 1600	26th Battery fired 68 A – Registrations	
			92nd — do — 133 A, 30 AX } — do —	
		1700 – 1800	13th — do — 63 A, 8 AX } — do —	
	21st		26 Bty, 92 –, 13 – } more registration. no details	
	22nd		13th Battery fired 53 Beaucourt Sta. Bois d'Hollande. — — 61 Beaucourt Trench. and one S.E of it } Registration	

Instructions regarding War Diaries and Intelligence Summaries are contained in F. S. Regs., Part II. and the Staff Manual respectively. Title Pages will be prepared in manuscript.

WAR DIARY
or
~~INTELLIGENCE SUMMARY~~
(Erase heading not required.)

Army Form C. 2118

(5)

Place	Date	Hour	Summary of Events and Information	Remarks and references to Appendices
ENGEL-BELMER.	June 22nd	1600	26th Battery fired 96 rounds in Registration	
			460th ——— 169 ———	
			92nd ——— 52 ———	
			On 22nd Right Group HQ and 17th Bde HQ moved from ENGELBELMER to dugouts in MESNIL VALLEY.	
MESNIL VALLEY	~~22nd~~ → ~~23rd~~		~~13th Battery – 428 rds – operations as per programme – [illegible] & wire registration.~~	
	~~24th~~	~~0800~~ ~~–1200~~	~~26th Battery. About 200 rds – do –~~	
			~~92nd – 213 – do –~~	
			Right Group Telephone Exchange was completed today – and the following batteries & stations connected up –	
			(1) 26 Battery (2) 92 – (3) 13 – (4) 460 – (5) 10 RGA (6) 370 – (7) 371 – (8) 8/243 RFA (9) A/241 – (10) Left Group (11) Mailly Exchange – to D.A. (12) 87th Bde. (13) Left Group, 36 D.A.	

1875 Wt. W593/826 1,000,000 4/15 J.B.C. & A. A.D.S.S./Forms/C. 2118.

Instructions regarding War Diaries and Intelligence Summaries are contained in F. S. Regs., Part II. and the Staff Manual respectively. Title Pages will be prepared in manuscript.

WAR DIARY
or
~~INTELLIGENCE SUMMARY~~
(Erase heading not required.)

(6)

Army Form C. 2118

Place	Date	Hour	Summary of Events and Information	Remarks and references to Appendices
METHIL VALLEY			The Brigade is in Right Group which consists of the following batteries – under the command of Lt Col W.P. Monkhouse C.M.G. M.V.O..	
			26th Battery, 92nd —, 13th —, 460th (How) Battery } 17 Bde RFA; 370th Bty. 132 Bde, 371st Bty. —; 10th Battery, 147 Bde; A/241, B/243 } 48th Division	
			Appendix IV of wire targets follows.	APPENDIX IV
	June 1916			B = 4.5 shrapnel
	24th	'U' Day	26 Battery expended 352 A on wire targets –	BX = -do- HE
		up to 12 noon	13 — — 444 A — } to 12 noon 25th	
			92 — — 422 A —	
			460 — — 404 BX —	
			[illegible]	

Instructions regarding War Diaries and Intelligence Summaries are contained in F. S. Regs., Part II. and the Staff Manual respectively. Title Pages will be prepared in manuscript.

WAR DIARY
or
~~INTELLIGENCE SUMMARY~~
(Erase heading not required.)

RFA.

Army Form C. 2118

Place	Date	Hour	Summary of Events and Information	Remarks and references to Appendices
MESNIL VALLEY	June 1916		The bombardment programme is as follows.	
	24th	'U' Day	~~4.5 (How) Bs~~	
		—	U Day - 0500 - 2100 ~~18 pdr batteries (except 40th) Bs~~ — WIRE.	
			U Night. 2100 - 0500. ~~WIRE~~ ——— - NIGHT WIRE TARGETS.	
	25th	V	Day — 0500 - 2100 WIRE	
			Night — 2100 - 0500 NIGHT WIRE	
	26th	W	Day. 0500 - 0830 - WIRE -	Each battery allowed 800 rounds per 24 hours.
			0900 - 1030 - Special Bombardment M.Gs & OPs upto STATION ROAD. B.F 40".	
	27th	X	Day. 0430 - 0550	
			0555 - 0600 - Special Bombardment M.Gs & OPs upto STATION ROAD. BF 40" HE.	460 Bty _ 640 rounds.
			0630 - 2100 - WIRE	
			Night 2100 - 0500 - NIGHT WIRE.	
	28th	Y	Day 0500 - 0530 - WIRE	for expenditure see APPENDIX I
			0600 - 0730 - MGs and OPs upto STATION RD. B F 40"	
			0800 - 2100 - WIRE	
			Night. 2100 - 0800 - NIGHT WIRE	
	29	Y1	Day & Night Same as Y	
	30	Y2	— do — Same as Y - Batteries take on any strong points when wire finished.	

1875 Wt. W593/826 1,000,000 4/15 J.B.C. & A. A.D.S.S./Forms/C. 2118.

Instructions regarding War Diaries and Intelligence Summaries are contained in F. S. Regs., Part II. and the Staff Manual respectively. Title Pages will be prepared in manuscript.

WAR DIARY
or
INTELLIGENCE SUMMARY
(Erase heading not required.)

Army Form C. 2118

Place	Date	Hour	Summary of Events and Information	Remarks and references to Appendices
			(I) Wire cutting map attached - APPENDIX IV	
			~~[illegible]~~	
			(II) List of Officers attached - APPENDIX II	
			(III) Ammunition expended in wire cutting attached - APPENDIX I	
			(IV) List of Casualties, and postings attached - APPENDIX III	
			The above diary compiled by me. A.G. Leadbetter Lt RFA	
			Adjutant 17th. Brigade R.F.A.	
			W.P. Monkhouse Lieut Colonel RFA	
			Commanding 17 Bde RFA	
			8/7/16	

1875 Wt. W593/826 1,000,000 4/15 J.B.C. & A. A.D.S.S./Forms/C. 2118.

APPENDIX I

Army Form C. 2118

WAR DIARY
or
INTELLIGENCE SUMMARY
(Erase heading not required.)

Instructions regarding War Diaries and Intelligence Summaries are contained in F. S. Regs., Part II. and the Staff Manual respectively. Title Pages will be prepared in manuscript.

Place	Date	Hour	Summary of Events and Information	Remarks and references to Appendices
MESNIL VALLEY	June		AMMUNITION EXPENDED during wire bombardments	

Date	Letters denoting the 7 days wire cutting and special bombardments	26th Bty A	26th Bty AX	92nd Bty A	92nd Bty AX	13th Bty A	13th Bty AX	460 Bty B	460 Bty BX	10th Bty B	10th Bty BX	370 Bty A	370 Bty AX	371 Bty B	371 Bty BX	A/241 A	A/241 AX	B/243 A	B/243 AX	Total Group
June 24–25	Noon U Day – Noon V Day	552	–	729	35	708	–	~~44~~	404	~~616~~	–	543	–	562	·	–	·	–	–	
25/6	— V — — W —	629	134	587	128	640	88	–	645	669	1119	462	77	519	120	–	–	–	–	
26/7	— W — — X —	608	156	613	383	838	10	–	880	192	114	273	112	659	126	–	–	–	–	
27/8	— X — — Y —	387	416	788	46	630	215	–	580	1000	524	731	207	414	200	–	–	–	–	
28/9	— Y — — Y1 —	500	350	496	99	461	75	–	640	499	[illegible]	762	28	489	28	75	–	92	–	
29/30	— Y1 — — Y2 —	201	412	297	384	256	312	–	976	244	374	332	400	267	514	–	–	–	–	
July 30th to 1st 0500	Noon Y2 – 0500 Z Day –	104	11	69	43	102	82	52	257	90	29	162	–	33	–	–	–	–	–	
		2981 A	1479	3579 A	1078	3635 A	2282	52 B	4382 BX	3310 A	1190	3265 A	824	2941 A	768	75 A	–	92 A	–	~~[illegible]~~ 7621

52 B 4382 BX

19,878 A 7,621 AX

The above table gives Group Expenditure by Batteries up to 0500 on 1st July – the end of the wire cutting.

19,878	18 pr. shrapnel
7,621	18 pr. H.E.
4,382	4.5" H.E.
52	4.5" shrapnel
31,933	rounds.

[signature] Adjutant 17th Brigade R.F.A.

APPENDIX II

Army Form C. 2118

WAR DIARY
or
~~INTELLIGENCE SUMMARY~~
(Erase heading not required.)

Instructions regarding War Diaries and Intelligence Summaries are contained in F. S. Regs., Part II. and the Staff Manual respectively. Title Pages will be prepared in manuscript.

Place	Date	Hour	Summary of Events and Information	Remarks and references to Appendices
			APPENDIX I	
	24th June		LIST of OFFICERS – 17th Bde – on 1st day ('U' day) of the Bombardment.	
			Headquarters :– Lieut. Col. W. P. Monkhouse CMG MVO. Commanding.	Commanding Rt Group 29 DA
			Lieut. A E G Leadbetter RGA. Adjutant.	
			2/Lieut H R Remington RGA (SR) S.O. Right Group.	
			2/Lt T. C. Ratsey RGA (T) Orderly Officer	
			Captain F. Harris RAMC. Medical Officer	
			detached at A.C.H.Q.D.A. – Captain Magill AVC Veterinary Officer	
			M. C. Lejeune – Interpreter.	
			26th Battery RGA	
			Captain D. Daly RGA	
			2/Lieut. R. Chalkley RGA.	
			— D. F. Davis RGA (T)	
			— G E Russell (T)	
			— A H Lake (T)	

1875 Wt. W593/826 1,000,000 4/15 J.B.C. & A. A.D.S.S./Forms/C. 2118.

APPENDIX II (cont.)

Army Form C. 2118

Instructions regarding War Diaries and Intelligence Summaries are contained in F. S. Regs., Part II. and the Staff Manual respectively. Title Pages will be prepared in manuscript.

WAR DIARY
or
INTELLIGENCE SUMMARY
(Erase heading not required.)

Place	Date	Hour	Summary of Events and Information	Remarks and references to Appendices
			92nd Battery RFA — Major R. C. Williams DSO RFA	
			Lieut. R. Marx RFA	
			Lieut. M. Pleith RFA (SR)	
			2/Lieut. A.W. Pewtress RFA (T)	
			2/Lieut. H. McCrory RFA	
			13th Battery RFA — Captain R.L. Leach RFA	
			2/Lieut. W. Dalziel RFA (T)	
			2/Lieut. F. Eggleton RFA (T)	
			2/Lieut. D.M. Ely RFA (SR) — on leave.	
			2/Lieut. Martin RFA (T)	
			2/Lieut W.E. Tibbs RFA (T)	
			460th Battery — Major J.H. Gibbon DSO RFA	
			Lieut M. Staveley RFA	
			2/Lieut C.P. Duff RFA (T)	
			— T. Stewart RFA (T)	
			— Tyrrell RFA (T)	Adjutant 17th Brigade R.F.A.

APPENDIX. III

Casualties during the Month of June & 1st July

(1) Officers Wounded

Rank	& Name	Unit	Nature of Casualty	Remarks
Major	R.C. Williams	92nd Batty R.F.A.	Severely wounded on chest by Gunshot 27-6-1916	PREMATURE
2/Lieut.	D. F. DAVIS.	26th Battery R.F.A	Gunshot wound on right forearm 1st July 1916	
-"-	H McCrory	92nd Bty	Bullet wound in Thigh 1st July 1916.	

(2) Other Ranks Killed

Regt No	Rank	Name	Unit	Nature of Casualty	Remarks
110793.	Gunner	Flack A.E.	17th Brigade Hd Qrs	Killed in Action on 23rd June 1916	

(3) Other Ranks Wounded

Regt No	Rank	Name	Unit	Nature of Casualty	Remarks
59066	Sergt	Shearing J.	460th Bty	wounded on thigh 5/6/16	by a Premature
15353	Gunner	Bypore J.	-"-	wounded on calf and head 5/6/16	-"-
66711	-"-	Rawling F.	-"-	wounded on left forearm, Stomach & head 5/6/16	-"-
35747	Driver	McDonald R.	17th Brigade Hd Qrs,	wounded on Elbow on 25/6/16	-"-
80809	Act/Bdr	Goodwright S.	460 Bty	wounded by Gunshot 27-6-16	
53812	Gnr.,	Fitch F.	-"-	wounded by Gunshot 27-6-16	
32953	-"-	Hurst	-"-	wounded by Gunshot 27-6-16	
42383	-"-	Robinson. A	-"-	wounded in Stomach by GUNSHOT 26-6-1916	
24273.	Bdr	Ellis J.	26th Batty R.F.A	wounded on head by Shrapnel 28/6/16	

APPENDIX III (1)

OFFICERS POSTINGS

Rank	Name	Unit	Remarks
2/Lieut.	R.E.R. Webster R.F.A	92nd Bty 17th Brigade R.F.A.	Posted from No 2 Secn, ~~29th D.A.C~~ 29th D.A.C 18th June 1916
-"-	H. McCrory	92nd Battery R.F.A	rejoined 17th Brigade from Egypt on 21-6-16
Lieut.	R.E.R Webster, R.F.A	I Battery	Posted away - 23/6/16
Lieut.	F.E. Mocatta	92nd Battery	Granted extension of sick leave - Struck off strength 7/6/16

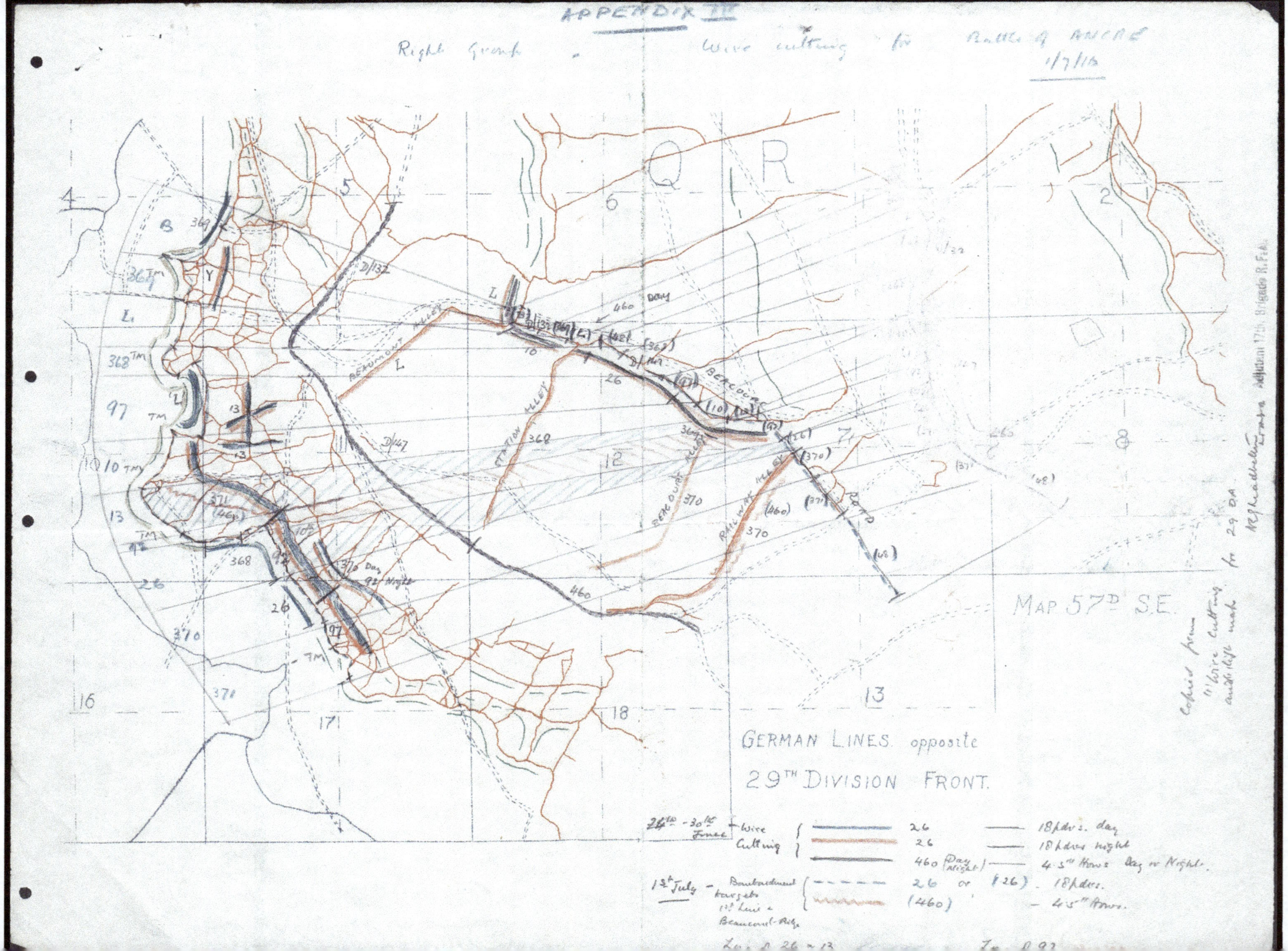
APPENDIX II
Right Group - Wire cutting for Battle of ANCRE 1/7/16
GERMAN LINES opposite
29TH DIVISION FRONT.
MAP 57D S.E.
Q
R
BEAUMONT ALLEY
STATION ALLEY
BEAUCOURT ALLEY
RAILWAY ALLEY
BEAUCOURT
ROAD
460 Day
24th - 30th June - Wire Cutting
26 — 18 pdrs. day
26 — 18 pdrs night
460 (Day/Night) — 4.5" Hows Day or Night.
1st July - Bombardment targets 1st Line & Beaucourt Ridge
26 or (26) 18 pdrs.
(460) - 4.5" Hows.
Copied from "Wire cutting" ... map for 29 DA
Adjutant 17th Brigade R.F.A.

29th Division.

17th BRIGADE

R. F. A.

J U L Y 1916

Appendices attached;-

Programme of lifts.
Casualties.

Instructions regarding War Diaries and Intelligence Summaries are contained in F. S. Regs., Part II. and the Staff Manual respectively. Title pages will be prepared in manuscript.

WAR DIARY
or
~~INTELLIGENCE SUMMARY.~~
(Erase heading not required.)

Army Form C. 2118.

17 Bde RFA
Vol V

29

Place	Date	Hour	Summary of Events and Information	Remarks and references to Appendices
	JULY 1916		17th Brigade R.F.A.	
			JULY 1916	
			ACTION on July 1st. (including 460 Battery) - extracted from 29 DA HQ Diary.	
MESNIL VALLEY	1st	0500	At 0500 the 4.5" Howitzers (in 460 Battery) opened with a bombardment on selected points in the German front line, at the rate of 1 round per battery per minute. ~~of the three~~ with one section. The other section was employed in counter battery work throughout the day under 16th Heavy Artillery Group.	
		0605	At 0605 Howitzers ceased firing for 20 mins. to register on important points, and permit observation.	
		0625	At 0625 Howitzers again opened but with a quicker rate of 1 round per gun per minute on points in front line and supports, quickening at 0700	
		0700	to 2 rds a gun a minute.	
		0625	All 18 pdr batteries in the Division (except 3) opened on front line with HE. at 1 round per gun per minute. a total of 2½ How. Batteries and 11 18 pdr batteries. R[t] Group including 6 18 pdr batteries - (and 2 18 pdr. batteries of 48th Divisional Artillery A/241 - B/243 attached ~~which did not open till 0000 i.e. 0730~~) all started firing except A/241 {zero}	

T2134. Wt. W708—776. 500000. 4/15. Sir J. C. & S.

Instructions regarding War Diaries and Intelligence Summaries are contained in F. S. Regs., Part II. and the Staff Manual respectively. Title pages will be prepared in manuscript.

WAR DIARY
or
INTELLIGENCE SUMMARY.
(Erase heading not required.)

Army Form C. 2118.

Place	Date	Hour	Summary of Events and Information	Remarks and references to Appendices
	July 1916			
MEINIG VALLEY	1st	0625		
		0720	18 pdrs. quickened to 3 rds per gun per minute.	
		0730	(ZERO) ~~time~~ the 18 pdrs. lifted onto Support line and at	
		0732	lifted 100 yds every two minutes until the line 400 yds E. of STATION ~~and WAGON~~ ROAD was reached about 0750. At	
		0835	the barrage again lifted 100' every two minutes, reaching the BEAUCOURT ROAD about	
		0845	Reports received from time to time showed the bombardment and barrage to be most effective, and the programme as arranged (see	APPENDIX I)
			was adhered to until at 0845, Right Group received orders to bring the barrage back to the line 400 yds. E. of the STATION ROAD, and after several continuances of 30 mins on this line, fire was ~~changed~~ changed again at 1100.	
		1053	At 1053 orders were received to bombard German 3rd line 1100 – 1105 Support line 1105 – 1110 Front line 1110 – 1230	

T2134. Wt. W708–776. 500000. 4/15. Sir J. C. & S.

Instructions regarding War Diaries and Intelligence Summaries are contained in F. S. Regs., Part II. and the Staff Manual respectively. Title pages will be prepared in manuscript.

WAR DIARY
or
INTELLIGENCE SUMMARY.
(Erase heading not required.)

Army Form C. 2118.

Place	Date	Hour	Summary of Events and Information	Remarks and references to Appendices
MESNIL VALLEY			to support an attack by 88th Infantry Brigade at 1230. This was done.	
		1212	At 1212 orders were received to stop on front line till 1245, as our infantry had been unable to get ready to attack at 1230. This attack however did not materialize, although at the time we did not know that it was not taking place, and so at 1245 lifts were made as ordered – ie at 1247 – lift on to support line	
			1249 – lift 100 yds	
			1251 – lift to BEAUCOURT ROAD.	
		1317	Orders received to return to barrage on the front line at a slow rate.	
		1420	Ceased fire and stood by.	
			29th Division had failed to take the trenches allotted to them – 36th Division from ~~Thiepval~~ THIEPVAL who ~~took their first 2 objects~~ were more successful, but being enfiladed from the left had later to fall back. 4th Division on our left captured part of their objectives but likewise had to fall back.	
		2100	A barrage was opened and kept up to 2230 to allow infantry.	

Instructions regarding War Diaries and Intelligence Summaries are contained in F. S. Regs., Part II. and the Staff Manual respectively. Title pages will be prepared in manuscript.

WAR DIARY
or
INTELLIGENCE SUMMARY.
(Erase heading not required.)

Army Form C. 2118.

Place	Date	Hour	Summary of Events and Information	Remarks and references to Appendices
MESNIL VALLEY	1st		to bring in wounded -	
			2/Lt D. T. Davis, 26th Battery RFA, was forward with the 1st Inniskillen Fusiliers, as liaison officer. He was wounded by machine gun fire soon after leaving our front trench, at the same time as Col. Pearce, commanding the Inniskillens was killed.	
			2/Lt McCrory, 92nd Battery, was wounded by a bullet at the Battery position - neither wounds were serious.	
	2nd		By day the Brigade devoted its time to shelling communications. By night the usual night firing was carried out, special attention being given to preventing the enemy repairing their wire	
			2/Lt Ely 13th Battery struck off the strength.	
	3rd 4th		Brigade continued firing on day and night targets - with a view to preventing the enemy repairing trenches & wire	
	5th		2/Lts S. W. K Crawford (posted to 26th Battery) and H. R. Nuttall (posted to 92nd Battery) joined from England.	
		2130	26th Battery moved from MESNIL VALLEY position to old position infront	

T2134. Wt. W708—776. 500000. 4/15. Sir J. C. & S.

Instructions regarding War Diaries and Intelligence Summaries are contained in F. S. Regs., Part II. and the Staff Manual respectively. Title pages will be prepared in manuscript.

WAR DIARY
or
INTELLIGENCE SUMMARY.
(Erase heading not required.)

Army Form C. 2118.

Place	Date	Hour	Summary of Events and Information	Remarks and references to Appendices
MESNIL VALLEY	5th		of ENGELBELMER (Q26 b 10/30)	
		2200	Left Section 13th Battery moved from their MESNIL VALLEY position to a 36th Division Battery's position between MAILLY and AUCHONVILLERS. (Q8 d 10/10)	
		2200	92nd Battery moved from MESNIL VALLEY position to position on right of 26th Battery (Q26 b 10/40)	
	6th	0900 onwards	Brigade and Group HQ moved from MESNIL VALLEY to tents in an orchard to SW of ENGELBELMER (P24 d 80/20)	
			26th, 92nd, 13th Battery Wagon Lines moved from AMPLIER to ARQUEVES. 460th Battery wagon line having been up near ENGELBELMER for the operations of the 1st July returned to ACHEUX.	
			Batteries carried out Registrations throughout the day. Right Section 13th Bty joined Left Section.	
			2/Lt G. G. Russell, 26th Battery R.F.A. admitted to hospital (deafness).	
	7th		Batteries carried out shelling of definite objectives and movement seen during the day. ~~The~~ but night firing was the same as usual.	

T2131. Wt. W708–776. 500000. 4/15. Sir J. C. & S.

Instructions regarding War Diaries and Intelligence Summaries are contained in F. S. Regs., Part II. and the Staff Manual respectively. Title pages will be prepared in manuscript.

WAR DIARY
or
INTELLIGENCE SUMMARY.
(Erase heading not required.)

Army Form C. 2118.

Place	Date	Hour	Summary of Events and Information	Remarks and references to Appendices
ENGEL-BELMER				
	7th		460th Battery 11 [illegible] in Left Group and D/132 in Right Group	
	8th		Firing by day - on movement seen and definite objectives	
			by night - on communications.	
	9th		2/Lieut. R Chalkley (26th Bty) admitted to hospital (appendicitis)	
	9th	1600	26th Battery was shelled by 8" - only 4 being fired - One of these	
			killed Sergeant STYLES and wounded Sergt HAMBLEY.	
			2/Lieut. A.S. Leachars, 92nd Battery RFA, admitted to hospital (rheumatism)	
			2/Lieut. G. Leal joined from D.A.C., posted to 92nd Battery.	
			2/Lieut. A.W. Stanford, 370th Battery attached ~~from~~ to 26th Battery for duty.	
	10th		2/Lieut. A.T. Tulloch, joined from D.A.C. posted to 26th Battery	
	11th		Both normal days - usual firing carried out by all batteries.	
	12th			
	13th		Lieut.-Colonel W. P. Monkhouse on being promoted temporary Brigadier	
			General left the Brigade to command 19th Divisional Artillery.	
			Major N. H. C. Sherbrooke, D/132 Battery, assumed command of	
			17th Brigade RFA. Lieut.-Colonel HRW Marriott Smith, 132nd Bde	

T2134. Wt. W708—776. 500000. 4/15. Sir J. C. & S.

Army Form C. 2118.

Instructions regarding War Diaries and Intelligence Summaries are contained in F. S. Regs., Part II. and the Staff Manual respectively. Title pages will be prepared in manuscript.

WAR DIARY
or
INTELLIGENCE SUMMARY.
(Erase heading not required.)

Place	Date	Hour	Summary of Events and Information	Remarks and references to Appendices
Between ENGELBELMER - FORCEVILLE			RGA, assumed command of Right Group. Headquarters 132nd Bde became HQ Right Group as well, and took over the Headquarters of Rt Group from 17th Brigade in orchard (P24 d 80/20). Headquarters 17th Brigade moved to ruined farm (P23 c 00/70) ~~where 132nd~~ and took it over from 132nd Bde.	
			From this point onwards O. C. 17th Brigade had not tactical command of 17th Brigade Batteries. 26th, 92nd & 13th Batteries being under Right Group (Colonel Marriott Smith) and 460th Battery being under Left Group (Colonel Forman)	
	14th		2/Lt Patsey, Orderly Officer, detached with 132nd Bde as Group Signal Officer.	
	15th		2/Lt Salberg posted to 26th Battery, joined from England.	
	16th 17th		Nothing to report —	
	18th		2/Lt A.C.W. Stanford (attached to 26th Battery) rejoined 370th Battery.	
	19th		Nothing to report. 2Lt W E Tibbs, 13th Bty, admitted to Hospital.	

Army Form C. 2118.

Instructions regarding War Diaries and Intelligence Summaries are contained in F. S. Regs., Part II. and the Staff Manual respectively. Title pages will be prepared in manuscript.

WAR DIARY
or
INTELLIGENCE SUMMARY.
(Erase heading not required.)

Place	Date	Hour	Summary of Events and Information	Remarks and references to Appendices
Between ENGELBELMER and FORCEVILLE	20th		The C.R.A. placed his car at disposal of Major Sherbrooke, who took ~~Majors~~ three of the battery commanders down to FRICOURT and MAMETZ to see the result of our bombardment down there. The bombardment there was very successful, there being very little left of the German trenches. FRICOURT and MAMETZ are completely destroyed.	
			2/Lieut H.R. Remington left Headquarters to rejoin 26th Battery.	
			2/Lieut T.B. Dowley joined Headquarters from D/132 Battery to take over work as Adjutant	
	21st		Nothing to report.	
	22nd		2Lt. H Lake, 26th Bty, attached to 13th Bty.	
	23rd		Nothing to report	
	24th		Lieut M Staveley 460th Bty posted to command 370th Bty (132 Bde)	
	25th		nothing to report.	
	26th		25th Division Infantry completed relief of 29th Division Infantry, the 29th Divisional Artillery was organised into 3 Groups as the 25th	

T2134. Wt. W708—776. 500000. 4/15. Sir J. C. & S.

Army Form C. 2118.

Instructions regarding War Diaries and Intelligence Summaries are contained in F. S. Regs., Part II. and the Staff Manual respectively. Title pages will be prepared in manuscript.

WAR DIARY
or
INTELLIGENCE SUMMARY.
(Erase heading not required.)

Place	Date	Hour	Summary of Events and Information	Remarks and references to Appendices
Between ENGLEBELMER and FORCEVILLE	July 26th		Division were holding the line with 3 Brigades.	
			Lieut Col. N. H. C. SHERBROOKE commands RIGHT GROUP which consists of the following batteries :— FRONT COVERED	
			10th Battery RFA (Captain T. de C. Batten) Q18c 20/75 – Q17b 53/10	
			13th Battery RFA (Captain R. S. Leach) Q17b 53/10 – Point (O3)	
			26th Battery RFA (Captain D. Daly) Q24b 15/45 – Q18c 53/20	
			92nd Battery RFA (Captain R. Marx) Q18c 53/20 – Q18c 20/75.	
			D/132 (How) Battery RFA (Captain H. Gray) – whole of Group Front – Q24b 15/45	to Point O3.
			460th (How) Battery remains in Left Group.	
ENGLEBELMER		~~2230~~	~~13th Battery~~ Headquarters 17th Brigade moved from P23c 00/70 to orchard P24d 80/20.	
		2230 -2345	13th Battery were shelled with gas shell – respirators gave complete protection.	
	27th	1330	At 1330 the new groups came into force – and control was taken over. 2/Lieut. T. B. Darley from D/132 Battery RFA posted as	

T2134. Wt. W708–776. 500000. 4/15. Sir J. C. & S.

Instructions regarding War Diaries and Intelligence Summaries are contained in F. S. Regs., Part II. and the Staff Manual respectively. Title pages will be prepared in manuscript.

WAR DIARY
or
INTELLIGENCE SUMMARY.
(Erase heading not required.)

Army Form C. 2118.

Place	Date	Hour	Summary of Events and Information	Remarks and references to Appendices
ENGEZ BELMER	27th		Adjutant 17 Bde RFA. Lieut. HG Leadbetter posted to 460th Battery RFA, but remained attached to ~~at~~ Right Group Headquarters.	
	28th		Usual day and night firing. At 2330 on night 27th-28th traffic was	
		23	heard on STATION road fire was opened, and infantry report shouts and teams galloping. From which it seems fire was very effective.	
	29th		During the course of the morning "test CONCENTRATIONS" were carried out, and Barrage lines checked by O. C. Group.	
			CONCENTRATIONS are given when the enemy require retaliation. There are two concentrations (1) CONCENTRATE 'A' being given when Right Battalion wishes help, (II) CONCENTRATE 'B' being given for Left Battalion. In each case the 4 18 pdr. batteries fire 4 rounds gunfire (alternate HE and shrapnel) ~~[illegible]~~ at given time, wait 4 minutes, and fire 2 rounds gunfire. D/132 fires 2 rounds gunfire at same time, waits 4 mins, and fires 1 round gunfire. All fire on selected points in enemy front system, opposite the Battalion	

T2131. Wt. W708–776. 500000. 4/15. Sir J. C. & S.

Instructions regarding War Diaries and Intelligence Summaries are contained in F. S. Regs., Part II. and the Staff Manual respectively. Title pages will be prepared in manuscript.

WAR DIARY
or
INTELLIGENCE SUMMARY.
(Erase heading not required.)

Army Form C. 2118.

Place	Date	Hour	Summary of Events and Information	Remarks and references to Appendices
ENGEL-BELMER	29th	–	which requires help.	
			In order that one battery of the Group may always be firing every few minutes, 26th 92nd, 13th Batteries are placed on a roll for night and day firing each taking 3 hours at a time.	
			10th Battery cuts wire by day and does not fire by night.	
			1 gun 10th Battery moved to MESNIL VALLEY (Q16 c 20/00) in order to be able to cut wire more satisfactorily.	
	30th	–	Remaining 3 guns went up to MESNIL VALLEY during night 30th-31st.	
	31st	1000	10th Battery cut wire.	
		0500-0900	Batteries fired at intervals on their ~~night~~ barrage lines while the mist was down.	
		1730	10th Battery cut wire. Group HQ shelled by Germ gun at 2350 about 12 rounds.	

Instructions regarding War Diaries and Intelligence Summaries are contained in F. S. Regs., Part II. and the Staff Manual respectively. Title pages will be prepared in manuscript.

WAR DIARY
or
INTELLIGENCE SUMMARY.
(Erase heading not required.)

Army Form C. 2118.

Place	Date	Hour	Summary of Events and Information	Remarks and references to Appendices
			This Diary compiled by me – A G Leadbetter Lt RFA.	
			H Sherbrooke Lieut Colonel RFA	
			1/8/16 Commanding 17th Bde RFA	
			APPENDIX I – Original programme of lifts for 1st July 1916 –	
			II – List of casualties and re-inforcements – attached –	

T2134. Wt. W708–776. 500000. 4/15. Sir J. C. & S.

APPENDIX I

Right Group
29th D/Arty.
30/6/16

All 18 Pounder Batteries

Zero Time is 7.30 AM

– Programme of Lifts:–

From minus 65 to " 10. (N.B. not minus 15)	Fire on enemy Front Line Trench One Round per gun per minute HE
At minus 10 0720	Same objective. 3 rounds per gun per minute. Percussion Shrapnel – except 92nd 26th and 340th Batteries who fire Time Shrapnel according to instructions issued verbally.
At minus 3. Battery Fire 5 secs Percussion Shrapnel	One Section lifts to 2nd Line Trench or further if necessary for safety of our own infantry
At Zero. 0000. Battery Fire 7.30 5 secs	The Other Section lifts to 2nd Line Trench, or further if necessary and both Sections fire Time Shrapnel
At 0002 7.32 Battery Fire 5 Secs. Time Shrapnel 7.50	Lift your fire 100 yards every 2 minutes and continue to do so until your fire is 100 yards beyond STATION Road KEEP IT THERE UNTIL 0020
At 0020. and Until 0030. (Battery Fire 5 Secs T.S.) 7.50 and ~~7.60~~ 0800 0030 to 0105 Bursts 0~~8.00~~ T.S. 08.35	Lift your fire 100 yards every 2 minutes until your fire is 400 yards beyond STATION ROAD – and keep it there until 0105.

Continued over page

at 0105. T.S. B.F. 5 Secs. T.S.	Lift your fire 100 yards every 2 minutes until your fire reaches BEAUCOURT Road - BEAUCOURT CHATEAU Trench (Fire to reach Trench by 01.18)
at 0120 Bursts T.S.	(92nd 26th 340th 341st and B243rd) Lift your fire 200 yards and keep it there until 0130.
at 0130 B.F. 5 Secs. Then "Bursts".	Lift your fire 100 yards every 2 minutes to a "Barrage Line R4B2050 - R4B8020 - R8C1520 - and keep it there until 0240
at 0120 T.S. Bursts	(A241st, 10th and 13th) Lift your fire from BEAUCOURT ROAD TRENCH to Double line of Wire through R1C - R4A.
at 0135. T.S Bursts	Lift your fire to ground EAST OF Artillery Lane and keep it there until 0230.
at 0230. B.F. 5 Secs to ROAD. Then:- Bursts	Lift your fire 100 yards every 2 minutes as far as the PUISEAUX ROAD and keep it there until 0240.
at 0240 B.F. 5 Secs Then Bursts. T.S.	The 340th and 341st Batteries cease firing. Remainder (except 92nd Battery) lift your fire 100 yards every 2 minutes to a "Single line of Wire" through R2, A C and D. Batteries not on wire extend in line in own area - down to the RIVER and keep it there until 0300
at 0240 Bursts. T.S.	92nd Battery. Lift 100 yards every two minutes until your fire is 300 yards beyond the PUISEAUX ROAD and remain there until 0310

08.35 +30

At 0105. T. S., B.F. 5 Secs., T. S.	Lift your fire 100 yards every 2 minutes until your fire reaches BEAUCOURT ROAD – BEAUCOURT CHATEAU TRENCH. Fire to reach Trench by 01.18 0848+30
At 0120 0850 Bursts T. S.	(92nd 26th 370th 371st and B 243rd) Lift your fire 200 yards and keep it there until 0130 0900 +30
At 0130 0900 +30 B.F. 5 Secs, Then "Bursts"	Lift your fire 100 yards every 2 minutes to a Barrage line R.7 B2050 – R.7 B 8020 – R.8 C 1520 – and keep it there until 0240 1010 +30
At 0120 0850 + T. S. "Bursts"	(A 241st 16th and 13th) Lift your fire from BEAUCOURT ROAD TRENCH to Double line of wire through R.K – R.7A.
At 0136 0905 T. S. Bursts	Lift your fire to ground EAST of ARTILLERY LANE and keep it there until 0230 10.00 +30
At 0230 10.00 + B.F 5 secs ROAD then – "Bursts"	Lift your fire 100 yards every 2 minutes as far as the PUISEAUX ROAD, and keep it there until 0240 1010 + 30
At 0240 B.F. 5 Secs., then Bursts T. S. 10.10 +30	The 370th and 371st Battery cease firing. Remainder (except 92nd Battery) lift your fire 100 yards every 2 minutes to a Single line of wire through R.2 AC and D. Batteries not on wire extend in line in own area down to the RIVER and keep it there until 0300 10.30 +30
At 0240 Bursts, T. S. 10.10 +30	92nd Battery Lift 100 yards every two minutes until your fire is 300 yards beyond the PUISEAUX ROAD and remain there until 0310 10.40 +30

Lifts (Continued

30/6/16

At 0300 Bursts. T.S. +30 10.30 to 10.40	All Batteries (except 92nd) bring your fire back from the Single Line of Wire through "R2AC & D" down to the River to a line 300 yards beyond the Puiseaux Road and keep there until 0310.
At 0310 B.F. 5 secs. T.S. +30 10.40 to 1057	All Batteries lift your fire 100 yards every two minutes up to the FRONT PUISEAUX TRENCH and keep it there until 0327.
At 0327 BF 5 secs T.S. +30 1057 to 11.00	Lift to 2nd PUISEAUX TRENCH and keep your fire there until 0330
At 0330 Bursts +30 H.E. 11.00 to 12.00	Lift your fire to the Barrage (The SUNKEN ROAD) - R4A 4090 to R2B 8099 and fire on this until 04.30. NOTE CHANGE OF SHELL.
At 0430 Bursts +30 H.E 12.00 to 12.10	Lift 300 yards EAST OF SUNKEN ROAD and BAILLESCOURT until 0440
At 04.40 +30 12.10	CEASE FIRING and "Stand by"

Special to A241st and B243rd

From minus 65 to 0000 - rate of fire "BURSTS" - from Pt 50 along the BEAUCOURT CHATEAU TRENCH and the Wire in front of it - down to the RIVER.

~~50%~~ All HE.

After 0000 - Join in the programme at 0120

[signature] Lt Col
O/C Left Group
[illegible] Arty

Army Form C. 2118.

Instructions regarding War Diaries and Intelligence Summaries are contained in F. S. Regs., Part II. and the Staff Manual respectively. Title pages will be prepared in manuscript.

WAR DIARY
or
INTELLIGENCE SUMMARY.
(Erase heading not required.)

Place	Date	Hour	Summary of Events and Information	Remarks and references to Appendices
			APPENDIX II	
			Casualties during month of JULY.	
			Officers. wounded - 2. Major R.C. Williams 92nd Battery 1-7-16 ; Lieut D. F. Davis 26th Battery —	} reported in last months diary.
			Other ranks. killed - 1 Sgt. Styles 26th Battery R.F.A. - 9-7-16	
			wounded - 6	
			Reinforcements: — 3 officers, 17 O.R.	
			Brigade is now overstrength (1-8-16) 26 O. and 618 O.R.	
			[illegible]	

29th Division.

<u>17th BRIGADE</u>

<u>R. F. A.</u>

<u>AUGUST 1916</u>

Appendices attached;-

List of Officers.
Artillery Reports.

17th Bde R.F.A.

WAR DIARY ~~or INTELLIGENCE SUMMARY.~~

(Erase heading not required.)

Vol. 6

Army Form C. 2118.

Instructions regarding War Diaries and Intelligence Summaries are contained in F. S. Regs., Part II. and the Staff Manual respectively. Title pages will be prepared in manuscript.

Map Reference 57. d. S.E. 1/10,000 Beaumont.

Place	Date	Hour	Summary of Events and Information	Remarks and references to Appendices
August 1916				
ENGLEBELMER	1st	00.23	Concentration given to Right Battalion from 26th & 92nd Batteries, H.Q.S. were shelled & communication to 13th Battery cut.	
		05.00–09.00	26th Bty fired on barrage during night.	
		03.26	13th Battery saw 3 red rockets and opened as for S.O.S. – nothing came of it. 1 Gun (26th) Battery out of action (springs weak)	
	2nd		Usual night firing. 26th fired on transport in STATION ROAD probably with effect.	
	3rd	22.20	Concentration "A" given on Minenwerfers. 26th gun in action again.	
	4th		Usual day & night programme carried out –	
	5th		Usual day and night programme – following batteries cut wire –	
			26th Battery – Q18 a 00/03 – 76 rounds –	
			Q18 c 12/96 – 70 rounds – Cone cut	
			10th Battery – Q17 b 40/17 – 75 rounds 18pr; 100 rounds 4.5" How – ×Q/132 (1 How)	wire cut – but knife rests not damaged
			Q17 b 80/40 – 75 rounds	
			Q17 b 80/10 – 75 rounds	
			Q17 b 15/28 – 75 rounds	

Instructions regarding War Diaries and Intelligence Summaries are contained in F. S. Regs., Part II. and the Staff Manual respectively. Title pages will be prepared in manuscript.

WAR DIARY
or
INTELLIGENCE SUMMARY.
(Erase heading not required.)

Army Form C. 2118.

Place	Date	Hour	Summary of Events and Information	Remarks and references to Appendices
ENGELBELMER				
	5th		Good deal of movement on GRANDCOURT-MIRAUMONT road - 500 men and a battery reported moving along it. MILL POST was in hands of the enemy for a few hours but he was dislodged about	
	6th	0300	0300 6th. 3 concentrations during night 5th & 6th in retaliation to Enemy Trench mortar which was troubling our infantry. 9.2" How fired eventually and stopped T. M. 1 gun 13th Battery away to I.O.M.'s workshops requiring new springs. Lieutenant T. B Darley, Adjutant 17th Brigade RFA admitted to hospital, having met with an accident riding. He was suffering from concussion.	
	7th		1 gun 13th Battery still away, 1 26th and 1 92nd also away wanting springs. Wire cutting carried out - report attached× ~~APPENDIX~~	×APPENDIX II
	8th		Intelligence report attached* wire cutting report attached×	*APPENDIX III
	9th		Intelligence report attached* wire cutting report attached×	
			2/Lt D. G. Thomas V/29 H.T.M. Battery posted to 29th D.A.C.	
			2/Lt. G. Leal, 92nd Battery posted to V/29 H.T.M. Battery } attached 17th Brigade.	
			2/Lt. W. H. Craib, 10th Battery posted to V/29 H.T.M. Battery }	

T2134. Wt. W708—776. 500000. 4/15. Sir J. C. & S.

Instructions regarding War Diaries and Intelligence Summaries are contained in F. S. Regs., Part II. and the Staff Manual respectively. Title pages will be prepared in manuscript.

Army Form C. 2118.

WAR DIARY
or
~~INTELLIGENCE~~ SUMMARY.
(Erase heading not required.)

AEQL

Place	Date	Hour	Summary of Events and Information	Remarks and references to Appendices
ENGEL-BELMER				
	10th		Wire cutting* and Intelligence report attached*	*
			Captain A.C. Chapman posted to V/29 H.T.M. Battery from Base.	APPENDIX III
	11th		Intelligence report attached* – Wire cutting stopped.	
	12th		Intelligence report attached*	
	13th		Intelligence report attached*	
	14th		Intelligence report attached*	
	15th		Intelligence report attached*	
	16th		Intelligence report attached* 2/Lt W.K. Greg posted to 92nd Battery from 29. D.A.C.	
	17th		From 17th onwards copies of Intelligence reports are attached APPENDIX III.	
			13th Battery heavily shelled today. 5 men wounded – no badly. 2 men buried by collapse of dugouts but dugout all right. DR. HENNY, 13th Bty, afterwards awarded MILITARY MEDAL for good work in digging a man out, while under shell fire.	
			3 officers (Captain A.C. CHAPMAN, 2/LT LEAL, 2/LT CRAIB) and 35 O.R. V/29 T.M. Bty posted to D.A.C. – V/29 Bty – now on strength of D.A.C. and not of brigades.	
	18th		nothing to report	

T2134. Wt. W708–776. 500000. 4/15. Sir J. C. & S.

Instructions regarding War Diaries and Intelligence Summaries are contained in F. S. Regs., Part II. and the Staff Manual respectively. Title pages will be prepared in manuscript.

WAR DIARY
or
INTELLIGENCE SUMMARY.
(Erase heading not required.)

Army Form C. 2118.

Place	Date	Hour	Summary of Events and Information	Remarks and references to Appendices
ENGER BELMER				
	19th		Nothing to report.	
	20th		Nothing to report. 20th 4/Lt W.E. Tibbs rejoined 13th Bty	
	21st		Nothing to report. 21st 2/Lt W.E. Tibbs transferred to No 2 Sec DAC.	
	22nd		Nothing to report.	
	23rd		Nothing to report.	
	24th		"B" Grover, Hq 17 Bde, wounded by shell fire.	
	25th	0100	Bombardment in support of 18th Inf. Bde (14th DLI) raid to South of Pt 03. Wire had been cut in two lanes N. & S. of the MOUND Pt Q17 b 10/20. Infantry did not get in; but Germans did not retaliate heavily. Colonel Sherbrooke temporarily handed over to Major Uniacke RHA, and went away for a few days to convalesce.	
	26th 27th 28th		Nothing to report	
	29th		Colonel Cunrage took over from Major Uniacke. 11th D.A took over from Left Group. Centre Group became Left Group. Batteries disposed as follows:- Right Group 26th, 92nd, 13th, 10th, 370th, 377th, D/132 (Colonel Cunrage)	

T2134. Wt. W708-776. 500000. 4/15. Sir J. C. & S.

Instructions regarding War Diaries and Intelligence Summaries are contained in F. S. Regs., Part II. and the Staff Manual respectively. Title pages will be prepared in manuscript.

WAR DIARY
or
INTELLIGENCE SUMMARY.
(Erase heading not required.)

Army Form C. 2118.

Place	Date	Hour	Summary of Events and Information	Remarks and references to Appendices
ENGLEBELMER				
			Left Group - 'B' 'L' 'Y' 97th 368th, 369th 460th D/147	
	30		Right Group cut wire from Q 17 b 90.00 to the ANCRE.	
			Various bombardments.	
	31		Wire cutting continued – Attack postponed till September 1st, then 2nd and eventually till Sept. 3rd 1916 –	
			This Diary compiled by me.	
			[illegible] Lt RGA Adjutant 17 Bde RGA	
			[illegible] Lt RGA for Lieut Col RGA	
	1-9-16		Commanding 17th Bde RGA	

T2134. Wt. W708–776. 500000. 4/15. Sir J. C. & S.

Army Form C. 2118.

Instructions regarding War Diaries and Intelligence Summaries are contained in F. S. Regs., Part II. and the Staff Manual respectively. Title pages will be prepared in manuscript.

WAR DIARY
or
INTELLIGENCE SUMMARY.
(Erase heading not required.)

Place	Date	Hour	Summary of Events and Information	Remarks and references to Appendices
			LIST of OFFICERS serving on 31-8-16 APPENDIX I	
			Headquarters. Lieut.Col. HNC Sherbrooke	
			2/Lt T. C. Ratsey	
			Captain A.S. Phillips (attached from 29 D.A.H.Q)	
			Captain Harris RAMC.	
			Captain Magill AVC.	
			13th Battery: Captain R.S. Leach; Lieut. W. Dalziel; 2/Lieut F. Eggleton; — S.G. Martin; — Lake (T)	
			26th Battery: Captain D. Daly; Lieut H.R. Remington; 2/Lieut. E. Salberg; 2/Lieut. S.T. Crawford; — H.R. Tulloch	

T2134. Wt. W708—776. 500000. 4/15. Sir J. C. & S.

Army Form C. 2118.

WAR DIARY
or
INTELLIGENCE SUMMARY.
(Erase heading not required.)

Instructions regarding War Diaries and Intelligence Summaries are contained in F. S. Regs., Part II. and the Staff Manual respectively. Title pages will be prepared in manuscript.

Place	Date	Hour	Summary of Events and Information	Remarks and references to Appendices
			93rd Battery — Captain R. Marx.	
			" — Lieut. M. Skilt	
			" — 2/Lieut H.R. Nuttall	
			" — " W.E. Grey	
			" — " R. Pewtress	
			460th Battery — Major T.H. Gibbon	
			" — Lieut H.G. Leadbetter a/Adjutant	
			" — Lieut. C.P. Duff	
			" — 2/Lt. Terrell	
			" — " J. Steward	
			A/Lieut. T.B. Davley - invalided at present in ENGLAND. Adjutant 7 Bde.	
			H.G. Leadbetter Lt R.F.A.	

T2134. Wt. W708—776. 500000. 4/15. Sir J. C. & S.

APPENDIX
II

Wire cutting – 6th August

26th Battery

(i) Q 18 c 13/98 with 10' sweep either side of this –

(ii) 330

(iii) FOO reports the front part of the wire cut, but not right through – wire very thick and a lot of knife rests which need howitzers –

D/132 400

(i) Q 17 b 40/17

(ii) 400 18pr 100 4.5" How

(iii) Progress has been made damaging the knife rests but they are still thick –

WBS

HTM Battery

6th	1130	2	Q17b & Q18c
	1200	4	damaged
	2240	2	
7th	—	1	Q17b

retaliation at
request of
infantry.

Wire cutting - August 7th -

(A) 26th Battn reports
— ~~2 lanes~~

(i) Q 18 c 18/92
(ii) ~~150~~ rounds
(iii) lane cut

(i) Q 17 B 99/05
(ii) 150
(iii) lane cut

Q 18 c 13/98, Q 18 c 00/02 reported
cut on 6th given more attention
and partially cut on 5th
firing 131 rounds -

(B) 13th Battn (i) Q 17 b 10/10
(ii) 100 rds
(iii) pathway
cut but knife
rests still lying
about in it -

(C) 6th & D/132 -
(i) Q 17 B 40/17
(ii) 200 18 pdr 120 4.5 Hows
(iii) progress made -

(i) ~~100~~ Q 17 B 30/15
(ii) 100 new lane started

Wire cutting. August 8th.

(A) 26th Battery

(i) Q 18 c 12/92

(ii) 679 rounds

(iii) Lane cut through the wire itself, but knife rests remain. Some of these were blown up and have come down sideways leaving gaps, but the majority are not much damaged.

(B) (i) 13th Battery – Q17b 10/10

(ii) 200

(iii) went on with same place as yesterday – shooting very good – results poor as knife rests cannot be smashed

(C) (i) 10th & D/13 2 How

(i) Q 17 B 30/15

(ii) 200 18pr 170 (4.5" how)

(iii) enlarged to the left – good results –

Wire cutting. August 9th

(A) GCJA (13th Battery)

(i) Q17 b 10/10

(ii) 300 rounds

(iii) No lanes visible – light bad AAA

(10th & D/132)

(B) GCKA (i) Q17 B40/17 to Q17 b 25/13

and GCKD (ii) 812 18pr 288 4.5" How

(iii) good results – several lanes right through.

(C) GCJB (26th) ~~(i)~~

(i) $\frac{B}{21}$, $\frac{B}{23}$, $\frac{B}{25}$

(ii) 430

(iii) range correct good bursts. impossible to see whether wire cut as nearest place to observe from is JACOBS LADDER. AAA Too many ~~[illegible]~~ batteries on front line but it rather difficult to see 3rd line through dust.

[illegible]

29th DA

(A) 26th Battery - (i) Pt B/23
(ii) 517
(iii) results not possible to observe as light conditions very bad

(B) 13th Battery - (i) 2 places Q18 c 40/40 to Q18 c 35/35
(ii) 250
(iii) wire cut, but knife rests not damaged - no gaps visible. another battery firing at same place -

(C) 10th Battery (i) Q17 b 50/15 to Q17 b 35/12
(ii) 500
(iii) good results

(D) Y Battery (i) Fired on wire Q18 c 25 65 - Q18 c 40/40
(ii) 600
(iii) 3 small gaps cut about 5 yds wide
very thick -

29DA

Int. Report. 8th 9th August

APPENDIX III

(1.) Usual night firing – ~~chiefly~~ wire cutting yesterday evening and today AAA

(2.) Very quiet

(3.) Left Battalion reports Gaps in wire were kept open all night AAA No enemy T.M. fire AAA 22.30 Relief party made rather a noise at MILL in Q24a and were shelled in consequence AAA Our patrol got to Q 24 a 50/65 and heard enemy listening post at Q24a 70/70 AAA Wire in front of German 2nd line about Q 11 b 95/95 to Q 11 b 75/05 has been strengthened AAA New earth probable O.P. in Q 19 a 10/52 AAA Probable O.P. with slit and louver at Q 11 b 70/22 on the road AAA PICTURE DROME to PECKHAM STREET still incomplete and in poor condition.

4. Nil

5. Nil

6. 1 gun 10th Battery still away.

[illegible]

Intelligence Report - 9th to 10th

(1.) Wire cutting yesterday evening AAA 5 Concentrations during the night AAA D/132 Hows. was moved from KNIGHTSBRIDGE to rejoin battery AAA 1 gun 92nd Battery moved to near HAMEL AAA 1 gun 26th Battery still in MESNIL VALLEY AAA 'Y' Battery in action yesterday in Q28b 15/55 cutting wire AAA

Wire cutting difficult this morning and only possible on front line owing to bad observation conditions AAA

1640 Heavy T.M. Battery fired 2 rounds on Q18c

AAA (II) Enemy artillery not active AAA Trench mortars active from 2330 9th onwards. shelling front line from LOUVERCY ST. to RIVER throughout the night AAA retaliation given AAA no effect AAA 5.9" Hows. also fired a few rounds between 2400 and 0200 which hampered our working parties AAA FOO reports 4 minenwerfer to be the number firing AAA

(III) Traffic heard on STATION ROAD at 2200
~~(III)~~ Trench mortar at Q 18 c 30/65 AAA
work going on at Q 18 c 20/90 AAA
observation bad all day AAA
(IV) ~~AAA~~ shoots 13th Battery AAA (V) NIL AAA
(VI) 1 gun (13th Battery
1 gun (10th Battery) still away.

At Group

29 DA / Intelligence 10th 11th —

(I) 1615 onwards – usual wire cutting – usual night firing – AAA fired on wire during mist AAA Quiet afternoon AAA

(II) Very quiet – except between 2300 and 2400 last night when enemy shelled our infantry sector – AAA

(III) 1940 ~~Hostile~~ arc of flame over. AAA

New wire in front of communication trench R19a 50/55 to Q24 B 85/05 AAA New earth at Q18 b 90/90 at bottom of Railway Alley AAA Suspected O.P. or M.G. emplacement at Q24 B 60/30 – timber roof disclosed by 92nd Battery's fire. AAA

(IV) ~~AAA~~ Broken spring D/132 AAA

(V) 7 other ranks wounded – AAA 3 slightly wounded and at duty 4 wounded and at Field Ambulance – D/132 Battery premature AAA

(VI) 1 How D/132.

[signature]

29DA

Intelligence Report – 11th to 12th

AAA (I) Concentrations during the night AAA Usual firing during night AAA

(II) generally quiet. Infantry were shelled last night from 2400 onwards at intervals by minenwerfers and Van Hk. AAA

0530 – 0900 – 50 rds. 15cm. into ANCRE VALLEY lower end THIEPVAL WOOD

1455 50 rds 77mm on our front line from Q17b to Q18a 30/90 AAA

(III) 4 hostile planes over HAMEL this morning AAA

11am. Motor Ambulance proceeding from STATION to BEAUCOURT up RAILWAY ROAD AAA

(IV) Springs 13th Battery AAA

(V) NIL AAA

(VI) 1 gun 13th Battery & 1 how. D/132 sent to LOUVENCOURT

~~(VII) All buffers faulty~~

Right Group

29DA.

Intelligence Report_ 12th – 13th

AAA (i) Several concentrations during night
~~AAA~~ AAA D/132 Bombardment of 100 rds.
at 1500 AAA (ii) 10th Battery
shelled during last 24 hours by 4.2" Hows.
and a few 5.9" Hows, also
MESNIL VALLEY has gas shell fired
into it last night – AAA
Trench mortars active from
0000 – 0100 and again at
1300, ~~AAA~~ on LOUVERCY SAP AAA

(iii) ~~B~~ At 1130 3 men seen on
RAILWAY ROAD, ran out of
sight on 92nd Battery firing a shot
AAA

(iv) springs ~~28th Battery~~ – springs 2nd Hows D/132 AAA

(v) wounded slightly in finger Captain
J. de H. C. BATTEN AAA gassed
1 O.R. 10th Battery AAA

(vi) 26th Battery – 1 gun AAA
13th Battery 1 gun AAA
D/132 Battery – 2 Hows AAA

(vii) Buffers of all guns in
action are full

Right Group

Intelligence Report

13/8/16 – 14/8/16.

(i) Several Concentrations during the night, TIGER at 1145 to-day. Mesnil
(ii) & Mesnil Valley were heavily shelled.
10th Battery was shelled with 4.2" & 5.9" howitzers; one gun was badly damaged & has been sent to workshops for repair.
On fire front line in front of Thiepval Wood was shelled by a 5.9 How. Battery firing from L 36 A 1 7. A single 5.9" How. was firing into Mesnil from MIRAUMONT CEMETERY. Gordon trench is shelled regularly.
(iii) The Beaucourt-Serre Road is used during the day time; men seen carry timber up to the Beaucourt Redoubt.

(iv)

13	NIL
92	NIL
26	1
D/132	3
10	1

(V) 10th Battery
Captain Baxter wounded
NO 50682 Sgt. Holland wounded. F.

1 OR wounded 10th
1 OR missing but rejoined

(vi)

(vii) Buffers of guns in action are full

M G Leadbetter
Lt RA
RC Group 29 DA.

29 D.A.

(i) Intelligence 14th 15th AAA
from 1530–1630 D/132 120 rds on Q.18.c 60/50
Usual Routine firing. From 2300 onwards to 2345 3 concentrations of Howitzers of the D.A. were given. 2 18 pdr batteries (26th & 134th) also firing H.E. in retaliation to enemy heavily shelling LOUVERVAL and neighbourhood with all kinds of trench mortars and rifle grenades. The 11th Essex Regt. asked for these, and O.C. Right Group had the use of Left Group Hows. The Infantry say that the concentration was very effective, and shut up the enemy.

The same arrangement is being made for tonight on receipt of the word TIGER. and a similar concentration for the triangle in Q.18.c (centre) has been arranged to take place on the word LION

(ii) Hostile artillery quiet except as in (i)

(iii) 2320 Gas shells Lachrymatory for ½ an hour into MESNIL VALLEY

0000 - 0230   2½ hours of gas
    shelling in MESNIL VALLEY
    (poison gas)

4. ~~~~ Springs 92nd Battery gun.
5. Nil
6. Guns out of action

    1 92nd Battery
    1 26th Battery still away.
    1 D/132 still away.
    1 10th Battery still away.

H. G. Thwaites
Lt RGA
RA Group 29 DA.

29 DA

16 AAA

Intelligence 15th to 16th AAA

1. During night from 2315 – 02.00 various concentrations and retaliations were carried out at request of the infantry mostly on the front of the Right Battalion. AAA
During the 24 hours D/132 fired 240 rounds at front and support line in Q18c and at Q18c 60/52.
1230 – 1400 X29 fired 25 rounds on line Q18c

2. Enemy shelled [illegible] SAP, DECIME STREET with [illegible] and trench mortars between 2307 15th and 0208 16th.
AAA otherwise hostile artillery quiet.

3. 2100 – 2200 [illegible] enemy aeroplanes ~~[illegible]~~ tried to come over our lines but were driven back by AA guns.
1350 3 hostile aeroplanes approached but were chased away by our own AAA
Smoke evidently from a dugout observed in R19c 60/50 AAA

4. Springs 10th battery.

5. Nil

6. 2 guns 10th Battery

1 gun 92nd Battery

1 howitzer D/132

7. ~~Re~~ All buffers full of oil.

Right Grade

[illegible signature]

Intelligence Report. 17th.

(1) No concentration during the night. Usual firing

2)

0700 to 1000 about 100 28cm. shells burst at 13th Bty. position. Bearing of gun 100° magnetic. Hamel & Jacobs Ladder shelled slightly.

(3) 1200 onwards Enemy trench mortars were shelling our line in front of the Bastion. One hostile aeroplane crossed our line about the usual o'clock at 1000. One enemy aeroplane crossed Englebelmer at 1730 this evening.

4) 6 men 13th Bty. wounded

5) Nil.

6) 6C 5A Two guns temporarily out of action due to emplacements being damaged.
6C 5B One out of action.
6C 5C Nil
6C LD Nil

7) GCJA, B, C, } GCLD
all full } one full.

29 DA

18 -

(i) Casualties to guns and equipment - NIL

(ii) Casualties to personnel -
- Nil

(iii) Guns out of action - 1 26th Battery
still away. 1. 10 Battery still away
1 D/132 still away

~~(iv) All buffers full~~

12

13

16

D/132

Rt Group

29 DA — 18th AAA

Intelligence 1600 18th to 1900 18th AAA

(i) Usual expenditure 200 rds per battery on wire AAA Concentration for Left Battalion at 1600 AAA

(ii) Quiet day - very little hostile fire

(iii) Hostile working party out in Q 18 a central this morning about 10.15 am. - guns fired on, but owing to mist observation was impossible AAA Mist hung a long time this morning AAA Hostile aeroplanes not active

Right Group

2310

Concentrations given
at 2305 Con. 'B' 2 mins
2310 Tiger
2323 Tiger
2330 Conc. 'B' 1 min.

29 DA

Intelligence from 1900 18th
to 0700 19th AAA

1. Pre arranged concentrations on roads at 2215, 2250, 2335. AAA
4 rds gunfire on each occasion
~~[illegible] Group [illegible] [illegible] batteries 1 How. Bty~~
from whole group AAA
At 2355 4 rds gunfire from whole group on R7 d 30/90 AAA
Infantry requested retaliation and got it as follows
2305 Concentration 'B' for Left Battalion, 2 mins interval –
2310 Tiger for Rt Bn
2323 Tiger for Rt Bn
2330 Conc. 'B' for Left Battalion 1 min interval –

Firing on wire during night

2. Enemy severely shelled and trench mortared both Battalion fronts 2300 - 2330 - otherwise quiet

3. Items of interest - Nil - Rained at intervals throughout the night. bad light this morning

Rt. Group.

29 DA

19th

Casualty Return ~~...~~ 18th to 19th

RHA (i) Casualty to guns and equipment
1 gun 92nd Battery springs. 1
howitzer D/132 damaged by
premature 1 how D/132 springs.

(ii) Casualties to personnel ~~...~~ 2/Lt Morrice
slightly wounded at duty D/132
Bty RHA 1 O.R. killed & wounded
D/132 premature.

(iii) Guns out of action –
1 gun 92nd Battery.
2 howitzers D/132
1 gun 13th Battery still away – springs.

Rt Group

29 DA

20th

AAA

Intelligence 0700 – 19th to
0700 20th AAA

(i)

Bad light AAA
Usual routine firing AAA – retaliations throughout the day AAA wire cutting as ordered AAA result difficult to see. AAA Retaliation given for Rt Battalion 2340 AAA Retaliation given for Left Battalion at 0047. AAA 0030 Heavies asked to fire – Retaliation effective – AAA

(ii) Hostile artillery active on HAMEL throughout the day AAA 1025 – 1340. Intense retaliation by Germans on HAMEL with 77mm. AAA During night heavy trench mortaring and shelling of PERTH ST., ROBERTS TRENCH, and old front line at 2330 ~~[illegible]~~ and 0030 AAA Left company of left battalion trench mortared at 0030. AAA

(iii) Trench mortar firing yesterday is believed to be in Q 18 a 4/00 AAA X/29 T.M.B fired 25 rounds on wire at Q 17 C 50/50 AAA also 10 rounds in retaliation on night 8th/19th. –

R A Smith.

29 DA / 20th AAA

Casualty Report 20th August

AAA (I) Springs 1 gun 13th Battery AAA
springs 1 how D/132 Battery AAA

(II) Captain ~~H.C.~~ CHAPMAN V/29 H.T.M. Battery killed 1 other rank V/29 Battery killed 1 other rank V/29 wounded (slight) AAA

(III) guns out of action AAA

2 - 13th Battery AAA

1 - 92nd Battery still away but on its way back AAA

3 - Hows. D/132 Battery still away. AAA

(IV) All buffers full

Right Group

29 DA 20th AAA

Intelligence 0700 – 1900

20th instant AAA

(1) Usual firing, wirecutting and registrations. AAA X29 ? fired 30 rds. on wire Q17c 50/50 good results –

(2) Enemy quite in morning.
0900 30 rds 77mm shrapnel in frontline trench Q17C from direction of R7B 10/30 AAA 1000 20 rds 10.5 cm. burst in MESNIL AAA HAMEL and frontline and CHARLES AVENUE shelled this afternoon AAA Heavy Batteries G32 b 23/70 firing in the open in direction of POZIERES AAA Location corresponds with flashes seen last night by our Heavy Artillery AAA ~~Corps.~~ Heavies engaged them AAA

(3) Traffic seen this afternoon on road in rear of IRLES CHURCH (G32 b) – AAA movement both to and from IRLES AAA 1600 2 pair-horse wagons seen going up STATION ROAD AAA 13th Battery engaged them – effects not observed AAA 1710 and 1755 German planes over our lines AAA 2040

German plane over KI
position – firing machine gun –
went on South and disappeared
West – climbing higher AAA
One of our captive balloons
broke loose this evening and
drifted over German lines –
disappearing and apparently
coming to ground on far side
of IRLES in wrecked condition
AAA Observer landed by
parachute in our own country
AAA

(IV) 92nd Batter 1 gun returned from
A.O.D. now all in action
AAA D/132 1 How. returned
from A.O.D. now 2 Hows.
in action

Rt Group

29DA 21 AAA

Supplementary Intelligence 1900 20th to 0700 21st AAA

(I) Bombardment with 3 18pdr and 1 4.5" How Battery carried out between 2315 - 2345 and 0015 - 0045 of front line and supports in Q17B. AAA Ammunition 18pdr 300 rds. 4.5" How 60 rds.

2355 Concentration 'B' given to Left Battalion

~~0215 LEOPARD given~~

0130 - Concentration B given to Left Bn.

0215 - Lion 3 given to Rt Bn

0245 - Tiger 3 given to Rt Bn

(II) Enemy trench mortars active from 11.45 pm to 2.15 am. opposite Left Battalion and from 1 am. to 2.30 am. opposite Rt Battalion

(III) No items of interest.

Rt Graf

0825

Current
~~Intelligence~~ Report –

21/8/16.

1) Nil

2) GCLB one ~~horse~~ horse killed.

3) Guns out of action.

GCLB	Two,
GCJA	NIL
GCJB	one
GCSC	NIL
GCKA	NIL

4) All Buffers filled.

1/2

29 DA

22 AAA

Intelligence Report 0700 - 21st to 0700 22nd.

(1) Usual wire cutting and routine firing.
2315 - 2345 and 0015 - 0045 2 18pr.
batteries carried out bombardment under
O.C. Centre Group. AAA
During 20th inst. from 1630-1730 X/29
fired 25 rounds on wire Q17c 50/50.
good results. AAA
3 Concentrations given during the
night AAA

(2) Hostile Artillery quiet during the day and
afternoon.
1512 20th. 10.5 cm. howitzer shelled BASTILLE
POSITION (16th Battery's forward position)
(Q 22 a 20/80). then 12 cm. how.
joined in. 2 observation balloons were
up during this time near IRLES and
had seen the a wagon near the
position.
1945 onwards 21st enemy shelled 16th
Battery present position in ENGELBELMER
firing 50 4.2" shells and some 5.9"
AAA Damage nil AAA
11.45 to 13.15 MESNIL was shelled by 5.9" How.

2. ~~1 Hostile balloons visible during the day.~~

Enemy trench mortars and some shrapnel were active against Right Battalion between 2400 and 0200, opposite Left Battalion between 2315 and 2345

3 7 Hostile balloons visible during the day.

Right Group

29 DA

22 AAA

Casualty Report AAA

(i) 1 gun 10th Battery damaged by splinters last night at about 2000 AAA

(ii) No Casualties AAA springs D/132 Battery AAA

(iii) Guns out of action – AAA

1 gun 10th Battery

1 gun 26th Battery

3 hows. D/132 Battery AAA

(iv) All limbers full

Rt Group

29 DA

23rd AAA

Intelligence 0700 22nd - 0700 23rd AAA

(i) Wire cutting in battery zones. AAA
3 18 pr. and 1 How battery carried out short bombardment from 0150 - 0205. ~~[illegible]~~ on Q17b 63-16 to 23/38. AAA

(ii) Enemy shelled MESNIL and MESNIL valley yesterday putting in about 60 rounds 15 cm from R15. AAA

~~[illegible]~~

Very quiet night. a few trench mortars on left company Right Battalion front. AAA

2100 - 2200. About 20 shell on Victoria Street. AAA

(iii) Hostile working party on RAILWAY ALLEY in Q12d dispersed with casualties at 1315 by 13th Battery. AAA

Guns seen firing R15a 85/60, R15d 30,40.

On night of 21st 22nd 17th Siege Battery in AVELUY WOOD was shelled by 15 cm. using long delay action fuze. AAA Effect on personnel small. but goes through anything less than 6 ft of overhead cover

Rh Graaf.

29 OR   23   AAA

Casualty Report AAA

1. Nil AAA
2. Nil AAA
3. Guns out of action AAA
   1 Gun 10th Battery
   2 hows. D/132 Battery AAA
4. All buffers full

— Rt. Group

29 DA

24 AAA

Intelligence 0700 23rd to 0700 24th AAA

(1) Enemy minenwerfer at Q18 a 25/30 engaged by D/137 Battery AAA

Retaliation given AAA

Usual routine firing AAA 10th Battery cut wire at Pt Q17b 0828 and 26th Battery at Q 17 b 30/15. Effect on French cuts of wire seems to be only to shove them all up to far end of lane. ~~With the help of~~ 81st Siege, ~~110th~~ Battery and Y/29 these two batteries are confident in having large lanes cut today.

2340. Salvoes fired on RAILWAY STA. RAILWAY ROAD, STATION ROAD, and RIVER ROAD, as F.O.O. reported traffic and various noises behind German lines, ~~and~~ ~~at~~ An extremely quiet night.

0015 – 0030. Bombardment of Q17b63/16 to 23/38.

2\. 0925 Enemy trench mortar active from Q18 a 25/30 ~~and during the morning~~ – firing on Garden Trench.

The 5.9" Hows, firing on near 36th Battery were seen firing by 10th

Battery F.O.O. at 0705 but were
already being engaged by Heavies AAA

3. 1700 3 Hostile Aeroplanes
came over our lines and
carried out a reconnaissance -
without interruption

Pt Graf

29 DA 25th AAA

Intelligence 0700 24th – 0200 25th AAA

11 Usual routine firing AAA 1530 onwards 26th and 10th Batteries cut wire at Q17b 30/15 and 08/28 respectively. AAA Y/29 helped but most bursts were over AAA 460th Battery lent by Left Group shot at 08/28 – enlarging left gap. AAA 81st Siege expended 100 rds on MG emplacements blockhouses etc between these two points. AAA

0100 Bombardment started as per programme AAA 5 18 pdr batteries 4 rds per gun per min AAA 3 How. Batteries 3 rds per how per min. AAA

0105 Rate of fire of 18 pdrs doubled at request of infantry. AAA Subsequently slackened but increased at 0120 to 10 rds per gun per min AAA subsequently slackened AAA

0155 Stopped firing.

0200 Report received from infantry Bde that wire was no good – parties unable to enter...

1. 0730 – 1130 HARAUZ shelled at intervals by 5.9 cm hows. AAA

2. Very quiet night – no reply to said bombardment. AAA [illegible]

[illegible] 3. 1230 – Hostile plane was driven off by AA guns AAA

1630 – 2 hostile planes over our lines. AAA

1708 – 2 horse Red Cross wagon came down STATION Road.

Observation conditions good –

HQ Group

29 DA

25th AAA

Intelligence 0200 - 0700 26th AAA

1. Routine firing. AAA
2. Quiet night - at 2300 enemy shelled HAMEL AAA

3. Casualties in raid 9 men wounded. shrapnel. AAA All party got back safely AAA Conflicting statements as to what happened

[illegible]

25th

1. NIL [illegible]
2. NIL
3. 1 query [illegible] [illegible] care
4. all staff most helpful.

TC Raby

29 DA

26 Apr

Intelligence 0700 25th to 0700 26th AAA

(1) Very little counter firing carried out as expenditure on night 24th/25th was large AAA N/29 fired 28 rounds into wire Q17c 50/60 on 24th night for retaliation requested during night but yesterday HAMEL and Right sector came in for a good deal of shelling and concentrations were given during afternoon.

(2) Artillery active around HAMEL in afternoon of 25th. AAA Quiet night AAA 13th S Battery shelled by 5.9 in delay action throughout the day - no damage but 1 gun temporarily out of action as it would be unsafe to fire through danger of bringing down emplacement.

(3) Bad light yesterday AAA Light wind S.W. this morning

[illegible]

29 DA

26

Casualties AAA

(i) Nil AAA

(ii) Nil AAA

(iii) 1 Gunr 9 Lang Batty still away. AAA
1 Bdr D/132 Regt still away AAA

(iv) All buffers full ~~AAA~~

Right Group

29 D A

27 — AAA

Intelligence 0700 26th to 0700 27th AAA

(i) Routine firing.

(ii) Hostile artillery quiet AAA
~~1400~~ ~~[illegible]~~ 12 trench mortar bombs fell in GORDON TRENCH — only 2 exploded and both were in the wire AAA T. M. located at Q18 A 05.00 just in rear of front line trench AAA
0900. 30 rounds 10.5 Trench Mortars fell in GORDON TRENCH.

(iii) 0915 working party in trench near R1 03 were dispersed were evidently repairing damage caused by artillery support fire used on night 26th – 25th AAA
1600 working party seen at R 2 d 20/80 on PUISIEUX TRENCH AAA out of range heavies informed AAA

[illegible]

29 DA

27 APP.

Casualties 27th APP

(i) Springs for 10th Battery.

(ii) NIL

(iii) 1 gun 18th Battery
1 how D/132 still away

(iv) All buffers full

R L Evans

27 OA

28 AAA

Intelligence 0700 27th to 0700 28th AAA

(i) 10th & 13th Battery were [illegible] at 0.18 c 24/70
1 gun 9th Battery also [illegible] hour AAA
D/132 [illegible], also
370th and 371st Batteries – AAA
26th Battery keeping Blockhouse [illegible]

(ii) Hamel and O.P.s in
BROUCK BENEFIT shelled
by 5.9's yesterday afternoon AAA
METNIL church spire knocked
down – otherwise quiet AAA

(iii) Hostile plane over at 7.30 AAA
observation conditions:
variable

[illegible signature]

29th DA 28/8/16

Casualties

(I) ~~Casualties~~, Springs for 26th Battery

(II) Nil

(III) 1 gun 26th Battery

1 " D/132 Still away

(IV) All Buffers full

Rt Group

29 DA 29 AAA

Intelligence 0700 28th to 0700 29th AAA

(1) Single gun 91st, ~~single how. D/132~~, and 10th Battery wire cutting AAA D/132 single how. wire cutting at Q18c 70/42 (192 rounds) AAA 13th Battery cut two lanes at Q 18 c 30/65 AAA 26th Battery firing on special points

(2) Hostile artillery shelled OPs AAA Lansdowne received a good deal of attention. D/132's O.P. two direct hits no damage. AAA about 12 4.2" fell near PROSPECT Point at 1730 AAA Gordon trench shelled with 5.9's in afternoon AAA otherwise quiet. AAA

(3) Howitzer battery – 4 separate guns at R4a 52/12 R4a 67/15 R4a 90/12 and R4c 92/95 were shelling ANCRE VALLEY South of THIEPVAL WOOD from 1745 to 2030 AAA Our heavies shooting at them was badly observed, all falling to the North of Northern most gun AAA Activity on RAILWAY ROAD was engaged by 26th Battery AAA Red Cross

wagon also seen followed by
wounded men. AAA Ahead.
5 balloons up during the day

[illegible]

29 DA

29 - NTR

Casualties 29th

(i) NIL

(ii) NIL

(iii) ~~NIL~~ 1 gun 370th Battery still away.

1 how D/132 Battery still away.

1 gun 10th Battery still away.

(iv) All buffers full

RA Group

29 DA

30 AAA

Intelligence 0700 29th to 0700 30th AAA

(i) Wire cutting – conditions bad. 10th Battery ~~1515 Bombardment~~ very good progress on wire from Q17b 90/00 to Q18c 15/90 AAA 1515 Bombardment as per programme AAA Routine firing as laid down for 2100 to 0300 in Operation Order No 57 AAA

(ii) Below normal.

(iii) 1150 British aeroplane shot down by KNIGHTSBRIDGE by German aeroplane. Two hostile planes flew low over BEAUMONT HAMEL for 90 mins unmolested. AAA Weather conditions bad

[illegible signature]

29 D A

Casualties 30 —

(i). Nil

(ii) Nil

(iii) 1 26th Battery

(iv) 1 92nd Battery

There are both at LOUVENCOURT – can arrangements be made for them to be exchanged. Please

NAA D/132 have a how. out of action but have been instructed to exchange

RA Group –

29 D.A.

31 - AAA

Intelligence 0700 30th to 0700 31st.

(i) 0815. Bombardment carried out as per programme. AAA Several batteries out of telephonic communication AAA Rounds were fired by time AAA A certain amount of wire cutting done during the day. AAA During the night 2100 30th to 0300 31st Routine firing as ordered.

(ii) Enemy did not retaliate at 0815 - But about 1045 put over a very concentrated bombardment of ROBERTS TRENCH and up as far as SHOOTERS HILL AAA otherwise quiet in trenches AAA 4 MAILLY and ENGLEBELMER WOODS shelled at 1430, and again at 2030. Again very heavily at 0430 AAA A few casualties at 1430 and several to horses AAA not

known if any during observation

(iii) Weather very bad –

N.B. 26th Battery all guns in action.

R.C. Gray

29 DA

31 KAA

Casualties

(i) NIL

(ii) 2/Lt. E. A. BUTLER wounded shell stomach — KAA

~~[illegible]~~ 3 other ranks wounded shell

370 Bty KAA

(iii) 1 gun 371 Battery — will be back tonight.

~~[illegible]~~ KAA

~~[illegible]~~

(iv) All buffers full

[illegible]

29 . DA

Intelligence 0700 31st to 0700 1st AAA

(i.) [illegible] [illegible] [illegible] AAA
wire cutting during during the day.
good results

(ii.) Very quiet. except for some
shelling of MAMETZ and O.Ps
in RIDGE trench at 1100 AAA

(iii) Wagon lines were moved
yesterday out of MARLEY
WOOD, to near BECORDEL

[illegible]

29th Division.

<u>17th BRIGADE</u>

<u>R. F. A.</u>

<u>SEPTEMBER 1 9 1 6</u>

Instructions regarding War Diaries and Intelligence Summaries are contained in F. S. Regs., Part II., and the Staff Manual respectively. Title pages will be prepared in manuscript.

WAR DIARY
or
INTELLIGENCE SUMMARY.
(Erase heading not required.)

Army Form C. 2118.

Vol 7

Hour, Date, Place	Summary of Events and Information	Remarks and references to Appendices
Volume No. 18.	WAR DIARY of 17th Bde R.F.A. 1st to 30th Sept 1916	

(103.) Wt. 3699.—854. 50,000. 10/1914.—A. T. & Co., Ltd. Forms/C. 2118/10.

Army Form C. 2118.

Instructions regarding War Diaries and Intelligence Summaries are contained in F. S. Regs., Part II. and the Staff Manual respectively. Title pages will be prepared in manuscript.

WAR DIARY
or
INTELLIGENCE SUMMARY.
(Erase heading not required.)

SEPTEMBER

Place	Date	Hour	Summary of Events and Information	Remarks and references to Appendices
ENGLEBELMER	1.		Wire cutting was continued by Batteries and all Battle Zones carefully re-registered	T.J.C.
	2.		There is nothing new to report today.	T.J.C.
	3.	0510 - 0605	The bombardment was carried out as per programme and worked very well.	
			Between 0605 and 0710 the Artillery fire was brought back to the enemy Support Line and again lifted to his Reserve Line: this Barrage was kept on at varying rates till 1410, when the Batteries ceased firing and devoted their attentions to "Sniping" mainly.	
			During the whole of the operations our Barrage was most satisfactory and the G.O.C. 116th Infantry Brigade expressed himself as very pleased with the work of the Artillery. The German Barrage was very slow in opening and at first was very wild, altho' later on our Front Line was rather heavily shelled	T.J.C.
			In the course of the night MESNIL VALLEY was shelled by 5.9" H.E. and gas shells.	
	4.		Things were fairly quiet: two bombardments were carried out at 1245 and 1530 on enemy Communications in neighbourhood of ANCRE.	
			Orders were received concerning relief of 29th Divisional Artillery by 39th Div. Arty and movement of 29th Div. Arty.	T.J.C.
	5.		This evening 13th Bty and 460th Bty and one section each of 26th and 92nd Batteries pulled out	

T2134. Wt. W708–776. 500000. 4/15. Sir J. C. & S.

Instructions regarding War Diaries and Intelligence Summaries are contained in F. S. Regs., Part II. and the Staff Manual respectively. Title pages will be prepared in manuscript.

WAR DIARY
or
INTELLIGENCE SUMMARY.
(Erase heading not required.)

Army Form C. 2118.

Place	Date	Hour	Summary of Events and Information	Remarks and references to Appendices
			to their wagon lines.	
	6.		At 1800 the 39th Div! Arty took over the line from the 29th Div! Arty.	
			The Headquarters of the Brigade were included in a bombardment of tear shells this evening – for nearly four hours the enemy swept and searched all round the orchards near ENGLEBELMER.	T.J.C.
			The remainder of the Brigade was withdrawn from the line tonight.	
AUTHIEULE	7.		The Brigade concentrated today at AUTHIEULE.	T.J.C.
	8.		The march today was to CONCHY-sur-CANCHE.	T.J.C.
	9.		MONCHY-CAYEUX was the halting place this evening	T.J.C.
	10.		The Brigade was billeted in two villages tonight — REBECQ and CRECQUES.	T.J.C.
			Orders were received this evening as to re-organization of 29th Divisional Artillery: under the new scheme the 132nd Bde will be broken up, three sections of it coming to the 17th Bde to complete its Batteries to 6 guns, and 460th Bty will be transferred to 15 Bde R.H.A. while D/132 comes to 17th Bde. Lt Col N.H.C. SHERBROOKE will command 15th Bde R.H.A., while Lt Col H.R.W. MARRIOTT-SMITH D.S.O. takes over 17th Bde R.F.A.	T.J.C.
	11.		The Brigade marched today to WAEMARS-CAPELL.	T.J.C.
			Additional orders re re-organization were received.	

T2131. Wt. W708–776. 500000. 4/15. Sir J. C. & S.

Army Form C. 2118.

Instructions regarding War Diaries and Intelligence Summaries are contained in F. S. Regs., Part II. and the Staff Manual respectively. Title pages will be prepared in manuscript.

WAR DIARY
or
INTELLIGENCE SUMMARY.
(Erase heading not required.)

Place	Date	Hour	Summary of Events and Information	Remarks and references to Appendices
POPERINGHE	12		The Brigade moved into wagon lines near POPERINGHE: Headquarters were in the town itself, while the 13th Bty, augmented by Right Section of 370th Bty under CAPT M. STAVELEY, billeted near VLAMERTINGHE and 26th Bty, plus Left Section of 370th Bty under LT EPPENHEIM, 92nd Bty plus Right Section of 369th Bty under LT F.Y. BRIGHT and D/17 were situated on the N.E. outskirts of the town.	T.J.C.
			The actual time of the change in the Brigade was 0600 this morning	
	13		The standings into which the Batteries have moved are all in a very bad way and a great deal of work is necessary before they will be fit for the rough weather in winter.	T.J.C.
	14		The day was spent in routine work.	T.J.C.
	15		An officer and two telephonists per Battery proceeded to YPRES today to get in touch with the Batteries of the 4th Division which this Div.l Arty is relieving	T.J.C.
	16		Bde Headquarters were moved to HOUTKERQUE and the Batteries went into positions round YPRES	T.J.C.
	17 18 19		Nothing to report	T.J.C.
	20		Lt Col H.R.W. MARRIOTT SMITH D.S.O, took over command of Div.l Arty while Brig Gen PEAKE went on Leave.	T.J.C.

T2134. Wt. W708—776. 500000. 4/15. Sir J. C. & S.

Instructions regarding War Diaries and Intelligence Summaries are contained in F. S. Regs., Part II. and the Staff Manual respectively. Title pages will be prepared in manuscript.

WAR DIARY
or
INTELLIGENCE SUMMARY.
(Erase heading not required.)

Army Form C. 2118.

Place	Date	Hour	Summary of Events and Information	Remarks and references to Appendices
HOUTKERQUE	21-30		There is nothing to report for this period: ~~ex~~ 93 horses were evacuated and 71 received to make up the Brigade to Establishment.	T.J.C.
			Thos. J. Cummins Lt RFA Adjutant 17 Bde RFA.	

T2134. Wt. W708–776. 500000. 4/15. Sir J. C. & S.

29th Division

17th BRIGADE

R. F. A.

OCTOBER 1 9 1 6

20

Instructions regarding War Diaries and Intelligence Summaries are contained in F. S. Regs., Part II. and the Staff Manual respectively. Title pages will be prepared in manuscript.

WAR DIARY
or
INTELLIGENCE SUMMARY.
(Erase heading not required.)

Army Form C. 2118.

Vol 8

Place	Date	Hour	Summary of Events and Information	Remarks and references to Appendices
			WAR DIARY of 17th Bde R.F.A. from 1st Oct '16 to 31st Oct. 16. Vol No 19.	

T2134. Wt. W708—776. 500000. 4/15. Sir J. C. & S.

Instructions regarding War Diaries and Intelligence Summaries are contained in F. S. Regs., Part II. and the Staff Manual respectively. Title pages will be prepared in manuscript.

Army Form C. 2118.

WAR DIARY
or
INTELLIGENCE SUMMARY.
(Erase heading not required.)

Place	Date	Hour	Summary of Events and Information	Remarks and references to Appendices
	October			
HOUTKERQUE	1–4.		Nothing to report, except that CAPT MARX, Cdg 92nd Bty was slightly wounded on 4th.	T.J.C.
	5.		Orders re relief of 29th Div Arty. by 55th Div. Arty were received.	T.J.C.
	6.		Further instructions arrived – the 17th Bde R.F.A. will be relieved by the 277th Bde R.F.A.	T.J.C.
	7.[illegible]		No new developement.	T.J.C.
	8.		Half batteries were relieved today, the personnel travelling by train from VLAMERTINGHE to the wagon lines.	T.J.C.
	9.		The remainder of the relief was carried out. Headquarters and the Batteries (less 26th) moved to wagon lines at HERZEELE. The 26th Bty changed to a wagon line near HOUTKERQUE. The guns of the incoming batteries were taken over, but they were in rather a poor state.	T.J.C.
HERZEELE	10.		The Bde (less 26th Bty) entrained at ESQUELBECQ: the times of departure were arranged as follows — 13th Bty, 0330; 92nd, 0630 and HdQrs and D/17, 0930: the first two trains were late but the third started punctually. The 26th Bty left PROVEN at 0830. All the trains were late on the journey: the first three went to LONGUEAU and the fourth to SALEUX	T.J.C.
DAOUR	11.		The Batteries moved into Camp at DAOUR, the 13th and 92nd arriving late on the 10th	

Instructions regarding War Diaries and Intelligence Summaries are contained in F. S. Regs., Part II. and the Staff Manual respectively. Title pages will be prepared in manuscript.

WAR DIARY
or
INTELLIGENCE SUMMARY.
(Erase heading not required.)

Army Form C. 2118.

Place	Date	Hour	Summary of Events and Information	Remarks and references to Appendices
	11 (contd.)		and marching on to Camp "A", North of BUIRE, Squares 17 and 18 on the forenoon of the 11th. Hd Qtrs, 26th and D/17 did not reach DAOURS until the 11th and accordingly spent the night there	1/20,000 Map 57c S.W. T.J.C.
	12.		The Bde concentrated at Camp "A".	T.J.C.
			Orders re relief of 95th Bde R.F.A. near LONGUEVAL by 17th Bde R.F.A. were received.	
	13.		The Bde Commander with representatives from each Battery went forward in the morning to reconnoitre: in the afternoon half batteries proceeded up to the line.	T.J.C.
	14.		The remainder of the Bde Staff and Batteries went into position and Lt Col H.R.W. SMITH D.S.O. took command over from Lt Col FITZGERALD D.S.O. at 6 p.m.	
			Headquarters and the Batteries forming the Group were situated as follows:-	
			HQ, S17b 4.4 (LONGUEVAL CHURCH); 13th Bty, one Section at each of M 30c 55.45, S6d 72.60, S11b 28.50; 26th S11a 6.3; 92nd S11b 2.1; D/17 S11b 2.6; B/64 (CAPT HARVEY) S11b 0.6, with one Section at M36d 48; 460th M36b 9.2.	T.J.C.
			The Wagon Lines are all in the neighbourhood of A1 and F.6	
	15.		The situation was normal, the enemy shelling the neighbourhood of FLERS intermittently all day.	T.J.C.

T2134. Wt. W708—776. 500000. 4/15. Sir J. C. & S.

Instructions regarding War Diaries and Intelligence Summaries are contained in F. S. Regs., Part II. and the Staff Manual respectively. Title pages will be prepared in manuscript.

WAR DIARY
or
INTELLIGENCE SUMMARY.
(Erase heading not required.)

Army Form C. 2118.

Place	Date	Hour	Summary of Events and Information	Remarks and references to Appendices
	16		The 12th Divl Arty. took over from the 21st Divl Arty.	57c S.W. 1/20,000
			As the Heavy Artillery was carrying out a Bombardment, the Group co-operated ~~with~~ by shelling certain trenches in the Group Zone (Line joining N19a 3.0 to N1b 4.0 — Line joining M24 b.4.0 to N1a 5.0).	
			CAPT R. MARX R.F.A., Comdg 92nd Bty R.F.A. was admitted to Fd Ambce: his wound was not healing as quickly as he had anticipated.	T.C.
	17.		Some aeroplane ~~operations~~ registrations in connection with impending operations of 18th had to be cancelled this forenoon on account of the mist.	T.C.
			CAPT M. STAVELEY R.H.A. was temporarily attached to command 92nd Bty.	
	18.		Today the 30th Division co-operated with the 9th Division in an attack on the hostile trenches from M.18.c 2.4 to the West: in particular the 17th Bde Group supported the attack on BITE Trench and BAYONET Trench from N13c 80.15 to M24 b 35.90	
			Zero was fixed for 3.40 am. and the Infantry were to attack at 3.43 after an intensive barrage by the Field Artillery on the German Front Line.	
			Reports as to the actual progress of the fighting were difficult to obtain, but apparently the Infantry found difficulty in attaining their objective on our Front in spite of the fact that Tanks	T.C.

Instructions regarding War Diaries and Intelligence Summaries are contained in F. S. Regs., Part II. and the Staff Manual respectively. Title pages will be prepared in manuscript.

WAR DIARY
or
INTELLIGENCE SUMMARY.
(Erase heading not required.)

Army Form C. 2118.

Place	Date	Hour	Summary of Events and Information	Remarks and references to Appendices
			went out to BITE and BAYONET Trenches.	
			~~At 12.15 p.m.~~ The Infantry were reported to be going to attack at 12.15 p.m. but this was put off, altho' the Group had put a Barrage on.	
			In the late afternoon the S.O.S. line was ordered to be put back to its original place, the infantry who had been in the German Front Line having apparently come back.	
			There was a very little shelling by the enemy at zero altho' he did some promiscuous shelling at different places later on in the day.	
			The weather was not very favourable to operations, as there was a lot of rain during the night and early morning.	T.J.C.
	19.		The weather was very bad all day.	
			From 4.30 ~~p.m.~~ to 6 p.m. the Germans put a heavy barrage on our front line, but did not attack, although he was reported to have attacked our Left.	T.J.C.
	20.		There was a big improvement in the weather, frost having set in during the night, it was a most favourable day for observation.	
			About 9 a.m. there was an aerial fight, in which three enemy machines were driven down, two in their own lines and one in ours.	T.J.C.

Instructions regarding War Diaries and Intelligence Summaries are contained in F. S. Regs., Part II. and the Staff Manual respectively. Title pages will be prepared in manuscript.

WAR DIARY
or
INTELLIGENCE SUMMARY.
(Erase heading not required.)

Army Form C. 2118.

Place	Date	Hour	Summary of Events and Information	Remarks and references to Appendices
			About 4pm. our Infantry on the left made a small attack and about 4.45p.m. the S.O.S. Signal was seen to go up in that direction, but the firing soon died down.	T.J.C.
			The rest of the day was quiet.	
	21.		There was very hard frost in the morning, a clear day with good observation succeeding. About 5pm. the Germans put a barrage on the Front Line in the Group Zone, to which the Group replied with a slow barrage: at 5.40 the enemy fire had completely died away, so we ceased firing.	
			During the day and night 21/22 the batteries in DELVILLE VALLEY were shelled.	T.J.C.
			In order to verify that none of the Group Batteries were firing short, the S.O.S. Barrages were fired with an officer from each Battery in the Front Line; while up on this duty LT S.W.K. CRAWFORD, 26th Bty R.F.A. was wounded in the chest by a sniper.	
	22.		There was again a good deal of frost.	
			A German Section of 5.9" Hows was very active this forenoon against the Batteries in S.11.b: they were probably shooting chiefly at the 60-pounder battery in the neighbourhood which had been very active during the night. The personnel of the batteries were withdrawn, but one shell landing on the road near II/17 killed 4 other ranks and wounded 2 other ranks.	T.J.C.

Instructions regarding War Diaries and Intelligence Summaries are contained in F. S. Regs., Part II. and the Staff Manual respectively. Title pages will be prepared in manuscript.

WAR DIARY
or
INTELLIGENCE SUMMARY.
(Erase heading not required.)

Army Form C. 2118.

Place	Date	Hour	Summary of Events and Information	Remarks and references to Appendices
	22.		One shell pitched on an ammunition dump and exploded the ammunition with the result that the whole battery position was wrecked, three guns being completely destroyed and the fourth very badly damaged: the men lost nearly all their equipment and most of the battery stores and rations were destroyed. As the whole battery was put out of action the personnel ~~was~~ withdrawn to the Wagon Lines.	
			In the afternoon the batteries were again shelled but there were no further casualties	T.J.C.
			2/Lt H.N. HENNEY, 26th Bty R and 2/Lt W.D. HART, 13th Bty were both wounded slightly but remained on duty.	
	23.		The weather was very bad today for observation.	
			The shelling was less today but there were a few rounds still falling among the batteries. 2/Lt R.H. BEAVER, 13th Bty was wounded slightly, but remained on duty. Operations for the 25th were postponed 24 hours.	T.J.C.
	24.		A heavy mist made observation very poor and on the whole the day was quiet.	T.J.C.
	~~25.~~		Operations for the 26th were postponed to 28th October.	
	25.		The enemy shelling was above normal – infantry crossing the high ground in the open being the chief target. At 4 pm. the enemy put a barrage which lasted for about	T.J.C.

T2134. Wt. W708–776. 500000. 4/15. Sir J. C. & S.

Instructions regarding War Diaries and Intelligence Summaries are contained in F. S. Regs., Part II. and the Staff Manual respectively. Title pages will be prepared in manuscript.

WAR DIARY
or
~~INTELLIGENCE SUMMARY.~~
(Erase heading not required.)

Army Form C. 2118.

Place	Date	Hour	Summary of Events and Information	Remarks and references to Appendices
			twenty minutes on our front line, to which our batteries replied.	T. J. C.
	26.		The enemy put a barrage on our front line about 10 a.m. and 5 p.m., to which the Group replied.	
			Operations ordered for 28th were postponed to 30th.	T. J. C.
	27.		The enemy put up a heavy barrage from 4.15 to 4.50 p.m.	T. J. C.
			The roads are now in a very muddy condition and transport is very difficult.	
	28.		On the whole the hostile fire was below normal. Operations were again postponed to Nov. 1st.	T. J. C.
	29.		The bad weather of the last few days became even worse today – heavy rain falling nearly all the time.	
			This evening the rear section of the 13th Battery was moved up alongside the section in S6a.	
			One section of the 92nd Bty proceeded about half way on its journey to M 29.a, but had to halt and wait for daylight before completing its move.	T. J. C.
			The 26th Battery was also to have gone forward but could not get into position owing to the mud.	
	30.		While the forenoon was dry, the afternoon and evening were very damp.	T. J. C.

Instructions regarding War Diaries and Intelligence Summaries are contained in F. S. Regs., Part II. and the Staff Manual respectively. Title pages will be prepared in manuscript.

WAR DIARY
or
~~INTELLIGENCE SUMMARY.~~
(Erase heading not required.)

Army Form C. 2118.

Place	Date	Hour	Summary of Events and Information	Remarks and references to Appendices
	30 (contd)		One gun of the section of 92nd Battery was got into position. As it was impossible to drive over the crest in day time and very bad going in the dark owing to shell holes, CAPT M. STAVELEY, Comdg 92nd Bty, had the guns ~~[illegible]~~ dismounted, placed on trollies on a light railway running ~~[illegible]~~ S.E. from HIGH WOOD, run down close to the position and afterwards manhandled into action.	T.J.C.
			The day was very bad for observation. CAPT A.S. PHILLIPS, 26 Bty was admitted to Fd Ambce, sick.	
			Operations ordered for the 1st of November were postponed until further orders.	
	31.		The second gun of the 92nd Bty was moved into position.	T.J.C.
			Enemy fire was below normal.	
			The weather showed an improvement, as there were only two or three showers during the day.	
			No 15010 Cpl Bdr S.J. MAYO, 13th Battery R.F.A. has been awarded the Serbian Gold Medal.	T.J.C.
			Lt A.E. HAYNES, D/17 was transferred to 26th Bty and 2Lt W.L. D'A. HART, 13th to 92nd Bty	

T2134. Wt. W708—776. 500000. 4/15. Sir J. C. & S.

Instructions regarding War Diaries and Intelligence Summaries are contained in F. S. Regs., Part II. and the Staff Manual respectively. Title pages will be prepared in manuscript.

WAR DIARY
or
INTELLIGENCE SUMMARY.
(Erase heading not required.)

Army Form C. 2118.

Place	Date	Hour	Summary of Events and Information	Remarks and references to Appendices
			Since coming into action on the 14th of October, four officers have been wounded (three slightly and at duty), one officer has been admitted to Field Ambulance sick and one transferred to R.F.C. as Assistant Equipment Officer (Lt M. SKITT), five other ranks were killed and 10 other ranks wounded. Thos J [illegible] Lt R.F.A.	T/C
			The demeanour of all ranks during the past 2 weeks has been admirable and under conditions of considerable hardships the men have maintained the accustomed cheeriness of the British soldier. The difficulties of getting up supplies water and ammunition have been great and mostly have been carried on horseback on unimproved paths. The movement of the return of the 92nd Battery was an achievement worthy of great skill and resource. It was hardly possible to walk over much of the country.	
			[illegible] Lt Col R.F.A. Cmdg 17 Bde RFA	

T2134. Wt. W708—776. 500000. 4/15. Sir J. C. & S.

29th Division.

17th BRIGADE

R. F. A.

NOVEMBER 1 9 1 6

Instructions regarding War Diaries and Intelligence Summaries are contained in F. S. Regs., Part II. and the Staff Manual respectively. Title Pages will be prepared in manuscript.

WAR DIARY
or
~~INTELLIGENCE~~ SUMMARY
(Erase heading not required.)

Army Form C. 2118

Vol 9

Place	Date	Hour	Summary of Events and Information	Remarks and references to Appendices
			WAR DIARY OF 17th Bde R.F.A. from 1st Nov.'16 to 30th Nov.'16. Volume No. 20.	

1875 Wt. W593/826 1,000,000 4/15 J.B.C. & A. A.D.S.S./Forms/C. 2118.

Instructions regarding War Diaries and Intelligence Summaries are contained in F. S. Regs., Part II. and the Staff Manual respectively. Title Pages will be prepared in manuscript.

WAR DIARY
or
~~INTELLIGENCE SUMMARY~~
(Erase heading not required.)

Army Form C. 2118

November

Place	Date	Hour	Summary of Events and Information	Remarks and references to Appendices
LONGUEVAL	Nov. 1st		The enemy fire was more capricious than usual ~~today~~, rounds being fired almost at random over the country. About 640 pm. a heavy barrage was opened on our left, but it died down in about twenty minutes. Some minor operations were ordered for the 2nd of the month, but were postponed to the 3rd	FRANCE 57c S.W. T.J.C.
	2nd		The operations ordered for the 3rd were postponed until further orders. Hostile aeroplanes were very active in the afternoon. The weather which was very bad in the morning improved in the afternoon	T.J.C.
	3rd		Enemy artillery was more active than usual ~~[illegible]~~ and it seemed as if some new guns were being registered on the FLERS – LONGUEVAL Valley. CAPT R. MARX, 92nd Bty R.F.A. rejoined from Field Ambulance.	T.J.C.
	4th		Hostile balloons were very active this morning, when the observation was fairly good: from midday onwards, however, it became very misty. Orders were received from 12th Div. Arty (Amendment to Operation Order No 16) ~~[illegible]~~ for operations on 5th Nov. The Infantry were ordered to take BAYONET TRENCH and GIRD SUPPORT (N13c4.2 – M24b3.9 – M18d1.1 – M18a25.15): this practically comprised the operations which had been ordered for the second of the month, being rather less ambitious. Zero hour was fixed for 9.10 am. The Major operations which had been originally projected for 25th October were announced as probably going to take place on 7th November. CAPT M. STAVELEY rejoined "Y" R.H.A. after handing over the 92nd Bty to CAPT R. MARX.	T.J.C.
	5th		The morning opened fine but very windy, very strong squalls making shooting very difficult.	

1875 Wt. W593/826 1,000,000 4/15 J.B.C. & A. A.D.S.S./Forms/C. 2118.

Instructions regarding War Diaries and Intelligence Summaries are contained in F. S. Regs., Part II. and the Staff Manual respectively. Title pages will be prepared in manuscript.

WAR DIARY
or
~~INTELLIGENCE SUMMARY.~~
(Erase heading not required.)

Army Form C. 2118.

Place	Date	Hour	Summary of Events and Information	Remarks and references to Appendices
	5th		At 0910 the bombardment and infantry attack opened simultaneously: immediate information as to what was taking place was difficult to obtain and even later on no absolutely reliable opinion of the sequence of events was easily formed. The enemy barrage opened about 7 minutes after our bombardment commenced and was very capricious and ineffective: it stopped altogether at 11 am, and was only put on at odd intervals throughout the day and for very short periods.	
			Our Infantry – 7th Australian Brigade – were not troubled much by machine guns on their way across but suffered several casualties from snipers in shell holes: according to one account we obtained a footing in the whole of BAYONET TRENCH, but according to another we did not manage to get into the portion in M18d. At any rate in those parts where we did force an entrance the enemy, who were in strong numbers at the start, were reinforced and bombed our men out, our infantry beginning to come back at 1030.	T/C.
			Owing to some misadventure the Battalion which was to have attacked on our left did not arrive so that the reserve companies from others had to be taken to make up the attacking force: when the infantry arrived in the German Trench the companies closed in and thus left the enemy more chance to bomb them out. Our infantry carried too few bombs and S.A.A., did not know the ground, were tired through incessant fatigues for the week before and suffered as there was only one wave of attack	
			In the evening orders were received that an attack was to be made again on the sixth, but these	

Instructions regarding War Diaries and Intelligence Summaries are contained in F. S. Regs., Part II. and the Staff Manual respectively. Title pages will be prepared in manuscript.

WAR DIARY
or
INTELLIGENCE SUMMARY.
(Erase heading not required.)

Army Form C. 2118.

Place	Date	Hour	Summary of Events and Information	Remarks and references to Appendices
			were cancelled about midnight.	
	6th		There was the usual firing today. At 9.45 pm the S.O.S. went up, but all became quiet again in 15 mins.	T.J.C.
	7th		The enemy artillery was less active than usual.	
			The weather was very bad – a strong gale blowing and heavy rain falling.	T.J.C.
			One howitzer of D/17 was moved into position, M 35 a 7.5 – it had to be dismounted and ~~placed in~~ run down on trucks from HIGH WOOD and then mounted and manhandled into position.	
	8th		The weather was somewhat better today, but the wind was still strong and there were showers.	
			At midnight 7th/8th, 3.40 and 5.15 pm the enemy put a barrage on our line: the Group retaliated and in all three instances his fire ceased after about quarter of an hour	T.J.C.
	9th		CAPT. MADELEY R.F.A. joined 26th Bty R.F.A. and Lt ——— 92nd Bty	
			The hostile artillery were active all day, shelling a wide area.	T.J.C.
			In the afternoon enemy balloons were up in great number, as many as 24 being counted at once	
	10th		From 9 to 11 am the Heavy Artillery bombarded the Front Line and certain points close in rear: after this had ceased the Group searched communications.	
			A hostile aeroplane was brought down by A.A. gunfire about noon near GUEDECOURT	T.J.C.
	11th		Observation conditions were very bad all day.	

T2134. Wt. W708–776. 500000. 4/15. Sir J. C. & S.

Instructions regarding War Diaries and Intelligence Summaries are contained in F. S. Regs., Part II. and the Staff Manual respectively. Title pages will be prepared in manuscript.

WAR DIARY
or
~~INTELLIGENCE SUMMARY.~~
(Erase heading not required.)

Army Form C. 2118.

Place	Date	Hour	Summary of Events and Information	Remarks and references to Appendices
			2Lt F.H.S. CAIGER, 92nd Bty was killed in the detached section this evening by a 5.9" H.E.	T.J.C.
	12th		A very heavy mist made observation impossible.	T.J.C.
			2Lt A.H. LAKE was transferred from 13th to 92nd Bty.	
	13th		In co-operation with the Fifth Army a bombardment was carried out along our front. It began at 5.45 am and went on till 6.35 am, the targets being BAYONET TRENCH, with a lift, drop back, pause and front line again with a gradual lift.	
			Observation throughout the day was very bad.	T.J.C.
			12th Div. Arty Operation Order No 18 for operations on 14th was received.	
			2Lt F.H.S. CAIGER R.F.A. was buried at M35d7.9.	
	14th		At 6.45 a.m. the 2nd Australian Division attacked GIRD and GIRD SUPPORT trenches from M24b35.95 and M24b0.5 to M18a35.10 and M18c05.90. The 18 pdr Batteries were kept on BAYONET TRENCH with the exception of B/64 which swept up to WHEAT TRENCH from 7.5 onwards. It was very difficult to obtain information as to the progress of the action especially in the Maze to the West of the Junction of BITE and BAYONET Trenches; a small trench was dug on the night 13th/14th running from M24b9.7 to 7.9, which was used for "jumping-off." The infantry managed to get into GIRD trench but owing to its very wet state found difficulty in leaving it to attack GIRD SUPPORT. The infantry, who were trying	T.J.C.

T2134. Wt. W708—776. 500000. 4/15. Sir J. C. & S.

Instructions regarding War Diaries and Intelligence Summaries are contained in F. S. Regs., Part II. and the Staff Manual respectively. Title pages will be prepared in manuscript.

WAR DIARY
or
INTELLIGENCE SUMMARY.
(Erase heading not required.)

Army Form C. 2118.

Place	Date	Hour	Summary of Events and Information	Remarks and references to Appendices
			to join up M24 b 35.95 and M24 b 85.75 were held up by a new German trench ~~at~~ from M24 b 2.7 to 6.7.	
			It was reported that while the Centre and Left Battalions had gained their objectives, the Right Battalion, who had been held up, were going to re-attack M24 a 95.50 to M24 b 15.90 from M24 b 0.4 to M24 b 2.6 at 12.30 pm. at the same time the right of the Centre Battalion was said to rest on M18 d. 1.1. This attack actually came off at 4.45 pm and failed. At 5.5 pm. the S.O.S was seen, but no further developement took place.	
			At 7 pm. the situation was reported to be as follows – Centre and Left Battalions in possession of GIRD trench from M18 c 2 8 to M24 a 88: by orders of 12th Div Arty. the fire of 17th Bde Group was brought back to the ordinary night lines.	
			During the operations 2/Lt H.H. COX B/64 was wounded slightly but remained at duty, Lt A.E.G. LEADBETTER, 460th Bty was wounded in several places in the right leg, one other rank of B/64 was killed and one other rank of 460th Bty & two other ranks of B/64 were wounded.	
			One gun of 26th Bty was completely damaged by a premature and one gun of B/64 was damaged by a direct hit on the emplacement.	T.J.C.
			Enemy aeroplanes were very active all afternoon, sailing up and down our lines at a	

T2134. Wt. W708—776. 500000. 4/15. Sir J. C. & S.

Instructions regarding War Diaries and Intelligence Summaries are contained in F. S. Regs., Part II. and the Staff Manual respectively. Title pages will be prepared in manuscript.

WAR DIARY
or
~~INTELLIGENCE SUMMARY.~~
(Erase heading not required.)

Army Form C. 2118.

Place	Date	Hour	Summary of Events and Information	Remarks and references to Appendices
			very low altitude.	T.J.C.
	15		About 12.30 a.m. the enemy put up a heavy barrage but no action resulted.	
			Owing to a heavy mist observation was very poor all day. LT EPPENHEIM 36th Bty made a reconnaissance of front line.	T.J.C.
	16		From 3.15 to 6 a.m. FLERS and the vicinity were bombarded with gas shell	
			There was intermittent shelling of the back areas all day.	
			Two aeroplanes were brought down today – the observer in one was captured, while the pilot died of his wounds.	T.J.C.
	17.		Our infantry were forced out of GIRD TRENCH today back to the line held before the operations of 14th November.	
			The Group Zone was altered today as follows – the Divisional Zone was laid down as N13d6.3 to M18a0.0. "A" Zone covered by 62nd Bde Group, N13d6.3 to N13c0.2 and "B" Zone covered by 14th Australian Bde N13b02 to M24a75.95 were covered by 17th Bde Group.	T.J.C.
	18.		There was very thick mist all day rendering observation very poor.	T.J.C.
			The enemy artillery was quiet today.	
	19.		Another quiet day with visibility poor most of the time.	
			About 2.30 p.m. the enemy put up a slight barrage on the Group Front, to which we	

Instructions regarding War Diaries and Intelligence Summaries are contained in F. S. Regs., Part II. and the Staff Manual respectively. Title pages will be prepared in manuscript.

WAR DIARY

or

~~INTELLIGENCE SUMMARY.~~

(Erase heading not required.)

Army Form C. 2118.

Place	Date	Hour	Summary of Events and Information	Remarks and references to Appendices
			replied. About 6.40 pm. there was a great deal of firing to the North of the Group Zone, but things were quiet on our front – the Group kept a slow barrage on for about quarter of an hour: ~~the~~ by 7.30 pm all was quiet again.	T/C.
	20.		New Zones were allotted at midday today: the 17th Bde Group supported the Centre Battalion from N13c0.2 — N7c5.9 to N24b75.95 — N12b3.0. This re-organization was necessary on account of the 1st Division taking over from the 2nd Australian Division.	
			The enemy artillery was more active today on the forward areas.	T/C.
			One gun of B/64 was withdrawn from ~~the~~ the forward position on the night 19th/20th: one howitzer of D/17 was withdrawn	
	21.		There was a very thick fog all the forenoon – the only time ~~that~~ visibility was good being between noon and two thirty p.m.	
			The enemy twice put a light barrage on our front to which the Group replied.	
			2Lt R.C. CHALKLEY, R.F.A. and 2Lt C. FULFORD BROWN R.F.A. joined the Brigade today and were posted to 26th and D/17 Batteries respectively: the former previously served in the 26th Battery and was invalided home about three months ago.	T/C
			One gun of B/64 and one howitzer of D/17 were withdrawn.	
	22.		The enemy artillery was quiet in the early part of the day.	

Instructions regarding War Diaries and Intelligence Summaries are contained in F. S. Regs., Part II. and the Staff Manual respectively. Title pages will be prepared in manuscript.

WAR DIARY
or
~~INTELLIGENCE SUMMARY.~~
(Erase heading not required.)

Army Form C. 2118.

Place	Date	Hour	Summary of Events and Information	Remarks and references to Appendices
			Lt Col H.R.W. SMITH, D.S.O. proceeded on leave – MAJOR C.D. UNIACKE, "B" Bty R.H.A. was attached to the Brigade to command during the C.O's absence.	
			The S.O.S. went up about midnight, but nothing happened.	
			One howitzer of D/17 was withdrawn.	T.C.
	23.		The 1st D.A. took over from the 12th D.A. at 8 a.m.	
			At this time the 17th Bde Group ceased to be responsible for the line.	
			Two guns from the forward section, 13th Bty and one from 92nd Bty forward section were withdrawn.	
	24.		A very quiet day.	
			The fourth howitzer of D/17 was withdrawn and second gun from 92nd Advanced Section	T.C.
	25.		The batteries withdrew to their Wagon Lines today – this was an operation attended with great trouble on account of the bad state of the roads and very deep mud.	
			An advance party went on to CAVALRY CAMP, MEAULTE to take over from the 79th Bde R.F.A.	T.C.
			All day the rain came down very heavily.	
	26.		The Brigade moved today from the wagon lines to MEAULTE.	
			Owing to road restrictions the batteries had to be clear off the MONTAUBAN–CARNOY	

Instructions regarding War Diaries and Intelligence Summaries are contained in F. S. Regs., Part II. and the Staff Manual respectively. Title pages will be prepared in manuscript.

WAR DIARY
or
~~INTELLIGENCE~~ SUMMARY.
(Erase heading not required.)

Army Form C. 2118.

Place	Date	Hour	Summary of Events and Information	Remarks and references to Appendices
			Road by 7.30 am.: to do this the first battery had to march out at 4 a.m. While the batteries passed CARNOY before 7.30 they were held up between that place and FRICOURT, on account of road repairs, for over two hours (this closure had never been intimated). The Brigade arrived in Camp after one o'clock – the site was very muddy, the horse-lines being worse than those left. The accomodation for the men was very poor, only seven tents per battery being available at first, but later on five more per unit were issued.	A/C.
	27.		The weather was much better today.	
			Six more tents were issued to the Brigade today.	
			2/Lt J. MORRICE, who was evacuated wounded from D/132, joined the Brigade and was posted to D/17.	A/C.
			The day was occupied in the usual Camp Routine.	
	28.		The number of sick is higher than usual – owing to the bad conditions prevailing at present.	A/C
	29		The other Brigades of the Divisional Artillery moved out today to their new Wagon Lines.	A/C.
			There are Divisional Baths close to Camp, so that opportunity is taken to give all the men a bath and a complete change.	
	30.		2/Lt J. NOWELL, D/17 was attached to 147th Bde R.F.A. to help in the liaison duties	

Instructions regarding War Diaries and Intelligence Summaries are contained in F. S. Regs., Part II. and the Staff Manual respectively. Title pages will be prepared in manuscript.

WAR DIARY

or

~~INTELLIGENCE SUMMARY.~~

(*Erase heading not required.*)

Army Form C. 2118.

Place	Date	Hour	Summary of Events and Information	Remarks and references to Appendices
			while the line was being taken over from the French.	
			During the month the following awards were made:—	
			2Lt A.W. STANFORD, 92nd Bty R.F.A. — Military Cross (for courage and resource in moving forward the section of the 92nd Battery).	
			68200 Corporal F. Bush 13th Bty R.F.A. } Military Medal	TJC
			38083 Bombardier A. Patterson 13th Bty R.F.A. }	
			40495 Sergeant W. Brough 26th Bty R.F.A. }	
			68013 Bombardier J.H. Batt 26th Bty R.F.A. }	
			44209 Sergeant H. Powrie 92nd Bty R.F.A. }	
			54625 Corporal R.F. Waterson 92nd Bty R.F.A. }	
			38092 Bombardier C.D. Ewen 92nd Bty R.F.A. }	
			Thos Cummins Lt RFA	
			C.D. Cunliffe(?) Major R.H.A., Comdg 17th Bde R.F.A.	

T2134. Wt. W708—776. 500000. 4/15. Sir J. C. & S.

29th Division.

17th BRIGADE

R. F. A.

DECEMBER 1 9 1 6

Instructions regarding War Diaries and Intelligence Summaries are contained in F. S. Regs., Part II. and the Staff Manual respectively. Title pages will be prepared in manuscript.

WAR DIARY
or
~~INTELLIGENCE~~ SUMMARY.
(Erase heading not required.)

Army Form C. 2118.

Vol 10

Place	Date	Hour	Summary of Events and Information	Remarks and references to Appendices
			WAR DIARY OF 17th Brigade R.F.A. from 1st December 1916 to 31st December 1916.	
			Vol. No 21.	1

T2134. Wt. W708—776. 500000. 4/15. Sir J. C. & S.

Instructions regarding War Diaries and Intelligence Summaries are contained in F. S. Regs., Part II. and the Staff Manual respectively. Title pages will be prepared in manuscript.

WAR DIARY
or
~~INTELLIGENCE SUMMARY.~~
(Erase heading not required.)

December 1917

Army Form C. 2118.

Place	Date	Hour	Summary of Events and Information	Remarks and references to Appendices
MEAULTE	1.		The Brigadier General R.A., Commanding Corps Artillery paid an informal visit of inspection to the camp.	
			3 18 pdr guns were handed over to a Brigade of the Guards Divisional Artillery.	T.J.C.
	2.		The Camp was inspected this morning by the XIV Corps Commander: ~~in~~ in accordance with instructions received no alteration in ordinary routine took place.	T.J.C.
	3.		A Church Parade was held in one of the huts belonging to the Corps Signal School.	
			Lts H.N. HENNEY and H. TISLEY and 4 N.C.O's proceeded to DAOURS ~~to~~ the Artillery School.	T.J.C.
	4.		30 Other Ranks went to MERICOURT to the Rest-Billets: the party, who will stay for a week, are men, who have been "off colour" and suffer from bad feet.	T.J.C.
	5.		The usual routine is carried on — in addition, there is a great deal of fatigue work to be done in straightening up the rest of the Camp, cleaning up refuse left behind by other units.	T.J.C.
	6		Lt H. EPPENHEIM and 1 Other Rank joined Corps Signalling Course.	T.J.C.
	7.		The weather broke down today.	
			This evening 118 Remounts were drawn for Corps Heavy Artillery — this Brigade was detailed for the party as through some misunderstanding the recipients did not receive the order to draw the horses.	T.J.C.

T2134. Wt. W708—776. 500000. 4/15. Sir J. C. & S.

Instructions regarding War Diaries and Intelligence Summaries are contained in F. S. Regs., Part II. and the Staff Manual respectively. Title pages will be prepared in manuscript.

WAR DIARY
or
INTELLIGENCE SUMMARY.
(Erase heading not required.)

Army Form C. 2118.

Place	Date	Hour	Summary of Events and Information	Remarks and references to Appendices
	8		The weather was again very wild today and the condition of the horse lines became very bad.	T.J.C.
			MAJOR C.D. UNIACKE rejoined "B" Battery R.H.A. today.	
	9		LT COL H.R.W. MARRIOTT SMITH D.S.O. returned from leave.	T.J.C.
	10		The weather improved somewhat, but it was still so uncertain that a Church Parade which had been ordered was cancelled.	T.J.C.
	11		Billets were arranged in MORLANCOURT for the Brigade to move into on the 12th.	T.J.C.
	12		The Brigade marched from the CAVALRY CAMP to MEAULTE to MORLANCOURT, D/17 leaving at 9, 92nd Bty 10 26th Bty 11 am. and 13th Battery 1pm.	
			While there is not much furniture in the billets, conditions are very comfortable on the whole; the men are in barns mostly, with the exception of a few who are in huts. All the 13th Battery, one section of the 26th Battery and a few horses of the 92nd & D/17 Batteries are under cover; a good deal of work will require to be done in the way of getting proper stables erected.	T.J.C.
			The move was not carried out too soon, as the weather conditions in the morning were very severe, sleet falling continuously from 4 to 10 a.m.	
	13.		A beginning was made in the work of improving the accomodation and cleanliness of	

Instructions regarding War Diaries and Intelligence Summaries are contained in F. S. Regs., Part II. and the Staff Manual respectively. Title pages will be prepared in manuscript.

WAR DIARY
or
INTELLIGENCE SUMMARY.
(Erase heading not required.)

Army Form C. 2118.

Place	Date	Hour	Summary of Events and Information	Remarks and references to Appendices
			the billets.	TJC.
	14.		Usual routine followed. 2Lt T.C. RATSEY returned from leave.	TJC
	15.		do.	TJC
	16		A visit of inspection was made by the B.G. R.A. XIV Corps, who expressed himself as satisfied with the progress made.	TJC
	17		A Church Parade was held in the disused village Church.	TJC
			MAJOR D. DALY M.C. proceeded on leave	TJC
	18		CAPT T.H. GRAY proceeded to England on a Battery Commander's Course.	
	19.		Lt. Cummins left 17th Bde. to take over the work of Staff Captain 29th D.A.	
	20.		Lt Chalkley left 17th Bde to become A.D.C. to General Rahman commanding 29th D.A.	
	21.			
	22.		Started making preparations for men's Xmas dinner. Held	
	~~22.~~		Brigade race meeting. Capt Stanford won officers race	
	23.		Orders made out for move up to the line.	

T2134. Wt. W708–776. 500000. 4/15. Sir J. C. & S.

Instructions regarding War Diaries and Intelligence Summaries are contained in F. S. Regs., Part II. and the Staff Manual respectively. Title pages will be prepared in manuscript.

WAR DIARY
or
INTELLIGENCE SUMMARY.
(Erase heading not required.)

Army Form C. 2118.

Place	Date	Hour	Summary of Events and Information	Remarks and references to Appendices
	24.		General Ashmore Commanding 29 D.A. inspected wagon lines at Dernancourt.	
	25.		XMAS DAY. Ran hares in the morning. Men had usual Xmas dinners.	
	26.		Boxing Day. Most of the Brigade officers turned out and ran hares in the afternoon. Advanced parties of Brigade (1 officer and 4 signallers per battery) went up to the line.	
	27.		1 officer and 12 men per battery went up to the line to start the relief of 15th Bde. R.H.A.	
	28.		The whole Brigade moved up to relieve 15th Bde. R.H.A in the line. Gun detachments were taken to COMBLES in motor lorries. Wagons & wagon line parties marched to CARNOY.	
	29.		Usual day in the line	
	30.		Intense bombardment from 2 to 2-30 p.m.	
	31.		Ammunition dump blown up in BARASTRE. Usual firing.	

Instructions regarding War Diaries and Intelligence Summaries are contained in F. S. Regs., Part II., and the Staff Manual respectively. Title pages will be prepared in manuscript.

WAR DIARY
or
~~INTELLIGENCE SUMMARY.~~
(Erase heading not required.)

Army Form C. 2118.

Hour, Date, Place	Summary of Events and Information	Remarks and references to Appendices
	The end of the year finds the 17 Bde in action supporting the ~~captured~~ line captured by the French NW of SAILLY SAILLISEL. The positions are ~~better than~~ at LONGUEVAL - and the ground better. The health of the brigade suffered much when first withdrawn from Longueval owing to insufficient shelter. As many as 30 men a battery were out of action. The health slowly improved after moving to billets at [illegible] but is still not good. Their spirits are good and they show little sign of the prolonged strain of the Somme fighting. A good many are getting leave - communications are improving & the work is lighter.	
31. 12. 16.	[signature] Lt Col RFA. Cmdg 17 Bde RFA.	

29th Dn

War Diaries.

17th Brigade. R.F.A.

Jany – December 1917.

Vol XI

CONFIDENTIAL

WAR DIARY

17th BRIGADE RFA

FROM 1st JANUARY 1917

To 31st JANUARY 1917

[signature]

Lt Col

Comdg

17 Brigade RFA

Army Form C. 2118.

WAR DIARY
or
INTELLIGENCE SUMMARY.
(Erase heading not required.)

Instructions regarding War Diaries and Intelligence Summaries are contained in F. S. Regs., Part II. and the Staff Manual respectively. Title pages will be prepared in manuscript.

Place	Date	Hour	Summary of Events and Information	Remarks and references to Appendices
			WAR DIARY. of 17th Brigade RFA from 1st January 1917 to 31st January 1917	
			Vol. No 22	

T2131. Wt. W708–776. 500000. 4/15. Sir J. C. & S.

Instructions regarding War Diaries and Intelligence Summaries are contained in F. S. Regs., Part II. and the Staff Manual respectively. Title pages will be prepared in manuscript.

WAR DIARY
or
INTELLIGENCE SUMMARY.
(Erase heading not required.)

Army Form C. 2118.

Place	Date	Hour	Summary of Events and Information	Remarks and references to Appendices
LEUZE WOOD	1st		Bombardment from 2pm - 3pm by all batteries except D147 (How) Enemy made no reply, but sent up rockets from front line trenches. Observing officers report damage to enemy front line. One man was wounded in D.147 battery during night 31st Dec 1st January.	KL
	2nd		Hostile shelling of BOULEAU wood and LEUZE wood above normal. Hostile Kite Balloons seen above LE TRANSLOY and REINCOURT LEY BAPAUME.	
	3rd		Hostile fire below normal.	
	4th		Hostile aeroplanes over our lines. AA guns too late in retaliation. Brigadier General of the 59th Infantry Brigade whose	
	4th		headquarters adjoin HQ of 17th Brigade had a Conference with OC Left Group (Lt. Col MARRIOTT SMITH 17th Bde RFA and Lt Col. COURAGE, 147th Brigade RFA). Our front is to be moved slightly to the right and this necessitates new orders to batteries as to 'Retaliation' 'S.O.S' 'Counterpreparation'	

T2134. Wt. W708—776. 500000. 4/15. Sir J. C. & S.

Instructions regarding War Diaries and Intelligence Summaries are contained in F. S. Regs., Part II. and the Staff Manual respectively. Title pages will be prepared in manuscript.

WAR DIARY
or
INTELLIGENCE SUMMARY.
(Erase heading not required.)

Army Form C. 2118.

Place	Date	Hour	Summary of Events and Information	Remarks and references to Appendices
LEUZE WOOD.	4th		Complete agreement was arrived at.	
	5th		Beautiful clear day. Much air activity. several fights with German aeroplanes who were flying directly over our ~~two~~ gun positions. Arrangement made for 15th Brigade RFA to take over from 147th Brigade RFA on 14th. Shell blew an infantry dugout in near our mess, one infantry man wounded (for the third time).	Kl. Kl
	6th		From 5 pm. today our front extends from U.8.c.8.1 to U.1.d.6.6. 13th Battery has moved from its old position to T23.A.7.6. taking over from 5th Batt. RFA. New SOS lines & Counterpreparation arranged.	Kl
	7th		From 8 a.m. today 97th Battery is handed over to LEFT Group Artillery.	Kl
	8th		slight frost during the night. Bombardment carried out.	
	9th		Great complaints as to shells falling short. O.C. thinks it is chiefly due to the very strong wind, but he circulated a memorandum to B.C.s impressing on them the necessity of careful checking of sights & ranges	Kl

Army Form C. 2118.

Instructions regarding War Diaries and Intelligence Summaries are contained in F. S. Regs., Part II. and the Staff Manual respectively. Title pages will be prepared in manuscript.

WAR DIARY
or
INTELLIGENCE SUMMARY.
(Erase heading not required.)

Place	Date	Hour	Summary of Events and Information	Remarks and references to Appendices
			WARWICK RHA Battery (15th Bde) take up position previously held by them, then LEFT GROUP have one more 18pr battery at T 22 a 55.65	
LEUZE WOOD	10th		From 2pm today 20th Div. Artillery take over from Guards Div Artillery; Left Group report to 20th Div Arty. Heavy shelling today; some gas shells especially near 97th Battery last night where one other rank was gassed. An aeroplane (German) flew very low over battery positions N of Combles and over valley where HQ Left Artillery & HQ 59th Infantry Brigade is situated. No British aeroplanes appeared and the antiaircraft gun fire was very wide indeed. OC Left Group (Lt Col A BARRETT SMITH DSO 17th Bde RFA) visited batteries finding 26th Battery very short of men. Ks & they are being temporarily helped by 12 men from the Trench MORTARS. There are over 100 men away from the brigade on leave courses etc	KL leave courses etc
	11th		Cold & snow. CRA 20th Div Arty called to see OC Left Group. Very heavy artillery fire on our left; little activity in our zone owing to low visibility till evening when 59th Infantry Brigade reported 5.9 German shells being put into SAILLY CHATEAU. Retaliation was ordered at 6.35pm; no report as to retaliation credible (made	KL

T2131. Wt. W708—776. 500000. 4/15. Sir J. C. & S.

Instructions regarding War Diaries and Intelligence Summaries are contained in F. S. Regs., Part II. and the Staff Manual respectively. Title pages will be prepared in manuscript.

WAR DIARY
or
INTELLIGENCE SUMMARY.
(Erase heading not required.)

Army Form C. 2118.

Place	Date	Hour	Summary of Events and Information	Remarks and references to Appendices
LEUZE WOOD	12		CRA 20th Division visited batteries. OC Left Group called on OC Right Group to discuss "SOS" on South of our zone. Cold and rain.	KC
	13th		Dull and rain. Lt. Duff RFA - orderly officer to OC 15th Brigade arrived as advance party prior to 15th Brigade RHA relieving 147 Brigade RFA in the line.	KC
	14th		15th Bde RHA relieve 147th Brigade RFA: 'L' Battery is attached to 17th Div. for tactical purposes. Cold and wet. Several salvos of 4.2 German shells on COMBLES road and up valley in evening about T20 D00	KC
	15th		Freezing. Normal gun activity } Tried to arrange with 256 Tunnelling Co to build dugouts	
	16th		Freezing. Normal firing } but they will not build unless we carry the material & we are short of man	KC
	17th		Thick snow. During night 5 men of 'L' Battery who were acting as ration party were wounded in BOULEAU WOOD by HE. One man was v. seriously wounded. Arranged with No 256 Tunnelling Co RE to assist in digging OP at SAILLY. Great difficulty in supply of labour. This Brigade has 130 away on leave, course, attached	

T2134. Wt. W708—776. 500000. 4/15. Sir J. C. & S.

Instructions regarding War Diaries and Intelligence Summaries are contained in F. S. Regs., Part II. and the Staff Manual respectively. Title pages will be prepared in manuscript.

WAR DIARY
or
INTELLIGENCE SUMMARY.
(Erase heading not required.)

Army Form C. 2118.

Place	Date	Hour	Summary of Events and Information	Remarks and references to Appendices
LEUZE	17 Jan		20 men are being borrowed from DAC & a fatigue of 6 men from each battery is being levied.	KL
	18 Jan		Colonel OC & Adjutant left early to visit sites for OP. in SAILLY. Accompanied by Major Leach MC 13th Batt. Major [illegible] MC 92nd battery & Lts. MORRISH (13th batt) and [illegible] (92nd). Visibility very low – snow and fog. Met the Divisional Commander Maj Gen Sir B de Lisle KCB who was going round batteries. 2nd Lieut K LYON RFA is appointed Adjutant from 1st Jany 1917 with [illegible] rank of Lieutenant. Bombardment arranged [illegible] [illegible] the [illegible] [illegible] to bombard [illegible] trenches [illegible] [illegible] and around SAILLISEL. Br Gen CROWELL (20th DA) Br Gen E B ASHMORE (29th DA) and Br Gen WHEATLEY (27th DA) called to see OC 17 Bde but OC had not returned from tour at SAILLY	KL KL

T2134. Wt. W708–776. 500000. 4/15. Sir J. C. & S.

Instructions regarding War Diaries and Intelligence Summaries are contained in F. S. Regs., Part II. and the Staff Manual respectively. Title pages will be prepared in manuscript.

WAR DIARY
or
INTELLIGENCE SUMMARY.
(*Erase heading not required.*)

Army Form C. 2118.

Place	Date	Hour	Summary of Events and Information	Remarks and references to Appendices
LEUZE WOOD	19		Today 15th Brigade RHA moved from LEFT GROUP of Centre Artillery to Right Group of LEFT ARTILLERY with the exception of 460th (How) battery. Guns were left in position the personnel taking over the guns of A/78 + B/78 of 78th Bde RFA, the two latter batteries taking over from 'B' & Warwick Battery. 2 Lieut COULTHARD RHA from 78th Brigade took the place of Lieut C Duff RHA 15th Brigade as Signal officer Left Group Centre Artillery.	
	20		17th Brigade ordered to accommodate 24 men of 147th Bde at gun lines for 24, 25, 26 Jan and 50 men & 100 horses at wagon line from same Brigade at same time. The 147th Bde is being brought up in view of certain operations on our left for which Left Group is to provide a Flank barrage. [illegible] Keen frost and [illegible] snow in dull weather. The two How. batteries (D/17 & 460th) are reduced to 400 rounds ammunition & consequently cannot fire their tasks as CRA	KC

Instructions regarding War Diaries and Intelligence Summaries are contained in F. S. Regs., Part II. and the Staff Manual respectively. Title pages will be prepared in manuscript.

WAR DIARY
or
INTELLIGENCE SUMMARY.
(Erase heading not required.)

Army Form C. 2118.

Place	Date	Hour	Summary of Events and Information	Remarks and references to Appendices
	20		has advised that at least 100 rounds are to be kept at these batteries per gun. The ammunition situation is not clear: 20th Div Arty state that they cannot get 4.5" ammunition easily and yet orders have been received that guns are to fire their full allowance (62 shrapnel + 187 HE for 18 pr and 212 rds HE for 4.5 How per day) as there was abundance of ammunition. CRA & Bde Major 20th DA have been informed of this situation. Shells fell on stables of adjoining Infantry Brigade killed 5 mules & wounded one man. Normal firing.	[illegible]
	21		Sunday. The Chaplain (Rev. J.W. [illegible]) administered Holy Communion in Left Group HQ office at 8.30 a.m. Four officers & 7 men communicated. Service held at D/[illegible] battery at 11 a.m. & 26th (forward) battery at 2.30 pm. Cold & frosty. Observation clearer: there is very	

WAR DIARY
or
INTELLIGENCE SUMMARY.
(Erase heading not required.)

Army Form C. 2118.

Instructions regarding War Diaries and Intelligence Summaries are contained in F. S. Regs., Part II. and the Staff Manual respectively. Title pages will be prepared in manuscript.

Place	Date	Hour	Summary of Events and Information	Remarks and references to Appendices
LEUZE WOOD	21		Considerable movement of men behind the German line. A working party of 80 was dispersed by our fire; B/78 battery fired a slow barrage from 4.45 pm to 6 pm on what appeared to be a German relief going up to the front line, when the an German aeroplane flew over SAILLY & Yesterday an F.O.O. of Right Group was sniped when observing from SAILLY CHURCH. He was shot through the jaws. Enemy artillery Quiet Day.	KL
	22		Cold + snow: morning temperature 26° F. Bombardment by left group from 2.30-3.0-3.30 pm on Enemy front Line. Enemy retaliated and counter retaliation ordered at 5 pm. At 5.30 pm FOO reported enemy shelling front line with gas shells. All batteries were ordered to "stand to" at 5.30 pm and a slow barrage of 1 round per battery per minute ordered to be fired on Enemy front line at 5.35 pm. Telephone wires to Left Battalion are broken both from Left Group RA + Infy Bde H.Q.	

T2131. Wt. W708—776. 500000. 4/15. Sir J. C. & S.

Instructions regarding War Diaries and Intelligence Summaries are contained in F. S. Regs., Part II. and the Staff Manual respectively. Title pages will be prepared in manuscript.

WAR DIARY
or
INTELLIGENCE SUMMARY.
(Erase heading not required.)

Army Form C. 2118.

Place	Date	Hour	Summary of Events and Information	Remarks and references to Appendices
	20		has advised that at least 100 rounds are to be kept at these batteries per gun. The ammunition situation is not clear: 20th Div Arty state that they cannot get 4.5 ammunition easily and yet orders have been received that guns are to fire their full allowance (62 shrapnel & 187 HE for 18 pr and 212 rds HE for 4.5 How per day) as there was abundance of ammunition. CRA & Bde Major 20th DA have been informed of this situation. Shells fell on stables of adjoining Infantry Brigade killed 5 mules & wounded one man. Normal firing.	HL
	21		Sunday. The Chaplain (Rev J W Hick (N)) administered Holy Communion in left Group HQ office at 8.30 a.m. Four officers & 7 men communicated. Service held at D/7 battery at 11 a.m & 26th (forward) battery at 2.30 pm. Cold & frosty. Observation clearer than is very	

WAR DIARY
or
INTELLIGENCE SUMMARY.
(Erase heading not required.)

Instructions regarding War Diaries and Intelligence Summaries are contained in F. S. Regs., Part II. and the Staff Manual respectively. Title pages will be prepared in manuscript.

Army Form C. 2118.

Place	Date	Hour	Summary of Events and Information	Remarks and references to Appendices
LEUZE WOOD	21		Considerable movement of men behind the German Line. A working party of 80 was dispersed by our fire. B/78 battery fired a slow barrage from 4.45 pm to 6 pm on what appeared to be a German relief going up to the front line. An enemy aeroplane flew over SAILLY. 2/Lt [illegible] an F.O.O. of Right Group was sniped when observing from SAILLY CHURCH. He was shot through the jaw. Enemy artillery quiet. Quiet Day	KL
	22		Cold + snow: morning temperature 26° F. Bombardment by left Group from 2.30-3.0-3.30pm on Enemy Front Line. Enemy retaliated and counter-retaliation ordered at 5pm. At 5.30 pm FOO reported enemy shelling front line with gas shells. All batteries were ordered to "Stand to" at 5.30pm and a slow barrage of 1 round per battery per minute ordered to be fired on enemy front line at 5.35pm. Telephone wires to Left Battalion are broken both from Left Group RA + Infy Bde H.Q.	

Instructions regarding War Diaries and Intelligence Summaries are contained in F. S. Regs., Part II. and the Staff Manual respectively. Title pages will be prepared in manuscript.

WAR DIARY
or
INTELLIGENCE SUMMARY.
(Erase heading not required.)

Army Form C. 2118.

Place	Date	Hour	Summary of Events and Information	Remarks and references to Appendices
	23rd		Clear cold weather. Morning temperature 16° F. North wind. Preparations being made for Left Group to cooperate in an attack on left on 27th. One battery is to cut wire on our own front, but to register North of front so as to put up a flank Barrage. An enemy aeroplane fell in flames S of COMBLES	
	24		Clear & cold. Temperature at 7.30 am 14° F. The Adjutant (Lt K KYON) took advantage of a lorry provided by 29 DA to proceed to AMIENS to procure necessaries and unnecessaries for the officers mess. Enemy shelling below normal. Great aeroplane activity	
	25.		Temperature 14° F. German aeroplane forced to land about 400 yds from Group HQ; aviator captured unhurt by Infantry. British plane also landed owing to bullet in petrol tank, near HQ aviator unhurt. Enemy appear to have registered several of our batteries by aeroplane in the afternoon. A/78 battery was heavily shelled by 5.9 from Magnetic bearing 61°	

Army Form C. 2118.

Instructions regarding War Diaries and Intelligence Summaries are contained in F. S. Regs., Part II. and the Staff Manual respectively. Title Pages will be prepared in manuscript.

WAR DIARY.
or
INTELLIGENCE SUMMARY
(Erase heading not required.)

Place	Date	Hour	Summary of Events and Information	Remarks and references to Appendices
	26		Temperature at 5 a.m. 11° F. at 8.30 14° F. cold wind. Enemy battery still shelling A/78 heavily, telephone pit blown in and Corporal Signaller was killed. & many telephone lines disconnected. Operation orders received for attack on 27th.	
	27		29 Division attacked enemy's front from N.36.d.4.2 to N.35.d.8.0 [Map 57.C.S.W. 1/20000], the final objective being line N.46.d.4.2 to N.36.d.2½.4 – 0.3, – N.36.c.5.6. – N.35.d.8.0. Centre Artillery ([illegible], [illegible] battery [illegible] and A/78 B/78 [illegible] Right Artillery) assisted by putting a standing barrage on line N.36.d.7.1 to O.1.a.6.9.5 and on support line N.36.d.7.8 to O.2.a.0.1½. For this operation two batteries of Left Group – Centre Artillery viz. 'B' Battery RHA and 1/1 Warwickshire Battery RHA (of 15th Bde RHA) were lent to Left Artillery in exchange for A/78 & B/78 batteries: only the	[initials]

2449 Wt. W14957/M90 750,000 1/16 J.B.C. & A. Forms/C.2118/12.

Instructions regarding War Diaries and Intelligence Summaries are contained in F. S. Regs., Part II. and the Staff Manual respectively. Title Pages will be prepared in manuscript.

WAR DIARY
or
INTELLIGENCE SUMMARY
(Erase heading not required.)

Army Form C. 2118.

Place	Date	Hour	Summary of Events and Information	Remarks and references to Appendices
			personnel was exchanged, the guns being left in their positions	
			The duties of the Left Group Centre Artillery were	
			(a) to put up a special barrage	
			(b) to arrange for a special SOS barrage	
			(c) to carry out special Howitzer tasks.	
			(a) Special barrage.	
			(i) 2 batteries (A/78 & B/78) fired on front line N.36.d.7 1 – O.31.c.3½ 0 and on support line N.36.d.7 8 – O.31.c.0 5¼	
			Three guns fired on Front line and three on support line	
			(ii) 3 batteries (92nd, 13th, 20th) fired on front line O.31.c.3½ 0 – U.1.b.3 7 and on support line ~~[illegible]~~ U.1.b.6 4½ – O.31.c.7½ 3½	
			three guns of each battery fired on front & three on support line.	

2449 Wt. W14957/M90 750,000 1/16 J.B.C. & A. Forms/C.2118/12.

Army Form C. 2118.

Instructions regarding War Diaries and Intelligence Summaries are contained in F. S. Regs., Part II. and the Staff Manual respectively. Title Pages will be prepared in manuscript.

WAR DIARY
or
INTELLIGENCE SUMMARY
(Erase heading not required.)

Place	Date	Hour	Summary of Events and Information	Remarks and references to Appendices
			(c) Howitzer Tasks. 1 Battery (A 17) one section on High ground O 25 c one " Quarry O 31 a 5.9 1 battery (460th) fired on STAR TRENCH in O 1 a. and U 1 b. (d) S.O.S. New SOS lines for 3 batteries (A/78. B/78 + 92nd) were covered from zero to plus 48 hours, the lines being N 36 a 7.1 to U. 1 d. 4½ 8½ Zero time was 5.30 a.m and fire ceased at 7 a.m 18prs fired 130 rounds per gun 4.5 Howitzer 200 rounds per battery per from 5.30 – 8.30 a.m The attack was a complete success. 1st Border Regt and 1st Inniskilling Fusiliers attained their object and report received states that the barrage was most successful	JCL

Instructions regarding War Diaries and Intelligence Summaries are contained in F. S. Regs., Part II. and the Staff Manual respectively. Title Pages will be prepared in manuscript.

WAR DIARY
or
INTELLIGENCE SUMMARY
(Erase heading not required.)

Army Form C. 2118.

Place	Date	Hour	Summary of Events and Information	Remarks and references to Appendices
			6 German officers and 321 German soldiers were captured unwounded together with 2 machine guns. Our casualties were about 130; five infantry officers were killed by one shell.	
			The Germans made no counter attack, but shelled SAILLY rather heavily. At 5pm, 7pm, 9pm all the guns in the Corps that could reach LE TRANSLOY fired 3 rounds gunfire. Morning Temperature 14° F.	KL
	28		Temperature 14° F. Enemy shelled 26th, 92nd, 13th batteries heavily. One gun of 13th battery was badly damaged, one of the 92nd had a wheel broken and one of 26th the trail split. There were no casualties to personnel. 2nd Lt. C FULFORD BROWN - D/17 - wounded in face and ankle by H.E. while F.O.O.?	KL.
			17th Div Arty HQ relieved 20th Div Arty HQ at 10. a.m.	
	29		A/78 & B/78 batteries returned to their old positions, Warwickshire & "B" RHA batteries rejoining left group. Lt Col. SHERBROOKE OC 15th Bde RHA and his adjt Lt IDESON joined Left Group HQ.	KL

Army Form C. 2118.

WAR DIARY
or
INTELLIGENCE SUMMARY
(Erase heading not required.)

Instructions regarding War Diaries and Intelligence Summaries are contained in F. S. Regs., Part II. and the Staff Manual respectively. Title Pages will be prepared in manuscript.

Place	Date	Hour	Summary of Events and Information	Remarks and references to Appendices
	29		Enemy shelled COMBLES GUILLEMONT road and 26th battery. Very cold. Morning temperature 15° F.	KC
	30		Morning Temperature 14° F. Usual day and night firing.	
	31		Morning Temperature 15° F. No receipts of special notice as regards operations. As regards organisation, the decision to make 4.5 Howitzer batteries of 6 howitzers instead of 4 came in at 6 pm. D/17 is split up, right section with 2Lt PILLING, 2Lt NOWELL goes to 460th battery in 15th Bde RHA, and left section with Captain GREY and 2Lt ~~[illegible]~~ DISLEY go to D/147 battery at [illegible] which hitherto belonged to 147 Brigade RFA. D/147 now became D/17, with one section in action and 2 sections under Captain HOLMES in rest at MORLANCOURT. No movement of personnel or guns is to take place as yet, but from today the battery as reconstituted is administered by 17th Brigade RFA.	

2449 Wt. W14957/M90 750,000 1/16 J.B.C. & A. Forms/C.2118/12.

Instructions regarding War Diaries and Intelligence Summaries are contained in F. S. Regs., Part II. and the Staff Manual respectively. Title Pages will be prepared in manuscript.

WAR DIARY
or
INTELLIGENCE SUMMARY
(Erase heading not required.)

Army Form C. 2118.

Place	Date	Hour	Summary of Events and Information	Remarks and references to Appendices
			During the month the following awards were made	
			1st January Major R S LEACH Commanding 13th Battery, Military Cross	
			" Major A MARX " " 92nd " " "	
			" No 1031 Staff Sgt D.K. GLASS. ASC 17 Bde HQ D.C.M.	
			" No 5772 Corporal S E LAWRENCE. RA 17 Bde HQ D.C.M.	
			During the month the following officers joined the Brigade	
			2.1.17 2Lt. E H DIMMERMAN 13th Battery	
			" " 2Lt. A E THOMPSON " "	
			18.1.17 Capt. A S PHILLIPS " "	
			7.1.17 Lieut. J C LISTER 26th "	
			25.1.17 2Lt. J CAZENAVE 92nd "	
			" 2Lt. A E TERRY 26th "	

2449 Wt. W14957/M90 750,000 1/16 J.B.C. & A. Forms/C.2118/12.

Army Form C. 2118.

WAR DIARY
or
INTELLIGENCE SUMMARY
(Erase heading not required.)

Instructions regarding War Diaries and Intelligence Summaries are contained in F. S. Regs., Part II. and the Staff Manual respectively. Title Pages will be prepared in manuscript.

Place	Date	Hour	Summary of Events and Information	Remarks and references to Appendices
			During the month the following awards were made.	
			1st January. Major R S LEACH. Commanding 13th Battery, Military Cross.	
			" Major A MARK " " 92nd " "	
			" No 1031 Staff Sergt D K GLASS AOC, 17th Bde HQ D.C.M.	
			" No 5772 Corporal S E LAWRENCE. HQ 17 Bde HQ DCM.	
			During the month the following officers joined the Brigade.	
			2.1.17 2 Lt E H THONEMAN 13th Battery	
			" " 2 Lt H E THONEMAN " "	
			16.1.17 Capt. A S PHILLIPS " "	
			17.1.17 Lieut. J C LISTER 26th "	
			25.1.17 2 Lt. J CAZENAVE 92nd "	
			" " 2 Lt. A F TERRY D/17	

2449 Wt. W14957/M90 750,000 1/16 J.B.C. & A. Forms/C.2118/12.

29 Div

CONFIDENTIAL

WAR DIARY

of

17th Brigade RFA

from 1st February 1917

to 28th February 1917

Vol. No. 23

Vol 12

Instructions regarding War Diaries and Intelligence Summaries are contained in F. S. Regs., Part II. and the Staff Manual respectively. Title Pages will be prepared in manuscript.

WAR DIARY
or
INTELLIGENCE SUMMARY
(Erase heading not required.)

Army Form C. 2118.

Place	Date	Hour	Summary of Events and Information	Remarks and references to Appendices
			February 1917	
LEUZE WOOD T.20.D.4.0	1.2.17		Hard frost. Usual day and night firing. Corps orders that work on gun positions for overhead cover [illegible] be pressed on.	
	2.2.17		Usual day + night firing. 2nd Lt W. E. Russell 26th battery posted to Trench Mortars. 2Lt J.P. BOSMAN returns from [illegible] Trench Mortars & is posted to 26th Battery	

2449 Wt. W14957/M90 750,000 1/16 J.B.C. & A. Forms/C.2118/12.

Instructions regarding War Diaries and Intelligence Summaries are contained in F. S. Regs., Part II. and the Staff Manual respectively. Title Pages will be prepared in manuscript.

WAR DIARY
or
INTELLIGENCE SUMMARY
(Erase heading not required.)

Army Form C. 2118.

Place	Date	Hour	Summary of Events and Information	Remarks and references to Appendices
LEUZE WOOD T.21.d.4.0	3rd		Temperature 12½°F. Enemy shelled SAILLY heavily at 5-30pm – 5.45pm. Retaliation ordered by Left Group. No signs of Thaw: Special precautions have been taken to deal with difficulties arising from Thaw; special Iron rations held in readiness for whole Brigade at Wagon Line as French authorities will close roads to Lorries immediately Thaw sets in. Large amount of ammunition are being drawn by batteries while ground is hard, so that all [illegible] have well over 3000 rounds at the Gunpits	
	4th		Hard frost. Usual day and night firing. Batteries working on providing overhead cover for guns.	
	5th		Thermometer at zero. Nothing of importance. Lovely weather	

2449 Wt. W14957/M90 750,000 1/16 J.B.C. & A. Forms/C.2118/12.

Army Form C. 2118.

Instructions regarding War Diaries and Intelligence Summaries are contained in F. S. Regs., Part II. and the Staff Manual respectively. Title Pages will be prepared in manuscript.

WAR DIARY
or
INTELLIGENCE SUMMARY
(Erase heading not required.)

Place	Date	Hour	Summary of Events and Information	Remarks and references to Appendices
	6.2.17.		Left Group reserved to assist ~~left~~ artillery Right Group in forthcoming operation. Registration begun	
	7.2.17		Frosty. Registration completed for attack to begin on 8th	
	8.2.17		Frosty. Left Group put up standing barrage to support infantry attack. Infantry gain objective (Trench in U.15.c.05.70 – U.14.b.55.20) 63 prisoners and one machine gun captured. Enemy shell SAILLY SAILLISEL very heavily especially at 5pm & 8pm. Infantry at 8pm asked for S.O.S which was given very promptly by the artillery.	
	9.2.17		Still frosty temperature 12°F. SAILLY SAILLISEL shelled.	
	10.2.17		Frost continues. Enemy heavily shell 'L' battery of right group left artillery (L Batty RHA 15th Bde RHA) 2 guns destroyed. No artillery [illegible] BOSNIA Trench heavily for an hour.	

2449 Wt. W14957/M90 750,000 1/16 J.B.C. & A. Forms/C.2118/12.

Instructions regarding War Diaries and Intelligence Summaries are contained in F. S. Regs., Part II. and the Staff Manual respectively. Title Pages will be prepared in manuscript.

WAR DIARY
or
INTELLIGENCE SUMMARY
(Erase heading not required.)

Army Form C. 2118.

Place	Date	Hour	Summary of Events and Information	Remarks and references to Appendices
	11.2.17		Temperature rises but is still below freezing point. Intermittent bombardment by Left Group artillery on BOSNIA Trench during night	
	12.2.17		Temperature rises in day time above freezing point. Cold at night. Usual day & night firing. Enquiry held into alleged short shooting by artillery during action of 11th	
	13.2.17		Glorious day. Several officers of 17th & 75 Brigade attended lecture on Courts Martial at HEILLY. Lt Col H R W MARRIOTT SMITH DSO Comdg 17th Bde RFA proceeds on leave to England.	
	14.2.17		Nothing to report.	
	15.2.17		Usual day & night firing. Slight frost.	
	16.2.17		Thaw sets in. Ammunition dump at PLATEAU blown up by enemy aeroplane bombs. Explosions continue all day	

2449 Wt. W14957/M90 750,000 1/16 J.B.C. & A. Forms/C.2118/12.

Army Form C. 2118.

Instructions regarding War Diaries and Intelligence Summaries are contained in F. S. Regs., Part II. and the Staff Manual respectively. Title Pages will be prepared in manuscript.

WAR DIARY
or
INTELLIGENCE SUMMARY

(Erase heading not required.)

Place	Date	Hour	Summary of Events and Information	Remarks and references to Appendices
	17th		Warm and very rapid thaw. Transport difficult.	
	18th		Thaw precautions adopted. No lorries or wagons to move on roads other than those for supplies: all wagons to be drawn by 2 horses only and light loaded. Lt Col H. SHERBROOKE RHA (acting OC Left Group Centre artillery in place of Lt Col MARRIOTT SMITH on leave) reconnoitres for positions for 5 batteries to be brought in for an operation; arrangements being pressed on for building OPs in SAILLY and a forward HQ for Left Group Centre artillery.	
	19th			
	20th		Foggy. Col SHERBROOKE visits all batteries & Brigade & Battalion HQ & OP at SAILLY. Maj Gen Sir H de B de LISLE and Br Gen WARDROP reconnoitre forward positions. 2nd Lt Sackston RFA 13th Battery Ptn acting as Guide	

Army Form C. 2118.

WAR DIARY
or
INTELLIGENCE SUMMARY

(Erase heading not required.)

Instructions regarding War Diaries and Intelligence Summaries are contained in F. S. Regs., Part II. and the Staff Manual respectively. Title Pages will be prepared in manuscript.

Place	Date	Hour	Summary of Events and Information	Remarks and references to Appendices
	20.2		Bombardment of enemy trenches in U.8.b. from 3pm to 4pm. Enemy put up short barrage of HE & gas shell at 11.15 am and again at 2.15 pm across valley from HALL WOOD southwards. [illegible] 26th Battery cut wire for proposed operation.	
	21.2.17		Foggy. Arrangements made to move a section of Warwick Battery forward for wire cutting. Warwick Battery RHA and 26th Battery begin wirecutting.	
	22.2.17		Batteries of Army Brigades move into position to reinforce artillery for forthcoming operation. A/76 battery is attached to Left Group for this purpose. Registration very difficult owing to foggy weather.	
	23.2.17		Bombardment arranged for today is postponed. Still foggy.	
	24.2.17		Bombardment ordered for 23rd takes place: considerable damage done to Enemy Trenches.	

2449 Wt. W14957/M90 750,000 1/16 J.B.C. & A. Forms/C.2118/12.

Instructions regarding War Diaries and Intelligence Summaries are contained in F. S. Regs., Part II. and the Staff Manual respectively. Title Pages will be prepared in manuscript.

WAR DIARY
or
INTELLIGENCE SUMMARY
(Erase heading not required.)

Army Form C. 2118.

Place	Date	Hour	Summary of Events and Information	Remarks and references to Appendices
	24.2.17.		Wire cutting continues.	
	25.2.17		Wire cutting continues: observation difficult owing to mist. D/17 battery is moved up to forward position, two sections being brought up from MORLANCOURT to complete the battery. Bombardment of enemy trenches, postponed on 24th, takes place.	
	26.2.17		Registration for barrage on 28th completed: wire cutting continued: barrage lines are U.8.d.8.½ to U.8.d.4.6.	
	27.2.17		Final test for barrage to support Infantry on 28th carried out. wire cutting continues.	
	28.2.17		Operations begin: ~~at~~ 5.25 a.m. zero hour, and ~~bombardment~~ barrage opened at that time. Infantry of 29th Division carry objectives, 2 officers and about 60 prisoners taken. Later enemy recover a portion of PALZ trench and the line finally held by us extends from U.8.d.2.6 to U.8.d.6	

2449 Wt. W14957/M90 750,000 1/16 J.B.C. & A. Forms/C.2118/12.

Army Form C. 2118.

WAR DIARY
or
INTELLIGENCE SUMMARY
(Erase heading not required.)

Instructions regarding War Diaries and Intelligence Summaries are contained in F. S. Regs., Part II. and the Staff Manual respectively. Title Pages will be prepared in manuscript.

Place	Date	Hour	Summary of Events and Information	Remarks and references to Appendices
	20.2.17.		Enemy retaliate with very heavy barrage on SAILLY. 2nd Lieut W.F MORRISH RFA, 13th Battery acted as Liaison Officer with the infantry. ~~and~~ The Corps Commander congratulates the Infantry and the artillery, saying that the barrage was admirable. The ~~&~~ 17th Brigade suffered no casualties, but the 15th Brigade RHA lost two Officers and two men killed and 4 men wounded. The two officers were Captain G H BAILEY, 'L' Battery RHA and Captain D.A GYE, 'L' Battery RHA Lt Col HRW MARRIOTT SMITH DSO returned from leave in England	

Instructions regarding War Diaries and Intelligence Summaries are contained in F. S. Regs., Part II. and the Staff Manual respectively. Title Pages will be prepared in manuscript.

WAR DIARY
or
INTELLIGENCE SUMMARY
(Erase heading not required.)

Army Form C. 2118.

Place	Date	Hour	Summary of Events and Information	Remarks and references to Appendices
	February.		The three events of the month have been the prolonged hard frost which we have all preferred to unutterable wet and mud, the lamented severance from our old comrades of the 147 Bde who have become an army brigade — and the success of our own gallant infantry on the 27th. The end of the month finds us still very short of men — much important work being delayed thereby. Batteries have made progress in bomb proof cover [illegible] down for their men. Leave allotment has been more generous and the men who served since the landing in Gallipoli have now been home.	
			[illegible signature] Lt Col RFA. Cmdg 17 Bde RFA.	

2449 Wt. W14957/M90 750,000 1/16 J.B.C. & A. Forms/C.2118/12.

Instructions regarding War Diaries and Intelligence Summaries are contained in F. S. Regs., Part II., and the Staff Manual respectively. Title pages will be prepared in manuscript.

WAR DIARY
or
INTELLIGENCE SUMMARY.
(Erase heading not required.)

Army Form C. 2118.

Hour, Date, Place	Summary of Events and Information	Remarks and references to Appendices
Month of February 1917	The prolonged frost improved the health of the men. The ground is now dryer than it has been for months, and movement is correspondingly easier. Since the 20th the Bde has been supporting its own infantry for the first time since October. Progress in construction has been made. Nearly all men of detachments of gun batteries are now 30' below ground – & railways have been layed to the positions for the carriage of ammunition & sights during the month. 5 guns hit. v. few casualties. H. A. Smith Lt Col RFA Comdg 17 Bde RFA.	

Vol 13

CONFIDENTIAL

WAR DIARY

—

MARCH 1917

—

17th Brigade RFA

—

Vol. 24

Instructions regarding War Diaries and Intelligence Summaries are contained in F. S. Regs., Part II., and the Staff Manual respectively. Title pages will be prepared in manuscript.

Army Form C. 2118.

WAR DIARY
or
INTELLIGENCE SUMMARY.
(*Erase heading not required.*)

Hour, Date, Place MARCH		Summary of Events and Information	Remarks and references to Appendices
HQ. Left Group. CENTRE ARTILLERY T.20.D.4.0	1.	Germans make several attacks on our new trenches especially bombing attacks. Several calls for SOS which were quickly answered by our artillery.	
	2.	Continued bombing attacks: infantry consolidate the new trenches except for one portion	
	3	Nothing to report.	
	4	Usual day & night firing	
	5.	Snowy night. Left Group which was Centre Arty is reorganised, 15th Bde RHA being placed under Right Group Left Artillery, 17 Brigade RFA acting as subgroup to Left Group Rt. Artillery under Lt Col BUZZARD DSO.	

(103.) Wt. 3699.—854. 50,000. 10/1914.—A. T. & Co., Ltd. Forms/C. 2118/10.

Instructions regarding War Diaries and Intelligence Summaries are contained in F. S. Regs., Part II., and the Staff Manual respectively. Title pages will be prepared in manuscript.

WAR DIARY
or
INTELLIGENCE SUMMARY.
(Erase heading not required.)

Hour, Date, Place		Summary of Events and Information	Remarks and references to Appendices
T. 20. D. 4 0 Leuzewood	6.3.17	Very quiet: misty.	
	7.3.17	Much enemy sniping at our new trenches near SAILLY – an officer of Warwick RHA battery (2nd Lt Swan) being killed. Day & night firing as usual. Cold	
	8.3.17	Reft Group assist in bombardment of enemy trenches near 'BOSNIA'. Heavy artillery carrying out chief part. Frosty	
	9.3.17	Frosty & snowy. Nothing of importance. Visibility poor. Gen Evidence accumulating that Germans contemplate a retirement to ARRAS CAMBRAI S. QUENTIN Line Evidence chiefly from prisoners especially officers servants.	
	10.3.17		

(103.) Wt. 3699.—854. 50,000. 10/1914.—A. T. & Co., Ltd. Forms/C. 2118/10.

Instructions regarding War Diaries and Intelligence Summaries are contained in F. S. Regs., Part II., and the Staff Manual respectively. Title pages will be prepared in manuscript.

WAR DIARY
or
INTELLIGENCE SUMMARY.
(Erase heading not required.)

Army Form C. 2118.

Hour, Date, Place	Summary of Events and Information	Remarks and references to Appendices
Leuze Wood		
10.3.17	29th D.A. are warned to be ready to move. Necessary action as to reduction of surplus kit repair to wagons etc to be carried out.	
11.3.17	Batteries ordered to fire a small amount of ammunition only except in case of enemy attack	
12th + 13th	Very quiet indeed.	
14.3.17	No firing on marshy ground in front of recently captured trenches as Infantry patrols are being sent out into No mans Land to gather accurate information	
15.3.17	Infantry continue patrolling ground beyond new trenches. Very little firing. Evidence daily accumulating as to German	

Instructions regarding War Diaries and Intelligence Summaries are contained in F. S. Regs., Part II., and the Staff Manual respectively. Title pages will be prepared in manuscript.

WAR DIARY
or
INTELLIGENCE SUMMARY.
(Erase heading not required.)

Army Form C. 2118.

Hour, Date, Place	Summary of Events and Information	Remarks and references to Appendices
15 3 17	Proposals to retire. A captured document states that retirement is to be completely 25th March.	
16.3.17	Preparations being made by 17th Brigade for withdrawal. GOC has frequently been round wagon lines and the orders given by him as to making preparations for mobile warfare are being carried out.	
17.3.17	Glorious day – no shooting.	
18.3.17	Fine & warm. 17th Brigade RFA warned to be ready to move in 3 days time.	
19.3.17	Half of each battery is withdrawn from	

(103.) Wt. 3699.—854. 50,000. 10/1914.—A. T. & Co., Ltd. Forms/C. 2118/10.

Instructions regarding War Diaries and Intelligence Summaries are contained in F. S. Regs., Part II., and the Staff Manual respectively. Title pages will be prepared in manuscript.

WAR DIARY
or
INTELLIGENCE SUMMARY.
(Erase heading not required.)

Army Form C. 2118.

Hour, Date, Place	Summary of Events and Information	Remarks and references to Appendices
19.3.17	to wagon lines. No firing by remainder. Germans have apparently retreated well out of range - 2/Lt. Remington RFA, 26th battery, reached Le MESNIL & Le Transloy finding no Germans there. Cavalry patrols sent out.	
HQ CARNOY 20.3.17	Remaining half batteries move to wagon lines at CARNOY	
HQ MORLANCOURT 21.3.17	Brigade marches to MORLANCOURT, filling with ammunition at PLATEAU on the way.	
22.3.17	Preparations made for training Brigade in open warfare. Map reading, communication, ranging, reconnaissance etc carried out. Orders suddenly received at 4pm to move next morning	
23.3.17 HQ FRANVILLERS	Brigade marches to FRANVILLERS via TREUX MERICOURT.	

HQ FLESSELLES. 24. 3. 17. Brigade marches to FLESSELLES via VILLERS BOCAGE. orders were given to march via TALMAS & NAOURS, but owing to traffic this was found ~~poss~~ impossible. Summer Time adopted 11 p.m. 24th becoming midnight.

25. 3. 17 Rest day

HQ BEAUCOURT 26. 3. 17. Brigade marches to BEAUCOURT via CANAPLES. BERNAVILLE

27. 3. 17 Brigade marches to FREVENT area. 26th & 92nd battery billeting at Petit BOURET, HQ and 13th & D/17 billeting at HONVAL

HQ HONVAL

28. 3. 17. Brigade marches to its new wagon line at GOUVES, via AVESNE-LE-COMTE and HABARCQ. Advance party including Lt Col. H MARRIOTT SMITH DSO, two officers per battery + 25 men per battery move up to ARRAS.

~~HQ~~

HQ ARRAS.

29 3 17 17th Brigade with 15th Brigade RHA form 'Left Group Artillery' under 12th D.A. Br. Gen. WILLIS

30. 3. 17 Batteries prepare positions and draw ammunition

30. 3. 17 Batteries guns & Howitzers came up from wagon Line on
ARRAS night of 30/31

31. 3. 17 Batteries register their Zones. 17th Brigade is to advance during the battle if operations are projected are successful. Battle wagon Lines reconnoitred. Preparations as to rations & water made. On Zero day 3 days rations are to be at guns.

Five men from D/17 wounded [illegible] while working on ammunition.

General remarks An uneventful month except so far as fighting is concerned. The German retirement left the Combles area comparatively peaceful. Reconnaissance of German old lines showed them to be very wet and exposed to our fire. Many Germans ~~[illegible]~~ & men of 29th Div. Infantry were found unburied. The Brigade buried a considerable number. Health of troops very good and very few casualties sustained. The march from COMBLES to Arras was interesting and a pleasant change after Angouts.

Kenneth [illegible] Lt Col
[illegible] 17th RFA [illegible]

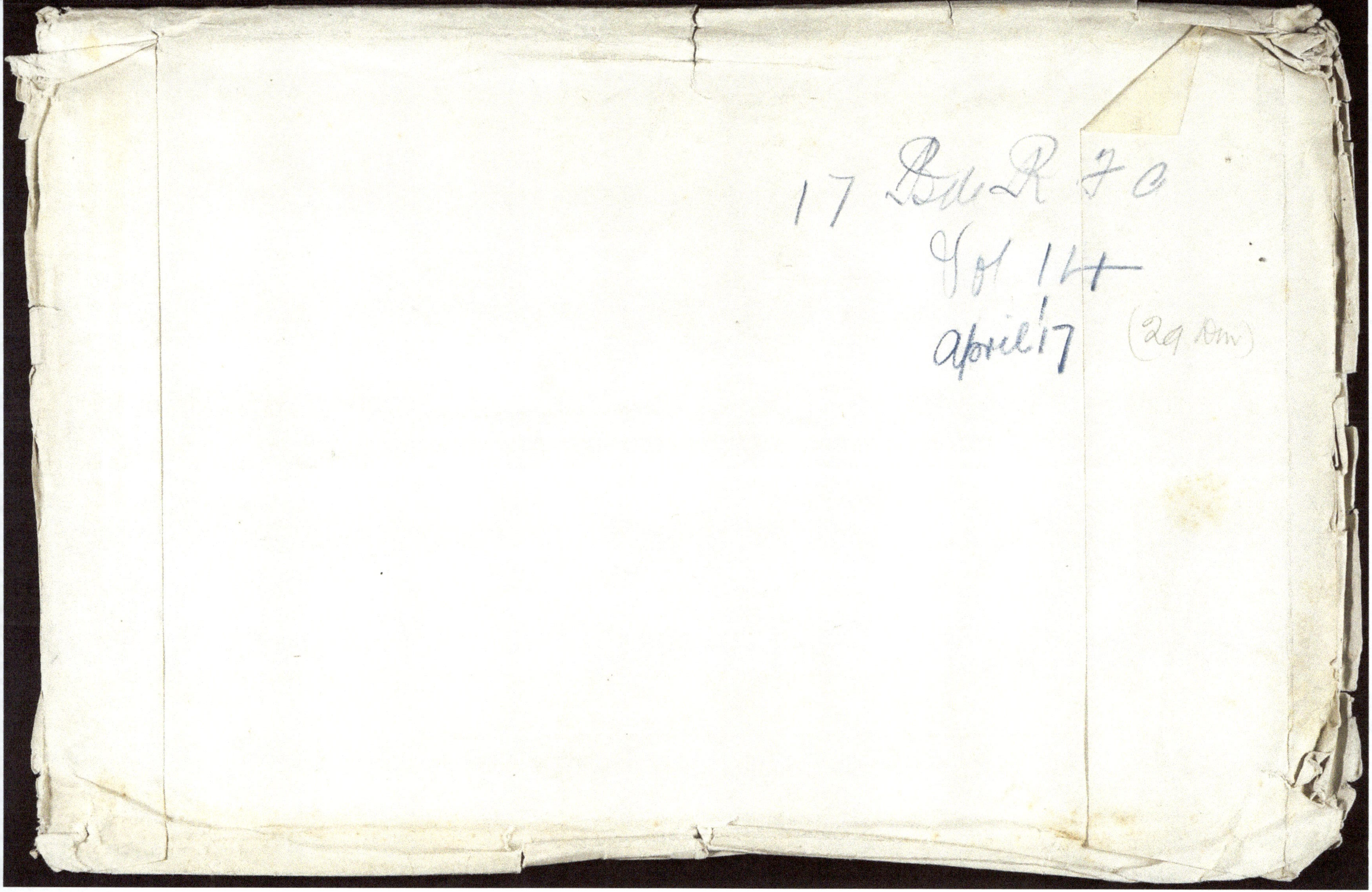
17 BdeR FC
Vol 14
April 17
(29 Dw)

On His Majesty's Service.

CONFIDENTIAL WARDIARY

—

17th BRIGADE RFA

—

APRIL 1–30

1917

Vol 25

H.Q. 4 Rue St BARBE. ARRAS.	April 1st 1917	17th Bde RFA with 15th Bde RHA form Left Group under 12th Div. Arty and will support attack on German lines by 12th Division with 15th and 3rd Division. Both Brigades will take part in preliminary bombardment for four days. On Zero Day, at zero + 2½ hours if the attack on the first German line is successful the 17th Brigade will limber up and advance to gun positions just in rear of our present front line. Batteries complete their gun positions, register and take in ammunition
	April 2nd	Registration continues. The track along which 17 Brigade will advance is prepared and artillery bridges laid across the trenches by 2Lt Hilary RFA 92nd Battery.
HQ Faubourg St SAUVEUR ARRAS	April 3rd	Lt Col HRW Marriott Smith DSO, 2Lt. TE Ratsey with servants and 6 signallers move to battle HQ. which is H.Q. of 36th Infantry Brigade (Br. Gen OWEN). All wires laid. The adjutant (Lt K Lyon RFA) with the adjutant of 15th Bde. RHA (Lt CP Duff) remains at 4 Rue St Barbe to deal with administration.

[illegible]

[illegible]

Ap. 3. A shell burst in the kitchen of 4 Rue St Barbe killing two men and wounding two men of 15th RHA Brigade.
Capt. V.O. Dolphin RFA arrives to take command of 26th Battery vice Major D. Daly MC RFA appointed Brigade Major 41st Dn. Capt. A.W. Stanford who had been transferred from 92nd battery to command 26th battery will continue to 'shoot' the battery during the battle as Capt Dolphin will not have time to get a complete grasp of the various details. Bombardment is to begin tomorrow 'V' day.

Ap 4. 'V' Day. Bombardment begins. Arrangements made for Brigade to have 3 days rations in hand on 'Z' day, and 2 days forage. The animals are being very hard worked and have been put on 13lbs oats.

Ap. 5. 'W' day. Bombardment continues. D/17 battery suffer casualties

2Lt C.D. COOPER wounded.
12976 Br GILL J. killed
50869 Sgt. RUSSELL W.H. wounded
26536 Sgt H. HEWITT H " "

[illegible]

Ap. 6 'X' day – Bombardment continues. Wire cutting appears good, but from aeroplane photographs ~~reveal~~ the second line works of the Germans do not appear very badly damaged. Enemy shell station + goods yard blowing up 5 limbers and wagons of D/17 battery. 'Z' day postponed and tomorrow is Q day. [Good Friday today].

Ap. 7 'Q' day. Bombardment continues. Batteries fire more shrapnel than hitherto.

Ap. 8 'Y' day. Tonight horses + wagon lines move from GOUVES to G.19.b just outside Arras, in readiness to move up to gun positions tomorrow. Batteries ~~are to~~ have had 12000 rounds of ammunition at their present gun positions and 3000 more at the forward positions to which they will move if the advance is a success.

Easter Sunday.

] See Map appendix. ARRAS. 57b NW3 Ed. 7a 1/10.000

Instructions regarding War Diaries and Intelligence Summaries are contained in F. S. Regs., Part II. and the Staff Manual respectively. Title pages will be prepared in manuscript.

WAR DIARY
or
INTELLIGENCE SUMMARY.
(Erase heading not required.)

Place	Date	Hour	Summary of Events and Information	Remarks and references to Appendices
HQ ARRAS.	9th		Easter Monday. The general attack by the III Army, postponed from Easter Sunday, took place at 5.30 am this morning. 29th Divisional Artillery supported the attack made by the 36th Infantry Brigade under Br Gen OWEN. 17th Brigade RFA together with 15th Brigade RHA formed a Group under Lt Col. HRW MARRIOTT SMITH DSO Comdg. 17th Brigade RFA. Lt EPPENHEIM 26th battery was Brigade FOO and went over the top with the infantry. The attack began in a storm of wind and sleet but was generally successful, the first objective known as 'BLUE LINE' being ~~took~~ captured according to programme, except where the Infantry were held up by strong points such as HERON WORK (see MAP attached), when the barrage got some distance ahead of them. 17th Bde RFA had orders to advance if possible two and three ~~[illegible]~~ hours after the attack began. The capture of BLUE LINE was to be the signal for the ~~attack~~ advance. At 8.50 am the teams,	

Instructions regarding War Diaries and Intelligence Summaries are contained in F. S. Regs., Part II. and the Staff Manual respectively. Title pages will be prepared in manuscript.

WAR DIARY
or
INTELLIGENCE SUMMARY.
(Erase heading not required.)

Army Form C. 2118.

Place	Date	Hour	Summary of Events and Information	Remarks and references to Appendices
			which had moved up during the night from GOUVES to an open field just W of ARRAS, behind the BUTTE de TIR, appeared at the gun positions, having suffered only one casualty, & that too from our own 18 pr premature firing from the Railway.	
			At about 11 am the order to advance was received and the guns were limbered up and advanced over a rough track and across trenches ~~bridge~~ roughly bridged the previous week by the gunners of the 92nd battery. The enemy shelled the batteries with 4.2 & some 5.9 shells, but only one man & 6 horses were wounded while advancing to the forward position which was soon left alone by the retreating enemy. Attached map shows ~~Al...~~ route and battery positions.	
			At 12 noon orders were received that the attack on the second objective (The BROWN LINE) would take place according to programme i.e. the barrage was to be put down at	

A7092 Wt. W128 9/M1293 750,000. 1/17. D. D & L Ltd. Forms/C2118/14.

Instructions regarding War Diaries and Intelligence Summaries are contained in F. S. Regs., Part II. and the Staff Manual respectively. Title pages will be prepared in manuscript.

WAR DIARY
or
INTELLIGENCE SUMMARY.
(Erase heading not required.)

Army Form C. 2118.

Place	Date	Hour	Summary of Events and Information	Remarks and references to Appendices
			12 10 pm. By this time 50% of the guns were in action, but owing to heavy going delaying the remainder, so that it was about 12 30 pm before all guns [illegible] ~~were again~~ in ~~action~~ could open fire, each number one as he came picking up the target according to timetable as he brought his gun into action. During the afternoon hostile fire on the battery ceased entirely and the enemy's retreat left the guns out of range. To the great regret of H.Q. staff No Gunner HARDINGHAM the Colonel's servant was killed during the afternoon by a piece of shell. He is buried in ARRAS Cemetery. Heavy snow fell during the evening and night.	
ARRAS ~~40th~~	10th midnight to 4 pm.		The capture of the Brown line during the afternoon of the 9th	

A7092 Wt. W128 9/M1293 750,000. 1/17. D. D & L. Ltd. Forms/C2118/14.

Instructions regarding War Diaries and Intelligence Summaries are contained in F. S. Regs., Part II. and the Staff Manual respectively. Title pages will be prepared in manuscript.

WAR DIARY
or
INTELLIGENCE SUMMARY.
(Erase heading not required.)

Army Form C. 2118.

Place	Date	Hour	Summary of Events and Information	Remarks and references to Appendices
HQ. N3a45 E. of TILLOY	10th	4pm.	made it possible for the guns to advance still further and orders were received to take up positions near the CAMBRAI Road beyond TILLOY LES MOFFLAINES, at about N 3 a 6. The batteries drove up in a snowstorm about 5pm and came into action behind a crest, officers & men sleeping by their guns or under hastily constructed cover. In the neighbourhood were numerous German battery positions – some with field guns in them intact – and deep dugouts. The possibility of being blown up by a booby trap in a deserted German dugout decided Brigade HQ to spend the night in an old German gun pit, but their caution was ill rewarded by two tanks during the night who having lost their way, and their wake hotly followed by German crumps, nearly obliterated HQ in their endeavour to find their way to the Cambrai road.	

A7092 Wt. W128.9/M1293 750,000. 1/17. D. D & L. Ltd. Forms/C2118/14.

Instructions regarding War Diaries and Intelligence Summaries are contained in F. S. Regs., Part II. and the Staff Manual respectively. Title pages will be prepared in manuscript.

WAR DIARY
or
INTELLIGENCE SUMMARY.
(Erase heading not required.)

Army Form C. 2118.

Place	Date	Hour	Summary of Events and Information	Remarks and references to Appendices
HQ N.3a 4.5 E of TILLOY	10th		at 11 pm 17 Bde RFA was ordered to cover front of 112th Infantry Brigade (HQ. FEUCHY CHAPEL)	
	11th	4 am	at 4 am orders were received to support an attack by 111th Infty Bde (37th Divn) on MONCHY. Little time was left to arrange programme for barrage as the attack was timed for 5 am.	
		5.5 am	The guns opened fire some minutes late. 2Lt A FIELD 26th Batt was wounded early in the day.	
		9 am	12th Div. Arty, under whom the Brigade still acted, ordered the O.C. to accompany the Brigadier as Liaison with the Infantry. He went to MONCHY and saw the vain attempts of the Cavalry to force their way through MONCHY, being only 300 yds away from the RHA battery ~~then~~ belonging to the Cavalry Division when its heavy shellfire compelled it to retire, leaving few	

A7092 Wt. W128 9/M1293 750,000. 1/17. D. D. & L. Ltd. Forms/C2118/14.

Army Form C. 2118.

Instructions regarding War Diaries and Intelligence Summaries are contained in F. S. Regs., Part II. and the Staff Manual respectively. Title pages will be prepared in manuscript.

WAR DIARY
or
INTELLIGENCE SUMMARY.
(Erase heading not required.)

Place	Date	Hour	Summary of Events and Information	Remarks and references to Appendices
			The enemy leaving five of its guns behind	
			The attack on MONCHY was successful, but the line NE of it was not very securely held. German Counterattacks were expected from either NE of MONCHY or GUEMAPPE.	
			In order to shorten range the O.C. Colonel decided to move the batteries further forward, and during the afternoon the batteries moved up from N3a to N4c	
	12th		The enemy began to shell us today. An operation is planned for tomorrow, when our group is to support infantry attack on high ground E & NE of MONCHY. Preparations made for the attack.	
	13th		Attack is postponed. Enemy shelled our positions heavily with gas shells; one man gassed but not seriously.	
	14th		Attack opened at 5.30 am. At first successful, but	

A7092 Wt. W128 9/M1293 750,000. 1/17. D. D & L. Ltd. Forms/C2118/14.

Instructions regarding War Diaries and Intelligence Summaries are contained in F. S. Regs., Part II. and the Staff Manual respectively. Title pages will be prepared in manuscript.

WAR DIARY
or
INTELLIGENCE SUMMARY.
(Erase heading not required.)

Army Form C. 2118.

Place	Date	Hour	Summary of Events and Information	Remarks and references to Appendices
			but at 11 am. a Counter attack was delivered which compelled us to withdraw to our original line. At 4pm Monchy was heavily shelled and 29th Group put down a barrage which broke up a German infantry attack. A trying day; the situation was not clear all morning and the Germans constantly counterattacked. Two men wounded	
	15.4.17.		The intelligence report sent into 29 DA HQ today was as follows. "Quiet night. Air activity below normal – low visibility."	
	16.4.17.		Enemy shelled us heavily at intervals: 3 men killed + 3 wounded one howitzer and one 18pr put out of action During the day Very heavy shelling between 7pm – 8pm. Difficult to say from what direction so that Counterbatteries do not know which battery is firing.	

A7092 Wt. W128 9/M1293 750,000. 1/17. D. D & L. Ltd. Forms/C2118/14.

Instructions regarding War Diaries and Intelligence Summaries are contained in F. S. Regs., Part II. and the Staff Manual respectively. Title pages will be prepared in manuscript.

WAR DIARY
or
INTELLIGENCE SUMMARY.
(Erase heading not required.)

Army Form C. 2118.

Place	Date	Hour	Summary of Events and Information	Remarks and references to Appendices
19. Maison Rouge	17.4		Positions heavily shelled 2am - 4am. Some gas shells. Our fire confined to registration. A Brigade O.P. manned from dawn to dusk has been established in front of our front line. One more gun of 92nd is out of action, and one howitzer was destroyed by shell. One man wounded.	
	18.4		Rain. Batteries very heavily shelled during night and early morning. 26th battery telephone pit blown up. 13th battery mess wrecked. 2 Lt. S.G. MARTIN of 13th battery killed: he was very severely wounded in the groin and died almost immediately. He is a great loss to the Brigade. One gun of 13th battery hit by shell, and four of 26th battery: this is in addition to the two 18pr + 2 howitzers already noted as out of action.	

A7092 Wt. W128 9/M1293 750,000. 1/17. D. D & I. Ltd. Forms/C2118/14.

Army Form C. 2118.

Instructions regarding War Diaries and Intelligence Summaries are contained in F. S. Regs., Part II. and the Staff Manual respectively. Title pages will be prepared in manuscript.

WAR DIARY
or
INTELLIGENCE SUMMARY.
(Erase heading not required.)

Place	Date	Hour	Summary of Events and Information	Remarks and references to Appendices
HQ near MAISON ROUGE E. of ARRAS N3a45	19 April		Enemy shelled battery positions heavily again during night & about breakfast time. 26th & 92nd batteries moved to new positions less advanced & further to the right, about N3b01. 26th Battery had 3 guns put out of action by shell fire during the night. 13th Battery lost 6 men killed at gun position early this morning: Cpl G DENNIS, Gr A HALLIDAY, a/Bdr J.B. COOK, Gr L HUGHES, Gr G.E. CROFT, Gr T.J. MORGAN This battery has now lost 11 killed since the Brigade moved from ARRAS. Tonight the detachment of the 13th were withdrawn for a rest & their front covered by 26 & 92 while 15th Bde RHA took over a wider front for SOS. Lt Col MARRIOTT SMITH reconnoitred new forward positions for guns near MONCHY (N6a&c) & Lt Col Duff of 15 Bde RHA reconnoitred new wagon lines for both Brigades near TILLOY. A large operation is to take place in a day or two when 29 Div. Infantry will attack, supported by 29th Div Arty & 12th Div Arty.	

A7092 Wt. W128 g/M1293 750,000. 1/17. D. D & L. Ltd. Forms/C2118/14.

Army Form C. 2118.

WAR DIARY
or
INTELLIGENCE SUMMARY.
(Erase heading not required.)

Instructions regarding War Diaries and Intelligence Summaries are contained in F. S. Regs., Part II. and the Staff Manual respectively. Title pages will be prepared in manuscript.

Place	Date	Hour	Summary of Events and Information	Remarks and references to Appendices
20. HQ. near MAISON ROUGE ARRAS. N3a45	20	ap.	Warmer day. Enemy still shell our batteries but change of position has relieved them considerably. 2Lt Rabey & Major Leach MC [illegible] make reconnaissance about our forward positions with a view to finding a suitable H.Q. Ammunition (2100 rds per battery) has to be sent up there on pack horses at night, an unpleasant job as the enemy puts down a barrage about 2 a.m. as a rule.	
			26th battery had another gun put out of action during the night. 92nd had one gun overturned by shell fire but not badly damaged.	
			D/17 had a direct hit on one howitzer – another gun has gone to IOM for repairs. It has just been reported that 13th battery lost another gunner on 13/18th: he had been missing since then, & is now reported died in Dressing station.	
	21	ap.	Further preparations for attack due to take place on 23rd. Bt Gen. E.B. Ashmore held conference at 17th Bde H.Q. in afternoon. Enemy shelled batteries very heavily again all last night	

A7092 Wt. W128 9/M1293 750,000. 1/17. D. D & L. Ltd. Forms/C2118/14.

Instructions regarding War Diaries and Intelligence Summaries are contained in F. S. Regs., Part II. and the Staff Manual respectively. Title pages will be prepared in manuscript.

WAR DIARY
or
INTELLIGENCE SUMMARY.
(Erase heading not required.)

Army Form C. 2118.

Place	Date	Hour	Summary of Events and Information	Remarks and references to Appendices
	22. April		Another bad night for the battery. The Counter groups do not seem to be able to put the German guns out of action. The men are very tired with hard work & lack of sleep. Registration carried out for attack. Parties from battery at work on the forward position to which our guns will move if the attack is a success. Difficulty found in getting up ammunition to forward position. It has to be carried up at night. there is no moon. the road is blocked and the enemy shells it with salvos of 5.9. Men & horses almost done up. The men make no complaint at all and have 'stuck' it well, but continual shelling and no sleep has told on them. 46 horses were evacuated today owing to 'debility'. This just cancels a draft of 45 received yesterday and leaves us with 90 short still.	

A7092 Wt. W128.9/M1293 750,000. 1/17. D. D & L. Ltd. Forms/C2118/14.

Instructions regarding War Diaries and Intelligence Summaries are contained in F. S. Regs., Part II. and the Staff Manual respectively. Title pages will be prepared in manuscript.

WAR DIARY
or
INTELLIGENCE SUMMARY.
(Erase heading not required.)

Army Form C. 2118.

Place	Date	Hour	Summary of Events and Information	Remarks and references to Appendices
4.45 am [illegible] RIDGE	23. April		The attack opened at 4.45 am. 29 our two artillery groups (29 & 12th) supporting the Infantry of 29th Division. The attack appeared to be successful, the Division on our right gaining the high ground which was to enable us to move forward the guns at 7.30 am; if the	
9.30 am HQ at LES FOSSES FARM on Cambrai Rd.		9.30 am	high ground on our right remained in German hands our forward gun positions (N.6 a & c) would be overlooked. This unfortunately is what happened, as a heavy Counter attack drove in our Right exposing our own guns to observation & machine gun fire. So serious did the situation appear to be that an order was received about 2.30 pm for the 15th Bde RHA to empty gun limbers, hook in horse teams and prepare to withdraw the guns. This order was cancelled, but the situation remained very obscure till 10.45 pm when the Brigade Major telephoned	

A7092 Wt. W128.9/M1293 750,000. 1/17. D. D & L. Ltd. Forms/C2118/14.

Instructions regarding War Diaries and Intelligence Summaries are contained in F. S. Regs., Part II. and the Staff Manual respectively. Title pages will be prepared in manuscript.

WAR DIARY
or
INTELLIGENCE SUMMARY.
(Erase heading not required.)

Army Form C. 2118.

Place	Date	Hour	Summary of Events and Information	Remarks and references to Appendices
	23.		that the guns were to remain where they were. This improvement in the situation appeared to be due to a further attack made by our troops at 6 pm which ultimately resulted in our regaining much of the high ground on our left right. Unfortunately Major R.S. Leach M.C. commanding 13th battery was wounded during the day, Captain F. Eggleton 26th battery being ordered to take his place. The 13th battery have had extraordinary bad luck during the past week as the 18th 2Lt. S.G. MARTIN was killed, on the night of 21st 2Lt. L.R.Fuzze MORRISH was gassed, but remained at duty, & on the night of 22/23rd Lt. R Beaver was wounded in the ankle while taking up ammunition forward. All these officers belonged to 13th battery	

Instructions regarding War Diaries and Intelligence Summaries are contained in F. S. Regs., Part II. and the Staff Manual respectively. Title pages will be prepared in manuscript.

WAR DIARY
or
INTELLIGENCE SUMMARY.
(Erase heading not required.)

Army Form C. 2118.

Place	Date	Hour	Summary of Events and Information	Remarks and references to Appendices
	23		2Lt RJ CAZEAUX and 2Lt R HENNEY, of the 92nd & 26th batteries were transferred to 13th batteries on 22nd & 24th respectively, to replace casualties.	
	24.		It is difficult to get accurate news but it appears that some progress is being made and during the night all our telephonists and HQ were kit moved up to Forward HQ. Two men ~~and~~ were killed & 13 wounded during yesterday and night. 13th battery had another gun put out of action.	
	25.		Enemy shelled our wagon line (near Bois de Boeufs) & killed one man, ~~killed~~ and 13 horses and wounded 10 horses. All the battery captains are agreed that it is desirable to move the lines back to Arras if possible, so as to give the men a rest from the continual shelling. 18 more horses evacuated today.	

A7092 Wt. W128 9/M1293 750,000. 1/17. D. D & L. Ltd. Forms/C2118/14.

Army Form C. 2118.

Instructions regarding War Diaries and Intelligence Summaries are contained in F. S. Regs., Part II. and the Staff Manual respectively. Title pages will be prepared in manuscript.

WAR DIARY
or
INTELLIGENCE SUMMARY.
(Erase heading not required.)

Place	Date	Hour	Summary of Events and Information	Remarks and references to Appendices
	26.		H.Q. moves across the Cambrai road from Les Fosses Farm to a cave occupied by the Infantry Brigade (H.Q.) which we are covering (the 76th Brigade) The cave reminds me of a witches haunt in a Drury Lane Pantomime, or a kind of hellish cathedral gloomy & smoky, with candles burning in the various alcoves as though before some Evil shrine.	
			Today 3rd Div. Arty H.Q relieve 29th Div Arty H.Q	
			The wagon Lines were removed to ARRAS to the great satisfaction of the men. Another gun of the 13th battery was damaged. They now have 3 guns in action but have borrowed one from 92nd to make four. This battery has had still further misfortunes as 2Lt Henney, recently transferred from 26th battery was killed by a piece of shell in the throat, while walking up to the O.P.	

A7092 Wt. W128 9/M1293 750,000. 1/17. D. D & L Ltd. Forms/C2118/14.

Instructions regarding War Diaries and Intelligence Summaries are contained in F. S. Regs., Part II. and the Staff Manual respectively. Title pages will be prepared in manuscript.

WAR DIARY
or
INTELLIGENCE SUMMARY.
(Erase heading not required.)

Army Form C. 2118.

Place	Date	Hour	Summary of Events and Information	Remarks and references to Appendices
	26		Henry's death is very sad. He had recently returned from leave to Scotland ~~to~~ to see his wife and child, which had been born a month or two before.	
			Lt Col. Smith went back to ARRAS today for a few days rest, Lt Col. Sherbrooke of the 15th Brigade RHA acting as Group Commander. As the batteries ~~of the 15th Bde~~ have been	
	27.		been heavily shelled, ~~as~~ Col. Sherbrooke asked CRA for permission to move them; ~~the only~~ area ~~available~~ ~~belongs~~ into which the batteries could move ~~...~~ belonged to the 15th Div. Arty and permission to move was refused.	
	27		Today it has been arranged that only one of our two Brigades should be permanently manned. The 17th Brigade will keep their guns manned, while 15th Bde will help by providing officers for OP work, signallers & linesmen.	
	28		Batteries & RONCHY shelled as usual	

Instructions regarding War Diaries and Intelligence Summaries are contained in F. S. Regs., Part II. and the Staff Manual respectively. Title pages will be prepared in manuscript.

WAR DIARY
or
INTELLIGENCE SUMMARY.
(Erase heading not required.)

Army Form C. 2118.

Place	Date	Hour	Summary of Events and Information	Remarks and references to Appendices
	29		Sunday. Comparatively quiet day, lovely warm sun. Gp Chaplain (Rev. J.W. HUNKIN) held services in the cave at HQ.	
	30		2Lt T.C. Ratsey is unwell & left HQ at the Cave for a rest at the Wagon Line. Lt. K Lyon, [illegible] from joined HQ at Cave to take his place. Bombardment of enemy trenches by 4.5 Howitzer with lethal and lachrymatory gas shell 9pm to 3am 1st May. Batteries not so heavily shelled during the day. A "Practice Barrage" is to be shot tomorrow at 4 am in view of a forthcoming operation. During the week at their MONCHY positions batteries have had a less unpleasant time so far as casualties to men is concerned, but they have been heavily shelled & several guns have been put out of action. At one time 13th battery were reduced to two guns & all the howitzers were out of action.	

Army Form C. 2118.

Instructions regarding War Diaries and Intelligence Summaries are contained in F. S. Regs., Part II. and the Staff Manual respectively. Title pages will be prepared in manuscript.

April

WAR DIARY
or
~~INTELLIGENCE SUMMARY.~~
(Erase heading not required.)

17 Bde R.F.A.

Place	Date	Hour	Summary of Events and Information	Remarks and references to Appendices
In Arras			This month has seen all the Batteries of the brigade continuously engaged in hard fighting and with varying success. The bearing of officers & men under conditions of great fatigue – hardships and danger has been splendid. The hardest ~~time~~ was in the neighbourhood of FEUCHY CHAPELLE when batteries were engaged day & night by heavy shell. The expenditure of ammunition has been enormous. The final advance to the neighbourhood of MONCHY was made under shell and machine gun fire. The brigade has been thanked for its services by G.O.C.s 36, 76 & 88 Inf Bdes – which it supported – and also by G.O.C. 29th Div. and G.O.C. 6th Army Corps. The losses have been 2 officers killed & 7 wounded, 28 men killed & 101 wounded. 44 horses killed & 43 horses wounded. Most of the losses fell on the 13th Battery.	
			[signature] Lt Col RA. Comdg 17 Bde RA.	

A7092 Wt. W128 9/M1293 750,000. 1/17. D. D. & L. Ltd. Forms/C2118/14.

Instructions regarding War Diaries and Intelligence Summaries are contained in F. S. Regs., Part II. and the Staff Manual respectively. Title pages will be prepared in manuscript.

WAR DIARY
or
INTELLIGENCE SUMMARY.
(Erase heading not required.)

Army Form C. 2118.

Place	Date	Hour	Summary of Events and Information	Remarks and references to Appendices
			92nd batten (continued) wounded Dr McINTOSH W JAMES H MEARS J DURHAM W James A. D/17 batten killed Bdr GILL D/17 batten wounded Sergeant SMITH F " RUSSELL " MILES " HEWITT Cpl S/S. EDWARDS J Bdr ALLEN J. a/Bdr CO BOND. Fitter ROGERS. Gr OLIVER. BIRD FREEMAN BELL WHEELDON THOMSON T BALDWIN J. Gr DOHERTY T " WOODS B. Dr SWAINE C " WESLEY A TERRY W Bdr SHELDON Gr GADSBY " PHILLIPS TAYLOR BROWN DEAN FEINSTEIN	

A7092 Wt. W128 9/M1293 750,000. 1/17. D. D & L. Ltd. Forms/C2118/14.

Army Form C. 2118.

Instructions regarding War Diaries and Intelligence Summaries are contained in F. S. Regs., Part II. and the Staff Manual respectively. Title pages will be prepared in manuscript.

WAR DIARY
or
INTELLIGENCE SUMMARY.
(Erase heading not required.)

Place	Date	Hour	Summary of Events and Information	Remarks and references to Appendices
			26th battery	
			Wounded	
			Sgt McMORROW J	
			SMITH G.W.	
			Br BATT E	
			Br BURGESS R	
			Corporal GAGE H.	
			Sgt WRIGHT W	
			THORPE H	
			ROBINSON S	
			PAGE	
			CHAPMAN T	
			Br BYGRAVE R	
			DALE W.	
			CONDON E	
			92nd battery	
			Killed	
			Driver JONES A	
			Wounded.	
			Gunner DUCKWORTH J	
			CAAN R	
			HALL G	
			EVANS W	
			COX J.H	
			JENKINS E.R	
			WILSON J	
			CRAMP J.S	
			TAYLER J.G	
			CATTERALL F	
			ROBSON W.	

A7092 Wt. W128 9/M1293 750,000. 1/17. D. D & L Ltd. Forms/C2118/14.

Instructions regarding War Diaries and Intelligence Summaries are contained in F. S. Regs., Part II. and the Staff Manual respectively. Title pages will be prepared in manuscript.

WAR DIARY
or
INTELLIGENCE SUMMARY.
(Erase heading not required.)

Army Form C. 2118.

Place	Date	Hour	Summary of Events and Information	Remarks and references to Appendices
			13th battery continued.	
			wounded	
			Gunner RODDAMS J	
			BARRACLOUGH S	
			PRETLOVE J.H	
			BAKER R.G	
			CRAWFORD R	
			Cooper G.A	
			COWAN C.	
			26th battery	
			Killed ABr HILL	
			Gr MASTERSON	
			Gr HARMSWORTH	
			wounded Cpl. ALEXANDER S	
			Gr TURNBULL	
			URTELL	
			RADFORD	
			Bdr. C.E. WOOD	
			Gr SKINNER	
			LYNCH	
			Bdr BATT	
			Gr REEKS	

A7092 Wt. W128 9/M1293 750,000. 1/17. D. D & L. Ltd. Forms/C2118/14.

Instructions regarding War Diaries and Intelligence Summaries are contained in F. S. Regs., Part II. and the Staff Manual respectively. Title pages will be prepared in manuscript.

WAR DIARY
or
INTELLIGENCE SUMMARY.
(Erase heading not required.)

Army Form C. 2118.

Place	Date	Hour	Summary of Events and Information	Remarks and references to Appendices
			NCO's and men	
			killed.	
			(1) 13th battery	
			Serjeant DOWNES	
			" " AMIOT	
			Corporal DENNIS	
			Bombdr MAYO S	
			a/Bombdr GIBBS	
			a/Bomb COOK	
			[illegible]	
			Gunner GOODMAN	
			HANKIN	
			ORD	
			STEPHENSON	
			Bde HQ. Gr Hardingham killed	
			Gr Dean wounded	
			Gr Brown. "	
			Gunner CROFT	
			" HALLIDAY	
			" HUGHES	
			" MORGAN	
			" O'NEILL	
			wounded	
			Serjeant CLAIR	
			Bombdr BARNES G (Gassed)	
			Gunner BOWEN	
			BYGRAVE	
			HURST A	
			TRAVIS W and Gassed	

A7092 Wt. W128 9/M1293 750,000. 1/17. D. D & L. Ltd. Forms/C2118/14.

Instructions regarding War Diaries and Intelligence Summaries are contained in F. S. Regs., Part II. and the Staff Manual respectively. Title pages will be prepared in manuscript.

WAR DIARY
or
INTELLIGENCE SUMMARY.
(Erase heading not required.)

Army Form C. 2118.

Place	Date	Hour	Summary of Events and Information	Remarks and references to Appendices
			The following casualties have been reported by batteries between 1st + 30th April 1917	
			Officers killed 2Lt. S.G. MARTIN 13th battery	
			2Lt. H.N. HENNEY 26th battery attached to 13th battery	
			Wounded Major R.S. LEACH M.C. 13th battery	
			Lieut R.H. BEAVER 13th battery	
			2Lt C.D. Cooper D/17	
			2Lt A.B. ENRIGHT D/17	
			2Lt L.R. FIFIELD 26th battery	
			2Lt L.R. FURZE MORRISH (Slightly at duty) 13th Bty	
			2Lt J.P. BOSMAN 26th battery – wounded slightly at duty)	

A7092 Wt. W128,9/M1293 750,000. 1/17. D. D & L. Ltd. Forms/C2118/14.

Army Form C. 2118.

29th

WAR DIARY
or
INTELLIGENCE SUMMARY.
(Erase heading not required.)

Instructions regarding War Diaries and Intelligence Summaries are contained in F. S. Regs., Part II. and the Staff Manual respectively. Title pages will be prepared in manuscript.

Vol 15

Place	Date	Hour	Summary of Events and Information	Remarks and references to Appendices
			WAR DIARY — 17th BRIGADE RFA — MAY 1 – 31 1917	—

Vol 26

A7092 Wt. W128 9/M1293 750,000. 1/17. D. D & L Ltd. Forms/C2118/14.

Instructions regarding War Diaries and Intelligence Summaries are contained in F. S. Regs., Part II. and the Staff Manual respectively. Title pages will be prepared in manuscript.

WAR DIARY
or
INTELLIGENCE SUMMARY.
(Erase heading not required.)

Army Form C. 2118.

Place	Date	Hour	Summary of Events and Information	Remarks and references to Appendices
HQ CAVE LES FOSSES FARM N' ARRAS N. of road	1. May		Practice barrage carried out at 4 a.m. preparatory to a forthcoming attack. Enemy replied very sharply. His Howitzers fired gas shell all night and again about noon. At 3.30 pm the roof of the cave in which we were living with HQ 76 Infy Bde fell in, buried the General's kit and all the Infy Brigade office together with much signal equipment. The General + Col Sherbrooke decided to move to a [illegible] which was [illegible] and [illegible] [illegible].	
HQ in Cave S. of the [illegible]		4.0 pm	In accordance with orders OC 2nd [illegible] RA (Col Sherbrooke) reconnoitred from the forward positions for our batteries with a view to [illegible] an attack by our [illegible] Infantry (29th DIV) from REMY to the COJEUL River	
Cave S. of Road	2 May		Enemy very active [illegible] extremely heavy barrage [illegible] [illegible] on MONCHY [illegible] about 4 pm. [illegible] our [illegible] in large [illegible] to take	

A7092 Wt. W125 9/M1293 750,000. 1/17. D. D & L Ltd. Forms/C2118/14.

WAR DIARY
or
INTELLIGENCE SUMMARY.
(Erase heading not required.)

Army Form C. 2118.

Instructions regarding War Diaries and Intelligence Summaries are contained in F. S. Regs., Part II. and the Staff Manual respectively. Title pages will be prepared in manuscript.

Place	Date	Hour	Summary of Events and Information	Remarks and references to Appendices
	2 May		Please summary see attached Barrage Maps and orders giving general scheme. Major Eddis (Comdg 460th Battery) to be liaison officer with 9th Infantry Brigade (3rd Div) whose attack our barrage is to support. For the duration as the number of Howitzers being so [illegible] owing to gun casualties Col Sherlocke organised the 2 How batteries (460th & D/17) as a How subgroup under the command of Major 460 Holmes (D/17). HQ 29th group RA and the mess of 'L' Battery RHA at Major Thorneycroft's [illegible].	
	3 May		During the night the enemy shelled our area N6 & N11 & N12 very heavily with gas shell (lethal and lachrymatory). The gas affected almost every one. One officer (Lt ST SALBERG 26th battery) and 5 men being very seriously gassed as a gas shell burst in their dug outs.	

A7092 Wt. W128 9/M1293 750,000. 1/17. D. D & L Ltd. Forms/C2118/14.

Instructions regarding War Diaries and Intelligence Summaries are contained in F. S. Regs., Part II. and the Staff Manual respectively. Title pages will be prepared in manuscript.

WAR DIARY
or
INTELLIGENCE SUMMARY.
(Erase heading not required.)

Army Form

Place	Date	Hour	Summary of Events and Information	Remarks and references to Appendices
	3. May.		The attack opened at 3.45 am. It was not successful. At 7.30 am the barrage was brought back according to orders 15th Brigade to 15/18 line & 9th Brigade to 46/54 line (see barrage map). As early as 5 am it was reported by our Observing officer that 9th Brigade (Right Co. of 13th Kings and Right Co. of ? Northumberland Fusiliers) could not get beyond German front line owing to machine gun fire. At 7.30 am our line ran along DEVILS TRENCH [illegible] between BOIS DES [illegible] towards KEELING COPSE [illegible] [illegible] REDOUBT and BOIS DU SART, the left Brigade of 3rd Division being between the two woods. 10.30 am The Infantry were reported E. of Infantry Hill	

A7092 Wt. W128 9/M1293 750,000. 1/17. D. D & L. Ltd. Forms/C2118/14.

Instructions regarding War Diaries and Intelligence Summaries are contained in F. S. Regs., Part II. and the Staff Manual respectively. Title pages will be prepared in manuscript.

WAR DIARY
or
INTELLIGENCE SUMMARY.

(Erase heading not required.)

Army Form C. 2118.

Place	Date	Hour	Summary of Events and Information	Remarks and references to Appendices
	3 May		3 pm Our line was reported by the FOO to be as follows ARROW TRENCH – SHRAPNEL TRENCH – North [illegible] line from O2a69 – O8a67 – Trench O?d15 – W[illegible] edge of Copse in O8 central – O8c68 – a Trench O2b07 – O2b42 & O2b69 – O2b80. By the evening we were practically back on our old front line. Unfortunately 2Lt E.H. THOMERSON of 13th Battery [illegible] Brigade FOO is missing [illegible] he attached himself to the 7th Buffs & one of his signallers was wounded [illegible] later in the day (8 pm) [illegible] having seen 2Lt THOMERSON during 4.45 am. Altogether not a good day. [illegible] affected everyone	

A7092 Wt. W128 9/M1293 750,000. 1/17. D. D & L Ltd. Forms/C2118/14.

Instructions regarding War Diaries and Intelligence Summaries are contained in F. S. Regs., Part II. and the Staff Manual respectively. Title pages will be prepared in manuscript.

WAR DIARY
or
INTELLIGENCE SUMMARY.

(Erase heading not required.)

Army Form C. 2118.

Place	Date	Hour	Summary of Events and Information	Remarks and references to Appendices
	4 May		Comparatively quiet day. Lt Col H R W Marriott Smith DSO relieved Lt Col H Sherbrooke in command of 19th Grp RA. Lt OPPENHEIM 2?th battery relieved 2Lt BROWN. HB (15th Bde RHA) as orderly officer at Group HQ.	
	5 May		[illegible] gas shell fired [illegible] during night. One man of 92nd was killed [illegible] gas shell and one was wounded. At 9pm orders were received that one battery per Brigade was to move out of the line and rest [illegible] [illegible] days. 92nd & B battery were withdrawn during the night. [illegible] [illegible] their guns but are [illegible] ready to move up at short notice. Group HQ moved from Caves to N 11 a 0 5 - old German Gunpits.	

A7092 Wt. W128 9/M1293 750,000. 1/17. D. D & L Ltd. Forms/C2118/14.

Instructions regarding War Diaries and Intelligence Summaries are contained in F. S. Regs., Part II. and the Staff Manual respectively. Title pages will be prepared in manuscript.

WAR DIARY
or
INTELLIGENCE SUMMARY.
(Erase heading not required.)

Army Form C. 2118.

Place	Date	Hour	Summary of Events and Information	Remarks and references to Appendices
HQ.	7. May.		Quiet day. Neighbourhood of les Fosses Farm intermittently shelled. Adjutant 15th Bde RHA relieves adjutant 17 Bde RHA as Staff Officer 29 Group RA. Two guns of 'L' battery damaged by shell.	
	8. May		Quiet day. Counterpreparation targets engaged twice during the day.	
	9 May		DEVILS TRENCH bombarded by 4.5 Hows. Lt Col. H Sherbrooke RHA takes Command of 29th Group relieving Lt Col. HRW Smith who goes to ARRAS to rest.	
	10.		Normal day and night firing. SOS lines tested by observation. DEVILS Trench bombarded by 4.5 Hows. 2 officers and 42 other ranks proceed to BOULOGNE for 14 days rest. (Major H.O. Holmes and 2 Lt K Ratez). 8.20 am. Infantry asked for SOS which was fired.	

A7092 Wt. W128 9/M1293 750,000. 1/17. D. D & L Ltd. Forms/C2118/14.

Instructions regarding War Diaries and Intelligence Summaries are contained in F. S. Regs., Part II. and the Staff Manual respectively. Title pages will be prepared in manuscript.

WAR DIARY

or

INTELLIGENCE SUMMARY.

(Erase heading not required.)

Army Form C. 2118.

Place	Date	Hour	Summary of Events and Information	Remarks and references to Appendices
HQ [illegible]	6. May.		A delightfully fresh sunny day. Communion service at HQ by 29 DA Chaplain [illegible] and [illegible] [illegible] much quieter than usual. CRA & BM [illegible] [illegible] [illegible] Lt Col [illegible] [illegible] & Major Clarke (29th Div HQ) called in the afternoon. Captain F HARRIS RAMC MO to 17 Bde went the wounded (gassed). He remains at duty. 2Lt P O BATTIN [illegible] sent to [illegible] [illegible] [illegible] [illegible]	

A7092 Wt. W128 9/M1293 750,000. 1/17. D. D & L. Ltd. Forms/C2118/14.

Instructions regarding War Diaries and Intelligence Summaries are contained in F. S. Regs., Part II. and the Staff Manual respectively. Title pages will be prepared in manuscript.

WAR DIARY
or
INTELLIGENCE SUMMARY.
(Erase heading not required.)

Army Form C. 2118.

Place	Date	Hour	Summary of Events and Information	Remarks and references to Appendices
	11. May		Practice barrage carried out and observed from front line. Lt Col. Sherbrooke wounded as he stepped out of H.Q. dugout. Lt Col. H.R.W. M. Smith comes up from Arras to relieve Col Sherbrooke in Command of Group.	
	12		Orders for attack on DEVILS Trench received. Practice barrage carried out and checked by FOO. 3 guns of Warwick battery knocked out by shell fire. Attack took place at 6.0 pm: barrage according to programme. No information as to what happened could be obtained during the evening or night. Batteries fired on new SOS lines over Devils Trench during night. Later information showed that the attack was not a success.	
	13		Quiet day. Church Parade of 29 DA at Wagon Line. Major Murray (Warwick RHA) in Command. CRA was present.	

Instructions regarding War Diaries and Intelligence Summaries are contained in F. S. Regs., Part II. and the Staff Manual respectively. Title pages will be prepared in manuscript.

WAR DIARY
or
INTELLIGENCE SUMMARY.
(Erase heading not required.)

Army Form C. 2118.

Place	Date	Hour	Summary of Events and Information	Remarks and references to Appendices
	14.		Adjt. 17th Bde RFA relieves Adjt. 15th Bde RHA as S.O. 29 Group. Counter barrage fired at 3.30pm: Considerable enemy fire. 87th Infy Bde. (29 Div) relieve 76th Bde (3rd Div) in the Monchy Defence.	
	15.		29 Group comes under orders of 29 Da. HQ which relieves 3rd Da HQ. Practice shoots on various targets.	
	16.		Enemy fire very active from 3.30 am. Two Eleven inch shell fell in MONCHY. Practice SOS fired by 29 Group. Destructive fire on DEVILS Trench carried out by 45 Hows. A new battery position is being prepared for L RHA and for 92nd RFA	
	17.		Orders received for all guns and howitzers to come up to Gunline for an Operation. Quiet day.	
	18		Warning order for Operation received: Personnel of	

A7092 Wt. W128 9/M1293 750,000. 1/17. D. D & L. Ltd. Forms C2118/14.

Instructions regarding War Diaries and Intelligence Summaries are contained in F. S. Regs., Part II. and the Staff Manual respectively. Title pages will be prepared in manuscript.

WAR DIARY
or
INTELLIGENCE SUMMARY.
(Erase heading not required.)

Army Form C. 2118.

Place	Date	Hour	Summary of Events and Information	Remarks and references to Appendices
	17.		Warwicks RHA and 92 RFA came up from wagon line and registration is begun. Enemy fire considerably below normal. Everyone talks of enemy retirement. QMG – Lt Gen. Sir J.S. Cowans KCB was expected at the wagon lines on a tour of inspection but did not appear. CRA inspected wagon line	
	18.		Little enemy artillery active today. Registration continued. Final orders received for operation on 19th (copy attached). British aeroplane fell near Monchy, both occupants killed.	
	19.		Very clear day. Practice barrage carried out – enemy still quiet.	
		9.pm.	29 Div. Infantry attacked according to orders under protective barrage. A smoke barrage was put down by artillery on our left + this blew back	

Army Form C. 2118.

Instructions regarding War Diaries and Intelligence Summaries are contained in F. S. Regs., Part II. and the Staff Manual respectively. Title pages will be prepared in manuscript.

WAR DIARY
or
INTELLIGENCE SUMMARY.
(Erase heading not required.)

Place	Date	Hour	Summary of Events and Information	Remarks and references to Appendices
	19		into our own men's faces making observation even from O.P. impossible. Two F.O.O.s went with the Infantry 2/Lt. A. Grant Suttie R.F.A. "D" Battery and 2/Lt. J.L. Lister R.F.A. 92 battery. Some messages by lamp signal were received from these officers but except for one all were sent too fast to read. It appears that the infantry were held up by machine guns from the start and never attained the objectives. At 3 a.m. G.O.C. Infantry Brigade asked us to bring back our S.O.S. lines to their original targets. 2/Lt J.L. Lister was killed between midnight & 3 a.m. by a bullet that came through parapet. 2/Lt M.A. Stephenson attached 92nd battery was wounded earlier in the day	

A7092 Wt. W128 9/M1293 750,000. 1/17. D. D & L. Ltd. Forms/C2118/14.

Instructions regarding War Diaries and Intelligence Summaries are contained in F. S. Regs., Part II. and the Staff Manual respectively. Title pages will be prepared in manuscript.

WAR DIARY
or
INTELLIGENCE SUMMARY.
(Erase heading not required.)

Army Form C. 2118.

Place	Date	Hour	Summary of Events and Information	Remarks and references to Appendices
HQ N.11.a 20.90	20.5.17		Quiet day. Usual day and night firing - 92nd battery sent to rest at Wagon Line	
	21.5.17.		Quiet day. Howitzer Group engage Machine Gun at junction of BIT LANE and DEVILS TRENCH. Orders received for that bombardment to take place at 3.14 am next morning. Gas was projected on BOIS du VERT and our batteries fired for four minutes on their SOS lines. Enemy did not reply. Adjutant 15th Bde RHA relieves adjutant 17 Bde RFA as SO 29 Group.	
	22.5.17		Very quiet day. Heavy rain and no observation possible	
	23.5.17		Quiet morning. During the afternoon Enemy shelled Group HQ (old German gun position) with salvos from 8 inch howitzers. A shell burst in the passage leading down to dugout and wounded Lt C P Duff RFA, adjutant 15th Bde RHA. Adjutant 17th Bde takes	

Instructions regarding War Diaries and Intelligence Summaries are contained in F. S. Regs., Part II. and the Staff Manual respectively. Title pages will be prepared in manuscript.

WAR DIARY
or
INTELLIGENCE SUMMARY.
(Erase heading not required.)

Army Form C. 2118.

Place	Date	Hour	Summary of Events and Information	Remarks and references to Appendices
			Lt. Auff's place as SO. 2q group	
H.Q. CAVE N12a2040.	24.5.17.		H.Q. moved to cave S. of Arras to CAMBRAI Road by Les Fosses Farm (N12a2040) 17th Bde batteries heavily shelled during morning. Major W. MURRAY (Warwick Batty RHA) took over command of Group from Lt Col Hanwell Smith DSO who returned to wagon line for a rest. Bombardment by howitzers of Long Trench	
	25.5.17		17th Bde RFA batteries heavily shelled during morning. CRA visits group H.Q. A small operation is to take place in a few days when 86th Bde are to capture HOOK TRENCH and organised shell hole.	
	26.5.17		Practice Salvos fired by 17th Bde 18pdrs over HOOK trench at 10.30pm + 12.30 am. These salvos are to be the signal for the infantry to go over as no barrage	

Instructions regarding War Diaries and Intelligence Summaries are contained in F. S. Regs., Part II. and the Staff Manual respectively. Title pages will be prepared in manuscript.

WAR DIARY
or
INTELLIGENCE SUMMARY.

(*Erase heading not required.*)

Army Form C. 2118.

Place	Date	Hour	Summary of Events and Information	Remarks and references to Appendices
	26.5.17.		will be put down. Continued bombardment of Hook and	
	27.5.17		Long Trench by 4.5 Hows on 26th and 27th. Orders received from 29 DA appointing 2Lt T.C. Ratsey RFA (Orderly Officer 17th Bde HQ) as acting adjutant to 15th Brigade RHA.	
	28.5.17.		Arrangements made for Lt K. LYON to act as adjutant to 15th Brigade and 2Lt TC Ratsey to remain at Group HQ and act as adjutant to 15th Bde. Lt Ratsey relieves Lt K. Lyon as SO 29 Group	
	29.5.17.		Operation was to take place tonight but was postponed. All spare guns & howitzers were sent up during night of 28/29 and necessary detachments left wagon line for gun line	
	30.5.17		A small attack by 29th Div Inf. not a success this time	
	31.5.17		A quiet Day.	

A7092 Wt. W128.9/M1293 750,000. 1/17. D. D & L. Ltd. Forms/C2118/14.

Army Form C. 2118.

Instructions regarding War Diaries and Intelligence Summaries are contained in F. S. Regs., Part II. and the Staff Manual respectively. Title pages will be prepared in manuscript.

WAR DIARY
or
INTELLIGENCE SUMMARY.

(Erase heading not required.)

Place	Date	Hour	Summary of Events and Information	Remarks and references to Appendices
			1210 Gnr Hornbuckle J -13th- Wounded in Action 4-5-17	
			Lieut H E THOMEMANN 13 Missing 4-5-17	
			115332 Gnr Worrall J 92 Wounded in Action 5-5-17	
			70836 Sgt O'Brien JW -92- Wounded in Action 5/5/17	
			217290 Dr Keswell W 92 Died of Wounds 5/5/17	
			~~75884 " Taylor H 92~~	
			175520 Gnr Morrison R 92 Gassed 5/5/17	
			14914 " Watson J 92 Gassed 5/5/17	
			92705 " Feinstein M D/17 Wounded in Action 4/5/17	
			32501 " Hall WH. D/17 do 4/5/17	
			Lieut J.O. BAIN D/17 Gassed 6/5/17	
			676074 Gnr Jones 10R 26 Killed in Action 12/5/17	
			160419 " Woodall R 26 Wounded in Action 13/5/17	
			4099 Br Saunders R 26 Gassed 5/5/17	
			38918 Gnr Blair G 13 Wounded in Action 15/5/17	

A7092 Wt. W128 9/M1293 750,000. 1/17. D. D & L Ltd Forms/C2118/14.

Instructions regarding War Diaries and Intelligence Summaries are contained in F. S. Regs., Part II. and the Staff Manual respectively. Title pages will be prepared in manuscript.

WAR DIARY
or
INTELLIGENCE SUMMARY.
(Erase heading not required.)

Army Form C. 2118.

Place	Date	Hour	Summary of Events and Information	Remarks and references to Appendices
			68062 Gnr Wooley W – 13th – Wounded in Action 15/5/17	
			13437 a/Br Davies W 13 – do 16/5/17	
			145825. Gnr Ransom E 92 do 12/5/17	
			178558 Gnr Lighton H. D/17 do 12/5/17	
			~~167379~~ " ~~Farnham J~~	
			2/Lieut AB ENRIGHT D/17 Died of wounds 11/5/17	
			8609 Dr Marsden JT. D/17 Wounded in Action 18/5/17	
			4393 Sergt Field H 13th attached from 3rd Huzzars } Killed in Action 21/5/17	
			55115 Gnr Calcan C 13th Wounded – " 23/5/17	
			174391 " Nickol J 13th do 23/5/17	
			2/Lieut J.G. Lister RGA 92nd Killed in Action 20/5/17	
			137579 Gnr Foster T D/17th Wounded in Action 19/5/17	

A7092 Wt. W128 9/M1293 750,000. 1/17. D. D & L. Ltd. Forms/C2118/14.

Army Form C. 2118.

Instructions regarding War Diaries and Intelligence Summaries are contained in F. S. Regs., Part II. and the Staff Manual respectively. Title pages will be prepared in manuscript.

WAR DIARY
or
INTELLIGENCE SUMMARY.
(Erase heading not required.)

Place	Date	Hour	Summary of Events and Information	Remarks and references to Appendices

Regt No	Rank	Name	Bty	Summary	Date
135928	Gnr	Manning. J	26th Bty	Wounded in Action	2-5-17
71893	"	Commerford B	"	do	2-5-17
82006	Bdr	Palmer, A.R.	92	do	2-5-17
23819	Gnr	Stewart H	26	Killed in Action	28-4-17
78453	Cpl	Harrison L J	26	do	27-4-17
67127	Gnr	Bailey H	26	Wounded in Action	27-4-17
74711	Gnr	Kane A	26	do	27-4-17
11305	Dr	Evans J	92	do	23-4-17
~~[illegible]~~	~~Gnr~~	~~Redding A~~	~~92~~	do	24-4-17
~~82006~~	~~Bdr~~	~~Palmer AR~~	~~92~~	do	2-5-17
155882	Gnr	Vane A	92	do	28-4-17
911	Sergt	Aston R	92	Killed in Action	29-4-17
159347	Gnr	Powell J	92	do	29-4-17
2099	Gnr	Turnbull F	92	do	29-4-17
35070	"	East E.	92	do	2-5-17
192577	"	Fraser J	26	do	4-5-17
69073	"	Livingstone D	26	Gassed	6-5-17
30613	"	Redding A	92	Wounded in Action	24-4-17

A7092 Wt. W128 9/M1293 750,000. 1/17. D. D & L. Ltd. Forms/C2118/14.

Army Form C. 2118.

Instructions regarding War Diaries and Intelligence Summaries are contained in F. S. Regs., Part II. and the Staff Manual respectively. Title pages will be prepared in manuscript.

WAR DIARY
or
INTELLIGENCE SUMMARY.
(Erase heading not required.)

Place	Date	Hour	Summary of Events and Information	Remarks and references to Appendices
			162047 Gnr Barlow G. 26th Gassed 6/5/17	
			Major Marx Wounded 29.5.17.	
			Capt Stamford " 27.5.17.	
			The month has grown quieter as it drew to its close, the [illegible] steering shifting to the North. One Open battery & 1/3 of the Howitzers are now kept in rest area and only go up for operations.	
			Batteries are still at v. close range 2400x about and get frequently shelled at times.	
			[illegible] Lt Col [illegible] Bde	

A7092 Wt. W128 9/M1293 750,000. 1/17. D. D & L. Ltd. Forms/C2118/14.

Instructions regarding War Diaries and Intelligence Summaries are contained in F. S. Regs., Part II. and the Staff Manual respectively. Title pages will be prepared in manuscript.

WAR DIARY
or
INTELLIGENCE SUMMARY.
(*Erase heading not required.*)

Army Form C. 2118.

Vol 16

Place	Date	Hour	Summary of Events and Information	Remarks and references to Appendices
			War Diary 17th Brigade RFA 1 June 1917 — 30 June 1917 Volume 27	

A7092 Wt. W128 9/M1293 750,000. 1/17. D. D & L. Ltd. Forms/C2118/14.

Instructions regarding War Diaries and Intelligence Summaries are contained in F. S. Regs., Part II. and the Staff Manual respectively. Title pages will be prepared in manuscript.

WAR DIARY
or
INTELLIGENCE SUMMARY.
(Erase heading not required.)

Army Form C. 2118.

Place	Date	Hour	Summary of Events and Information	Remarks and references to Appendices
H.Q. FOSSE FARM CAMBRAI Road nr MONCHY	1.6	17	Attacks on Hook Trench unsuccessful. Usual day firing	
	2.6	17	Harassing fire on Bois des Aubepines, [illegible] CT & back area.	
	3.6	17.	2Lt Hilary, H.J., 92nd Batt RFA very severely wounded at the battery. He was taken to DUISANS No 19 CCS but died the same evening about 7 pm. Major R Marx MC (his battery Commander) and Lt K Lyon (adjutant) saw him just before he died. He was unconscious the whole time. Mr Hilary is a great loss he left a very important post in India (Chairman of the Calcutta Port Trust) to enter the ranks as a cadet and became a 2 Lieutenant. He was 41 11/12 years of age	
	4.6	17.	2Lt Hilary was buried at Duisans Cemetery CRA, RO, Staff Captain, Battery Commander & adjutant were present.	

A7092 Wt. W128 9/M1293 750,000. 1/17. D. D & L. Ltd. Forms/C2118/14.

Instructions regarding War Diaries and Intelligence Summaries are contained in F. S. Regs., Part II. and the Staff Manual respectively. Title pages will be prepared in manuscript.

WAR DIARY
or
INTELLIGENCE SUMMARY.
(Erase heading not required.)

Army Form C. 2118.

Place	Date	Hour	Summary of Events and Information	Remarks and references to Appendices
	4.6.17.		Usual day and night firing.	
	5.6.17.		Arrangement made for several days continual and slow bombardment of enemy trenches and Infantry Hill with a view to Infantry attack on latter	
HQ Bois des Boeufs N2a4.6.	6.6.17.		HQ moves from Caverne les Fosses Farm to Bois des Boeufs just East of TILLOY and S. of CAMBRAI Road. A delightful spot, beautiful green trees and wild flowers (spotted palmate orchis and green man orchis found). The wood pigeons coo at the same time as a 15" Howitzer fires just behind us. We live in tents glorious hot weather. We have our mess in the open.	
	7.6.17.		Bombardment continues. 13th and 26th batteries prepare to move to a position 1000 yards in	

Instructions regarding War Diaries and Intelligence Summaries are contained in F. S. Regs., Part II. and the Staff Manual respectively. Title pages will be prepared in manuscript.

WAR DIARY
or
INTELLIGENCE SUMMARY.
(Erase heading not required.)

Army Form C. 2118.

Place	Date	Hour	Summary of Events and Information	Remarks and references to Appendices
	7.6.17		rear of their present position. Their new position is in the old German Brown Line (N of CAMBRAI Rd). They will be safer there from the regular shelling that came over MONCHY. Major V.O Dolphin commanding 26th battery was killed today just after he had returned from a reconnaissance with the Colonel. He had been with us since the beginning of April and was a man of great bravery and cheeriness	
	8.6.17		Lt Col Douglas Forman CMG has taken over Command of 15th Brigade RHA and came up to Bois des Boeufs today. Much work has to be done by batteries to complete their new positions and O.Ps. Difficulty is experienced in the provision of material as batteries will not take the trouble to salve stuff that	

Army Form C. 2118.

Instructions regarding War Diaries and Intelligence Summaries are contained in F. S. Regs., Part II. and the Staff Manual respectively. Title pages will be prepared in manuscript.

WAR DIARY
or
INTELLIGENCE SUMMARY.
(Erase heading not required.)

Place	Date	Hour	Summary of Events and Information	Remarks and references to Appendices
			is lying about. Bombardment Continues	
	9.6.17.		Bombardment Continues 300 rounds per day per 18pr battery & 400 per day per 4.5 How. The idea is to systematically destroy existing trenches and prevent enemy linking up fresh shell holes.	
	10.6.17		Bombardment and work on battery position and OP's Continues.	
	11 12		Gloomy weather. bombardment Continues. Nothing special to report. Orders received for operation on 14th (orders & map attached)	
	13		2Lt TR Ratsey (Orderly Officer) proceeds on leave to England	
	14		Attack on Infantry Hill successful.	Lt Col ARW M Smith DSO

A7092 Wt. W128 9/M1293 750,000. 1/17. D. D & L Ltd Forms/C2118/14.

Instructions regarding War Diaries and Intelligence Summaries are contained in F. S. Regs., Part II. and the Staff Manual respectively. Title pages will be prepared in manuscript.

WAR DIARY

or

INTELLIGENCE SUMMARY.

(Erase heading not required.)

Army Form C. 2118.

Place	Date	Hour	Summary of Events and Information	Remarks and references to Appendices
	14.6	17	acts as Liaison Officer with 76 Infy. Bde which carried out attack. In the afternoon the Germans counterattacked but was driven back by our artillery. One enterprising brigade fired smoke shell for SOS with the result that nobody could see anything as it screened the German advance. Our Infantry held up to the 'mound'. No damage luckily resulted.	
	15.6	17	and is tender night Capt T Grey D/17 battery relieves Col Smith as Liaison Officer. Germans attack during the day & we fire SOS frequently at slow rate. Some of our advanced posts driven in	
	16th		Further fighting for Infantry Hill. Lt Col Sherbrooke Liaison Officer. Major W.A. Murray commands 17th Bde RFA in absence of Col Smith who proceeds on leave to England. Batteries fire 60 rounds per hour all day	

Instructions regarding War Diaries and Intelligence Summaries are contained in F. S. Regs., Part II. and the Staff Manual respectively. Title pages will be prepared in manuscript.

WAR DIARY
or
INTELLIGENCE SUMMARY.
(Erase heading not required.)

Army Form C. 2118.

Place	Date	Hour	Summary of Events and Information	Remarks and references to Appendices
HQ: German Gunpit E of Bois des Boeufs	17 June		Batteries fire all day: HQ shelled in Bois des Boeufs and is moved to old German Gunpits 400 yds further East	
			1 Lt Lyon leaves new Group work to 2Lt & Brown RHA and proceeds to wagon line.	
	18		Infantry Brigade re-establish themselves in Infantry Hill	
	19 June		Quiet Day: batteries are to come out of the line in a day or two	
	20 June		Batteries relief postponed. Very quiet day	
HQ AGNY	21 June		Batteries come out of action & return to wagon line at AGNY.	
	22 June		March to MONTENESCOURT	
	23 June		Training & refitting. CRA visits the batteries	

Instructions regarding War Diaries and Intelligence Summaries are contained in F. S. Regs., Part II. and the Staff Manual respectively. Title pages will be prepared in manuscript.

WAR DIARY
or
INTELLIGENCE SUMMARY.
(Erase heading not required.)

Army Form C. 2118.

Place	Date	Hour	Summary of Events and Information	Remarks and references to Appendices
			Generally the month was much quieter and casualties dropped to below normal except that the Brigade lost a Battery Commander on 7 June and a subaltern on 3 June. The weather was glorious and the wagon lines very comfortable; the latter gave batteries an opportunity for a real rest to their officers & men. Leave was opened during the whole month a relief much appreciated. A good draft of NCOs (including 18 bombardiers) was received. The guns themselves ~~were~~ got badly worn out and needed careful overhaul (one gun used to shell the OP occasionally) owing to the heavy work during April & May and the dam hastily repaired damage. [illegible]	

A7092 Wt. W128 9/M1293 750,000. 1/17. D. D & L Ltd. Forms/C2118/14.

Instructions regarding War Diaries and Intelligence Summaries are contained in F. S. Regs., Part II. and the Staff Manual respectively. Title pages will be prepared in manuscript.

WAR DIARY
or
INTELLIGENCE SUMMARY.
(Erase heading not required.)

Army Form C. 2118.

Place	Date	Hour	Summary of Events and Information	Remarks and references to Appendices
HQ MONTENESCOURT	24 June		Church Parade for 29 Div Arty at Montenescourt. C.R.A. present. The padre preached about "HARIZON" & the piano (brought in on a G.S. wagon) was dreadfully out of tune.	
			Training. Guns overhauled by 10th	
	25			
	26		Training.	
			2Lt Rotter returns from leave. Lt Kay on proceeds on leave.	
	27		2Lt R Chalk goes on in advance to BOESINGHE to prepare O.Ps. Batteries continue training. Arrangement made for 29 D.A.	
	28		Sport to be held on 30 June. Glorious weather.	
	29		As on 28th	
	30		Wet day. Sport held though no jumping was possible owing to state of ground.	

A7092 Wt. W128 9/M1293 750,000. 1/17. D. D & L. Ltd. Forms/C2118/14.

GUEMAPPE
3/6/17

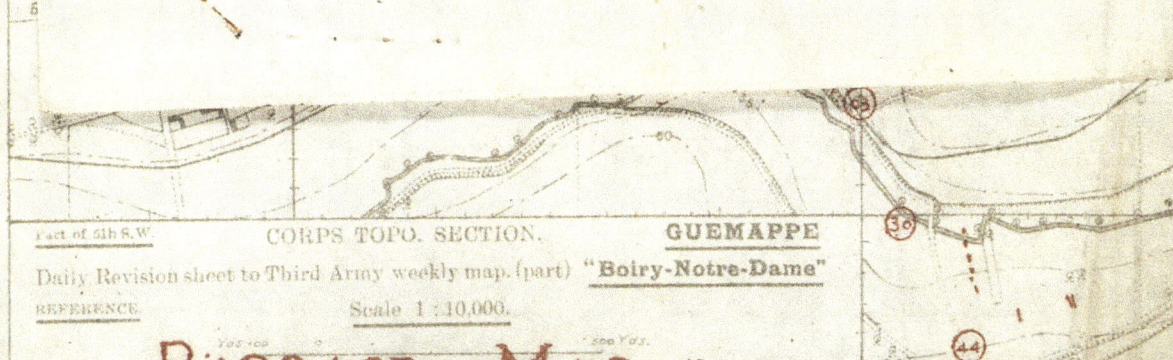

Part of 51b S.W.
CORPS TOPO. SECTION.
GUEMAPPE
Daily Revision sheet to Third Army weekly map. (part)
"Boiry-Notre-Dame"
REFERENCE.
Scale 1 : 10,000.
BARRAGE MAP
U. No 156 3-6-17
JUNGLE ALLEY
3rd Field Survey Co., R.E.
Note—Magnetic Variation from Grid N. is 12° 16' W.
May, 1917.
20

Mount Pleasant Wood
Rœux
la Scarpe River
Dulbar Wood
Junction Copse
Pelves
Pelves Mill
Lone Copse
Sandpit
Splinter Copse
Jigsaw Wood
Hatchet Wood
Keeling Copse
Clear Copse
Sack Wood
Bois du Sart
B. des Aubepines
B. du Sart
Bois des Chiens
Arrow Head Copse
Monchy-le-Preux
Infantry Hill
Green Work
B. du Vert
la Bergère
Cavalry Farm
St Rohart Factory
Guémappe
Hillside Work
Pont à trois Gueules
Vis-en-Artois
Twin Tr.
Infantry Lane
Canister Trench
Green Lane
Grape Trench
Saddle Trench
Cavalry Trench
Factory Trench
Pit Trench
Stirrup Lane
Jungle Alley
Cyclist Trench
Cambrai Road
Hill Lane
Bridge Lane
Bois Lane
Tool Trench
Long Trench
43rd Bde.
33 D.A.
9 D.A.
29 D.A.
12 D.A.
17 D.A.
61st D.A.
50th D.A.
H I
N O
I
CORPS TOPO. SECTION.
GUEMAPPE
Daily Revision sheet to Third Army weekly map (part) "Boiry-Notre-Dame"
Scale 1:10,000.
BARRAGE MAP
U. No 156. 3-5-17

6p

GUEMAPPE
3/6/17

Instructions regarding War Diaries and Intelligence Summaries are contained in F. S. Regs., Part II, and the Staff Manual respectively. Title pages will be prepared in manuscript.

WAR DIARY
or
INTELLIGENCE SUMMARY.
(Erase heading not required.)

Army Form C. 2118.

Vol 20

Place	Date	Hour	Summary of Events and Information	Remarks and references to Appendices
			17th Brigade RFA	
			War Diary	
			1 – 31 October 1917	
			Vol No 31.	

D. D. & L., London, E.C.
(A7883) Wt. W803/M1672 350,000 4/17 Sch. 52a Forms/C2118/14

Instructions regarding War Diaries and Intelligence Summaries are contained in F. S. Regs., Part II. and the Staff Manual respectively. Title pages will be prepared in manuscript.

WAR DIARY
or
INTELLIGENCE SUMMARY.
(Erase heading not required.)

Army Form C. 2118.

Place	Date	Hour	Summary of Events and Information	Remarks and references to Appendices
CHASSEUR FARM	1		Bombs dropped from aircraft last night. Boesinghe shelled.	
	2		Batteries fired harassing fire on ~~Front~~ Trenches & communications.	
	3		Intermittent bombardments by batteries on Hun Trenches. Night quiet	
	4		Infantry attacked at 6.0 AM. Batteries fired flank smoke barrage which was reported very effective, & finished with bombardment of new Hun line. Attack very successful. One counter attack at 3.0 PM, not effective. Two more SOS fired later. Rather doubtful if needed.	
	5		Bursts of fire by Batteries on SOS line etc. At night Batteries moved forward to Battery Copse. Considerable casualties amongst men & horses.	
Wood House	6		Brigade HQ moved up to Wood House. Both safe & comfortable. Batteries having a bad time. Working very hard getting up ammunition & improving positions. Batteries registered. Weather v. bad & mud worse. Many guns still stuck on road.	
	7		Weather frightful. We have all but two guns in position. These two hopelessly stuck. No casualties luckily. Batteries fired on Task. Other people's guns & ammunition wagons stuck everywhere.	
	8		A quiet day. Much [illegible] for the attack.	

A7092 Wt. W128 9/M1293 750,000 1/17. D. D & L. Ltd. Forms/C2118/14.

Army Form C. 2118.

Instructions regarding War Diaries and Intelligence Summaries are contained in F. S. Regs., Part II. and the Staff Manual respectively. Title pages will be prepared in manuscript.

WAR DIARY
or
INTELLIGENCE SUMMARY.
(Erase heading not required.)

Place	Date	Hour	Summary of Events and Information	Remarks and references to Appendices
Wood House	9th Oct		We attacked at 5.20 AM. The attack was completely successful & we gained all our objectives. Casualties very light as a whole, though the 15th Bde RHA got it very hot down in the 'Steenbeek. Several POs in the afternoon. Bad weather	
	10th		A very quiet day on our part of the line but apparently successful counter-attack on our left.	
	11th		In the afternoon what was apparently a "Travelling circus" of Boche guns engaged our own & other batteries, with intensive hate of all calibres. Our batteries took little damage by it. Wagon line also shelled. A few casualties	
	12th		A very successful attack all along the line. Boche gave quiet afterwards & [illegible] ing the attack. No counter-attack.	
	13th		A very peaceful day save that at 2.0 AM & midnight we were shelled a little. Orders have come for us to move forward again.	
	14th		BC's reconnoitred near positions. Whitworth Major Daly & the CO & Adj reconnoitred for new Brigade HQ.	

A7092 Wt. W128 9/M1293 750,000. 1/17. D. D & L. Ltd. Forms/C2118/14.

Army Form C. 2118.

Instructions regarding War Diaries and Intelligence Summaries are contained in F. S. Regs., Part II. and the Staff Manual respectively. Title pages will be prepared in manuscript.

WAR DIARY
or
INTELLIGENCE SUMMARY.
(Erase heading not required.)

Place	Date	Hour	Summary of Events and Information	Remarks and references to Appendices
PILCKEM	15/10/17.		A quiet day except for a few enemy bombs. That night Brigade got all guns into forward position in front of LANGEMARCK.	
"	16/10/17.		Visited Batteries in new positions which are in full view of the enemy and in a very desolate spot.	
LANGUEMARCK	17/10/17		Brigade Hd. Qrs. moved forward to MARTIN'S MILL north of LANGUEMARCK. Very dirty.	
	18/10/17		Got orders that we should have to move to CANNES FARM. Gassed between 9 pm and 1 am.	
	19/10/17		Moved to CANNES Farm where there were three old Hun dug-outs, very smelly and wet. Gassed again between 9 pm & 12.	

Instructions regarding War Diaries and Intelligence Summaries are contained in F. S. Regs., Part II. and the Staff Manual respectively. Title pages will be prepared in manuscript.

WAR DIARY
or
INTELLIGENCE SUMMARY.
(Erase heading not required.)

Army Form C. 2118.

Place	Date	Hour	Summary of Events and Information	Remarks and references to Appendices
CANNES FARM	20/10/17	–	Bombardment commenced at 6 am. Very little hostile shelling in the morning but hostile shelling increased in the afternoon when the enemy concentrated all calibres on LANGEMARCK and the Railway.	
	21/10/17		Bombardment continued. Major Eggleton commanding 17th Bty was killed while helping a wounded officer into a dugout. A very great loss and much felt by all officers and men. Bombardment increased in violence and at night fall our Heavies and the French on our left redoubled their efforts	
	22/10/17	5.35 am	With the French on our left and the 35th Division on our Right the 34th Division on our front advanced to the attack to try and capture the Southern edge of HOUTHOLST FOREST. 17th Brigade supported the Right Battalion with a creeping barrage. Enemy S.O.S. rocket was a white rocket bursting into two reds. The first down	

Instructions regarding War Diaries and Intelligence Summaries are contained in F. S. Regs., Part II. and the Staff Manual respectively. Title pages will be prepared in manuscript.

WAR DIARY
or
INTELLIGENCE SUMMARY.
(Erase heading not required.)

Army Form C. 2118.

Place	Date	Hour	Summary of Events and Information	Remarks and references to Appendices
			a heavy barrage between EGYPT HOUSE & PASCAL FARM 15th Cheshires took their whole of the Left Battalion but the Manchesters (Right Battalion) failed to take even their first objective. Casualties very heavy and medical arrangements not good many men being had to walk down Collapsed by CANNES FARM. (in the evening) Enemy Counter attacked at 4.55 and drove the Cheshires out of MARECHAL Farm. Line remained like this for the rest of the night	
CANNES FARM	23/10/17		O.C Brigade & Adjts 250 Bde R.F.A. arrived at 5am. to commence relief of our batteries. Relief completed by 6pm when all except Lt RAMSEY & two men per Sub. Section of our D/? had marched down to wagon lines. Officers of 9 & 10/17 also left behind.	

A7092 Wt W128 9/M1293 750,000. 1/17. D. D & L. Ltd. Forms/C2118/14.

Instructions regarding War Diaries and Intelligence Summaries are contained in F. S. Regs., Part II. and the Staff Manual respectively. Title pages will be prepared in manuscript.

WAR DIARY
or
INTELLIGENCE SUMMARY.
(*Erase heading not required.*)

Army Form C. 2118.

Place	Date	Hour	Summary of Events and Information	Remarks and references to Appendices
PROVEN	24 } 25 }		Batteries entrained at 4 hours intervals for DOULLENS miserable weather trains 6 hours late and very slow consequently all Btties. kept waiting on the road.	
AOTHIEULE	26		By 6 pm all Btties arrived and marched into billets in AOTHIEULE (two miles S.E of DOULLENS) weather miserable, horses and men wet and tired through long journey, billets fair	
	27		Batteries spent this day trying to rest the men	
	28.		Batteries sent their guns to ARRAS for overhaul.	
	29		Cleaning up, sports committee formed.	
	30		Batteries still cleaning up. weather fine many sick with colds.	
	31.		30 men and one officer per Battery went by train to assist to [illegible] fighting gun positions	

T. C. R[illegible]
LIEUT.-COLONEL. R.F.A.
COMDG., 17TH BDE., R.F.A.

A7092 Wt. W12S.9/M1293 750,000. 1/17. D. D & L. Ltd. Forms/C2118/14.

H.Q.,
17TH BRIGADE,
R.F.A.
No. ....
Date 31.10.17

Casualties for Month of October 1917.

Regt No.	Rank	Name	Unit	Killed	Wounded	Missing	Remarks
	2nd Lt.	Cazeaux R J	13th Bty		1		Gassed - To hosp.
	Lieut.	Ely D.M.	" "		1		Wounded leg - At duty.
32443	Corpl.	Noble H	" "		1		Wounded forearm - To hosp.
39135	Gnr	May J	" "		1		Gas Blisters - To hosp.
42444	Corpl.	Avis J	" "		1		Gas Blisters - To hosp
	Major	Eggleton	" "	1			Killed in Action
33568	Corpl.	Holmes A.C			1		Wounded back + legs To hosp.
38086	Gnr	Groves J.G			1		Wounded thigh - To hosp.
745322	Gnr	Pooley G.W.			1		Wounded thigh - To hosp.
13437	Bdr	Davies W			1		Wounded - gassed At Duty
38089	Gnr	Triggs H.			1		Wounded face At duty
	2nd Lieut	D'Arcy-Hart W.	26th Bty		1		Wounded
111777	Corpl.	Bell H.S			1		"
165365	Gnr	Rudler J.			1		"
630131	"	Gordon B		1			Killed in Action
204199	"	Smith S M			1		Wounded
745505	"	Scowcroft H		1			Killed in Action
61665	Dvr.	Emmerson A.			1		Died of Wounds
73269	"	Livesey A			1		" " "
12234	Gnr	Cook H			1		Wounded.
45367	Dvr.	Onslow A		1			Killed in Action.
131635	"	Davies J R			1		Wounded
235286	Gnr	Skerry H.V.			1		"
770372	Dr	Gaffing G		1			Killed in Action
218423	Gnr	Walker J			1		Wounded
205281	"	Bosson B			1		"
L45389	Dvr.	Chapman T			1		"
845063	"	Wren H			1		"
134489	Gnr	Spear G			1		"
901067	Dvr	Eastwood A			1		"
5689	Gnr	Dohney P			1		" At duty
69688	Corpl.	Newman C			1		Accidental Injury
34523	"	Needham H.			1		Wounded
Total		33		5	28		

P.T.O

2.

Casualty for Month of October 1917 – (Contd)

Regl No	Rank	Name	Unit	Killed	Wounded	Missing	Remarks
	a/Lieut	Smith J W.	92nd		1		Gassed
70179	Gnr	Simpson R.		1			Killed
112896	Gnr	Raynor J.B.			1		Wounded
40374	a/Bdr	Longfoot R.			1		"
906409	Gnr	Sidebotham J.			1		"
192677	"	Ferguston J			1		"
47785	Dvr	Greenway H			1		"
170467	"	Barnes G			1		"
116040	a/Bdr	Gillespie R.			1		" Retd to duty
67089	Sgt	Davis A			1		"
98821	Gnr	Logan T			1		"
81551	"	North W.			1		"
30357	"	Rowe R			1		" Retd to duty
44209	Sgt	Powrie H			1		"
47316	Bdr	Hodgson W.			1		"
38092	"	Ewen C B.			1		"
45686	Dvr	Thorpe T			1		" Retd to duty
47000	Bdr	Blake H			1		"
830263	Gnr	Harris J W.			1		" Gassed
222822	"	Lawson J H			1		" "
5458	"	Marsh W.			1		" "
76202	"	Oram J G			1		" "
202120	"	Thomas J S			1		" "
168551	"	Styles J			1		" "
227596	"	Mitchell G			1		" "
63392	"	Kirkhope A	Attd 92nd Bty		1		" "
50740	Sgt	Bennett C	92 "		1		" Shell Shock
45914	Corpl	Brown W	"		1		" " "
212692	Gnr	Poat W. A	"		1		" " "
	Lieut	Bedford-Pim E W	D/17		1		Wounded leg.
103551	Gnr	Standhope P.J.	"		1		" by Bomb Explosion
36535	Dvr	Brewer J. H	"		1		Wounded
53757	Dvr	Turner C J	[illegible]	1			Killed in Action
Total (page 1–2)				7	59		

[illegible signature]

Lt RFA

Adj 17 Bde RFA

H.Q.,
17TH BRIGADE,
R.F.A.
No ....
Date 31.10.17.

Casualties for Month of October
17 Brigade R.F.A. Head Qrs

Regt No	Rank	Name	Unit	Killed	Wounded	Missing	Remarks
	Lieut. Col	W. A. Murray DSO R.F.A.	Hd Qrs		1		To hosp Gassed,
56156	Gnr	Davis W	" "		1		30/9/17
792	"	Alcock L	13th Bty		1		" " Gassed
50689	Sapper	Barnett E	29 R.E. att Hd Qrs		1		" " "
15545	Cpl	Bradley O	" "		1		" " "

Instructions regarding War Diaries and Intelligence Summaries are contained in F. S. Regs., Part II, and the Staff Manual respectively. Title pages will be prepared in manuscript.

WAR DIARY
or
INTELLIGENCE SUMMARY.
(Erase heading not required.)

Army Form C. 2118.

Vol 21

Place	Date	Hour	Summary of Events and Information	Remarks and references to Appendices
			War Diary.	
			17th Brigade. R.F.A.	
			From 1st November 1917 to 30th November 1917	
			Vol, No. 32.	

D. D. & L., London, E.C.
(A7883) Wt. W803/M1672 350,000 4/17 Sch. 52a Forms/C/2118/14

Instructions regarding War Diaries and Intelligence Summaries are contained in F. S. Regs., Part II, and the Staff Manual respectively. Title pages will be prepared in manuscript.

WAR DIARY
or
INTELLIGENCE SUMMARY.
(*Erase heading not required.*)

Army Form C. 2118.

Place	Date	Hour	Summary of Events and Information	Remarks and references to Appendices
AUTHIEULE.	1/11/17	–	All teams and limbers under Lt ELY proceeded to ARRAS to pick up guns to proceed to the ranges at FRICOURT.	
"	2.		One picked gun detachment per Bty: ~~—~~ proceeded to ALBERT to calibrate guns of the Brigade. Capt BALL M.C 15 Brigade RHA in charge of ranges which were at FRICOURT. Guns brought down from ARRAS via BAPAUME to FRICOURT. 2Lt RATSEY reconnoitred forward wagon lines with Staff Captain at SAPIGNIES. Orders given and cancelled by 29 D.A. many times until we are all in a whirl.	
"	3.		Orders to move to MAILLY MAILLET & BEAUSART on 5/11/17. When the guns were to meet us from ALBERT after calibration. Guns calibrating.	
"	4.		Orders cancelled again. Billeting party already gone to MAILLY MAILLET. Guns proceeded to MAILLY MAILLET but remainder of wagons etc. remained at AUTHIEULE.	
	5.		~~Guns returned~~ Orders for Bde. to concentrate here	

D. D. & L., London, E.C.
(A7883) Wt. W803/M1672 350,000 4/17 Sch. 52a Forms/C/2118/14

Instructions regarding War Diaries and Intelligence Summaries are contained in F. S. Regs., Part II. and the Staff Manual respectively. Title pages will be prepared in manuscript.

WAR DIARY
or
INTELLIGENCE SUMMARY.
(*Erase heading not required.*)

Place	Date	Hour	Summary of Events and Information	Remarks and references to Appendices

AUTHIEULE 5. Guns returned from MAILLY MAILLET but two snipers of our digging party.

6. Digging party returned from gun position. Came by train to BELLE EGLISE from where they had to march. Brigade are once together after having been scattered nearly all over FRANCE for a week. Colonel in bed sick with bad cold. Major Daly takes charge.

7. Weather fine. Spent in preparing for C.R.A's inspection tomorrow. One of those obliging Field Cashiers refused to pay out any money for paying the men, giving no other reason than he had no money. The men will therefore have to go for another week without pay.

8. Brigade turned out in drill order and marched through ORVILLE, SARTON, THIEVRES and back through ORVILLE and AMPLIER to AMPLIER. C.R.A inspected us just short of SARTON, not too satisfactory. Rained most of the time which

Instructions regarding War Diaries and Intelligence Summaries are contained in F. S. Regs., Part II. and the Staff Manual respectively. Title pages will be prepared in manuscript.

WAR DIARY
or
INTELLIGENCE SUMMARY.
(Erase heading not required.)

Army Form C. 2118.

Place	Date	Hour	Summary of Events and Information	Remarks and references to Appendices
AUTHIEULE	8.		did not add to the general enjoyment. Colonel Richwarden went to a hospital to see why his cold would not improve and was told that he was suffering from gas which had only just escaped affecting his heart. He may have to leave us ~~again~~ for ten days.	
	9.		Colonel & Doctor warned by A.D.M.S. that they would have to go to the CANADIAN Hospital DOULLENS for a short while as they were both suffering from gas shell poisoning. A filthy day.	
	10.		C.R.A. saw Brigade Staff horses at 10 a.m. Bde. Staff played Div. Arty. at football we lost 2-nil. Colonel & Doctor departed in an ambulance to hospital. Very cold.	
	11		Normal day in rest at AUTHIEULE.	
	12		Prepared for march to forward area.	
	13		Marched to BUIRE on night of 13/14. Arrived BUIRE at	

D. D. & L., London, E.C. (A7883) Wt. W803/M1672 350,000 4/17 Sch. 52a Forms/C/2118/14

Instructions regarding War Diaries and Intelligence Summaries are contained in F. S. Regs., Part II. and the Staff Manual respectively. Title pages will be prepared in manuscript.

WAR DIARY
or
INTELLIGENCE SUMMARY.
(Erase heading not required.)

Army Form C. 2118.

Place	Date	Hour	Summary of Events and Information	Remarks and references to Appendices
MANNANCOURT			6.30 am. Rest of Brigade got lost in Albert. Major Daly in command of Bde. Colonel Culhane[?] sick.	
	14.		Spent at BUIRE.	
	15		Night of 15/16 marched to HENNOIS WOOD near MANNANCOURT. Orders were to have all vehicles in the wood by dawn but as we were held up on the road by Bde. Brigade we did not get in until 7 am.	
	16.		Spent in camp at HENNOIS WOOD very uncomfortable 7 tents only per Battery. Started taking up ammunition up to gun positions.	
	17.		Guns of 13" Bty. went into action on night of 17/18. Position one mile N.E of GOUZEAUCOURT.	
	18.		Remaining Batteries went into action in the same area. All "silent" Batteries	
	19.		On night of 19/20 wagon lines moved forward to	

D. D. & L., London, E.C.
(A7883) Wt. W803/M1672 350,000 4/17 Sch. 52a Forms/C/2118/14

Instructions regarding War Diaries and Intelligence Summaries are contained in F. S. Regs., Part II. and the Staff Manual respectively. Title pages will be prepared in manuscript.

WAR DIARY
or
INTELLIGENCE SUMMARY.
(*Erase heading not required.*)

Army Form C. 2118.

Place	Date	Hour	Summary of Events and Information	Remarks and references to Appendices
			new wagon lines East of Gouzeaucourt Wood. Firing	
GOUZEAUCOURT	19		Battery wagons taken up to gun line. Brigade Headquarters moved to 15 Ravine between Gouzeaucourt and Villers Plouich. Very miserable as we had only a small tarpaulin over our heads.	
	20.		THE DAY. Attacked at 6.20 am. Everywhere successful LA VACQUERIE, RIBECOURT, MASNIERES MARCOIGNE all ours by 11 am. Batteries moved forward a mile beyond Hindenburgh line, no shelling. Aided by party of Tunnellers and Gunners made a good road over all trenches. Tanks everywhere, some derelict, but on the whole doing excellent work. Batteries came into action in L33, Bde. Headquarters with 87th Infantry Brigade in Chateau at MARCOIGNÉ. Strong enemy resistance on MARCOIGNÉ-BEUREVOIR and held 29th Division. This was first real resistance made by the enemy who up to this time had been	

D. D. & L., London, E.C.
(A7883) Wt. W809/M1672 350,000 4/17 Sch. 52a Forms/C/2118/14

Instructions regarding War Diaries and Intelligence Summaries are contained in F. S. Regs., Part II, and the Staff Manual respectively. Title pages will be prepared in manuscript.

WAR DIARY
or
INTELLIGENCE SUMMARY.
(Erase heading not required.)

Army Form C. 2118.

Place	Date	Hour	Summary of Events and Information	Remarks and references to Appendices
MARCOIGNE	20		Completely taken by surprise. 4000 Prisoners taken	
	21.		Enemy still quiet. Attack by 87th Bde. and 9 Tanks made on RED LINE where the Germans were holding out. Attack repulsed by machine Gun fire from FLOT FARM. Bde. Headquarters moved into dug-outs just behind MARCOIGNE. Colonel Murray D.S.O. returned.	
	22.		Normal day nothing done. All Batteries have been registered. Two Batteries moved 200 yds on night 22/23.	
	23.		Brigade Headquarters moved to good dug-outs near Battery positions. Deep dug-outs, elephant huts. All happy	
	24.		Slight shelling of Battery positions with 77 mm. H.E & mm 13' 13½'. Wounded. Weather remains fine with intermittent heavy showers.	
	25.		Normal day. Hun still inactive. Reconnoitred forward position for section of 92nd Battery by NINE WOOD. Decided	

Army Form C. 2118.

Instructions regarding War Diaries and Intelligence Summaries are contained in F. S. Regs., Part II, and the Staff Manual respectively. Title pages will be prepared in manuscript.

WAR DIARY
or
INTELLIGENCE SUMMARY.
(Erase heading not required.)

Place	Date	Hour	Summary of Events and Information	Remarks and references to Appendices
			in position by NINE WOOD in Quarry from where we can get a good enfilade fire on to the RED LINE.	
	26.		93rd Bty (Hows.) started digging at NINE WOOD. Hope to be ready to put Section in tomorrow morning. Weather much colder.	
Marcoing	27.		Supported an attack by the Corps on our left. A normal day.	
	28.		Gun of 26th Battery received direct hit and blown to pieces. 10 casualties caused. Lt GOODWIN posted to the Brigade.	
	29.		Germans slightly more active. A fine day.	
	30.		About 8.30 am information received that the enemy had broken through on our right. Shortly confirmed by Major Holmes and Major Stanford at the O.P. who could see the enemy advancing, and Major Stanford opened fire with the Battery Lewis Gun. Two guns of 9.2 D/17	

D. D. & L., London, E.C.
(A7883) Wt. W803/M1672 350,000 4/17 Sch. 52a Forms/C/2118/14

Instructions regarding War Diaries and Intelligence Summaries are contained in F. S. Regs., Part II. and the Staff Manual respectively. Title pages will be prepared in manuscript.

WAR DIARY
or
INTELLIGENCE SUMMARY.
(Erase heading not required.)

Army Form C. 2118.

Place	Date	Hour	Summary of Events and Information	Remarks and references to Appendices
			were turned right round to try and check the advance of the enemy. These guns undoubtedly did good work as the enemy were held. 29 Division who were holding MARCOING & MASNIERES fought magnificently not only holding the enemy in their own front but also throwing out a defensive flank on their right to try and cover the gap where the Germans had broken through. 15 Brigade R.H.A. on our right after a magnificent fight at point blank range were forced to abandon their guns thus necessitating our covering a much larger front. 232 A. Field Brigade then came under the command of Colonel Murray which helped us a lot. Batteries firing continuously all day. Batteries & Brigade Headquarters under M.G. fire almost all day. Fighting in Masnieres very heavy.	

R Parcell Lt RFA
a/Adjt. for. Commanding 17th Bde RFA

D. D. & L., London, E.C.
(A7883) Wt. W893/M1672 350,000 4/17 **Sch. 52a** Forms/C/2118/14

H.Q.,
17TH BRIGADE,
R.F.A.

No.
Date

Vol 22

War Diary
of
17th Brigade R F A.
From 1st December 1917 to 31st December 1917

Vol No 33

Instructions regarding War Diaries and Intelligence Summaries are contained in F. S. Regs., Part II, and the Staff Manual respectively. Title pages will be prepared in manuscript.

WAR DIARY
or
INTELLIGENCE SUMMARY.
(Erase heading not required.)

Army Form C. 2118.

Place	Date	Hour	Summary of Events and Information	Remarks and references to Appendices
Marcoing	1/12/17		Enemy continued his assaults on Marcoing. Batteries fired continuously all day. During the night 9/2.12.17 retired to new positions in front of RIBECOURT.	
Ribecourt	2		Situation obscure 29 Division fighting splendidly and still holding on. That night we evacuated Marcoing. 13 & 26 Batteries retired to positions by 9/2.12.17. Brigade Headquarters also retired to Headquarters just outside Ribecourt.	
Ribecourt	3.		The Brigade retired to positions behind Ribecourt. This night the front line was brought back to the Hindenburgh support line with an outpost line 500 yards in advance. This was accomplished in good order.	
	4.		Normal day. Batteries registered from new positions	
	5		Capt Reynolds & Lt Richardson wounded. Brigade H.Q. were in dug outs in Hindenburgh line. Batteries digging in in new positions.	

D. D. & L., London, E.C. (A7883) Wt. W803/M1672 350,000 4/17 Sch. 52a Forms/C/2118/14

Instructions regarding War Diaries and Intelligence Summaries are contained in F. S. Regs., Part II. and the Staff Manual respectively. Title pages will be prepared in manuscript.

WAR DIARY
or
INTELLIGENCE SUMMARY.
(Erase heading not required.)

Army Form C. 2118.

Place	Date	Hour	Summary of Events and Information	Remarks and references to Appendices
Ribecourt	6.		Lt Williams detached from Brigade Headquarters to take over temporary command of 26th Battery. [illegible] attached to that Battery for duty as they were short of officers.	
	7		Capt Chaldecott rejoined 26 Battery & so Lt Williams was able to return to Headquarters. A quiet day. [illegible] attached to 26 Divisional Artillery.	
	8.		Normal day.	
	9.		Quiet day but hostile attacks anticipated. Higher Commands very uneasy although we do not feel very worried. Much ammunition is expended now daily at dawn to forestall the Huns attack(?).	
	10.		A quiet day. The Brigade is in need of relief as we are very short of stores and the men are tired.	
	11.		The Group here consists of 17th Brigade R.F.A. and two Batteries of 5th Brigade R.H.A. these Batteries are O & Z.	

D. D. & L., London, E.C. (A7883) Wt. W803/M1672 350,000 4/17 Sch. 52a Forms/C/2118/14

Instructions regarding War Diaries and Intelligence Summaries are contained in F. S. Regs., Part II. and the Staff Manual respectively. Title pages will be prepared in manuscript.

WAR DIARY
or
INTELLIGENCE SUMMARY.
(Erase heading not required.)

Army Form C. 2118.

Place	Date	Hour	Summary of Events and Information	Remarks and references to Appendices
Ribecourt	12.		Quiet day. The enemy has devoted the whole of his artillery fire to shelling the roads at night so we haul ammunition up by day.	
	13.		We are informed that we will change over positions with 153rd Brigade RFA in order that this latter Brigade may ~~[struck out]~~ come under their own Division and Divisional Artillery. On looking at our new positions we find that they are very bad indeed which makes all ranks down-hearted as so much work has been done in positions which we have to hand over in place of these bad ones.	
	14		This change takes place. We now cover with very few guns a large front between Ribecourt and Flesquieres. The Batteries we have just taken over from are in a pointless condition as regards guns and stores as (1) of the former they are very	

D. D. & L., London, E.C.
(A7883) Wt. W809/M1672 350,000 4/17 Sch. 52a Forms/C/2118/14

Instructions regarding War Diaries and Intelligence Summaries are contained in F. S. Regs., Part II, and the Staff Manual respectively. Title pages will be prepared in manuscript.

WAR DIARY
or
INTELLIGENCE SUMMARY.
(Erase heading not required.)

Army Form C. 2118.

Place	Date	Hour	Summary of Events and Information	Remarks and references to Appendices
Marcoing	1/12/17		Enemy continued his assaults on Marcoing. Batteries fired continuously all day. During the night 92 & 93 Btys retired to new positions in front of RIBECOURT.	
Ribecourt	2		Situation obscure 29 Division fighting splendidly and still holding on. That night we evacuated Marcoing. 13 & 26 Batteries retired to positions by 92 & 93. Brigade Headquarters also retired to Headquarters just outside Ribecourt.	
Ribecourt	3.		The Brigade retired to positions behind Ribecourt. This night the front line was brought back to the Hindenburgh Support line with an outpost line 500 yards in advance. This was accomplished in good order.	
	4.		Normal day. Batteries registered from new positions.	
	5		Capt Reynolds & Lt Richardson wounded. Brigade H.Q. came in the day into Hindenburgh line. Batteries shifting in to new positions.	

D. D. & L., London, E.C. (A7583) Wt. W807/M1672 350,000 4/17 Sch. 52a Forms/C/2118/14

H.Q.,
17TH BRIGADE,
R.F.A.

No.............

Date...........

Vol 22

War Diary

of

17th Brigade R F A.

From 1st December 1917 To 31st December 1917

Vol No 33

Instructions regarding War Diaries and Intelligence Summaries are contained in F. S. Regs., Part II. and the Staff Manual respectively. Title pages will be prepared in manuscript.

WAR DIARY
or
INTELLIGENCE SUMMARY.
(Erase heading not required.)

Army Form C. 2118.

Place	Date	Hour	Summary of Events and Information	Remarks and references to Appendices
Ribecourt	14		doubtful as to where some are (2) of the batteries they have gone. Bde. H.Q. remains where it was before.	
	15.		Registered guns from new positions and tried to repair some of the new guns that were out of action.	
	16.		At 3pm we are informed that we must pull out and be in our wagon lines by 5pm. As this is impossible we obtain permission to stay in until the morning. Only D/[illegible] pulls out that night.	
	17		We pull out to wagon lines at dawn and march on from there to billets at Beaulencourt near Bapaume. Billets which are in Nissen Huts are very cold. It has snowed and frozen hard so we have not got much hope of good roads in the morning.	
	18.		March to Bernancourt just behind Albert and although it is 8am when we start the condition of	

D. D. & L., London, E.C. (A7883) Wt. W803/M1672 350,000 4/17 Sch. 52a Forms/C/2118/14

Army Form

Instructions regarding War Diaries and Intelligence Summaries are contained in F. S. Regs., Part II. and the Staff Manual respectively. Title pages will be prepared in manuscript.

WAR DIARY
or
INTELLIGENCE SUMMARY.
(Erase heading not required.)

Place	Date	Hour	Summary of Events and Information	Remarks and references to Appendices
			the roads which frozen hard and the blocks in	
			the traffic delayed us so much that it is 6pm. before	
			all the Batteries are in the village, even then	
			the baggage and supply wagons did not arrive	
			until 9 pm. and some were left in the road.	
	19.		Remained in Dernancourt where everyone is	
			busy shoeing the horses to try and compete with	
			these frozen roads. Billets are bad	
	20.		Marched to Forceville. Roads in a terrible	
			condition as they are covered with ~~[illegible]~~ ice	
			Busy all night re-shoeing in order to be able to march	
			in the morning. Still very cold.	
	21.		Marched to DOULLENS and billeted in the town. Arrived	
			3pm.	
	22.		Remained at Doullens.	

D. D. & L., London, E.C.
(A7883) Wt. W803/M1672 350,000 4/17 Sch. 52a Forms/C/2118/14

Instructions regarding War Diaries and Intelligence Summaries are contained in F. S. Regs., Part II. and the Staff Manual respectively. Title pages will be prepared in manuscript.

Army Form C. 2118.

WAR DIARY
or
INTELLIGENCE SUMMARY.
(Erase heading not required.)

Place	Date	Hour	Summary of Events and Information	Remarks and references to Appendices
	23		Marched to FILLIEVRES. Arrived at 2pm. Roads very bad.	
	24		Marched to BEAURANVILLE area. Arrived at 1.30pm. Roads still bad. HQrs and D/17 Battery in MARESQUEL 26th & 92nd Batteries in LESPINOY and 13th Battery in MARENLA.	
	25		Stayed in the above mentioned villages. Batteries training and cleaning up.	
	26		— do —	
	27		— do —	
	28		— do —	
	29		— do —	
	30		— do —	
	31		— do —	

H Parcell 2/Lieut RFA
a/Adjt. 17th Bde RFA.

D. D. & L., London, E.C.
(A7883) Wt. W809/M1672 350,000 4/17 Sch. 52a Forms/C/2118/14

H.Q.,
17TH BRIGADE,
R.F.A.
No. B257
Date 15/2/18

Vol 23

War Diary
of
17th Brigade R.F.a.

From 1—1—18 To 31—1—18.

Vol. No 34.

Instructions regarding War Diaries and Intelligence Summaries are contained in F. S. Regs., Part II. and the Staff Manual respectively. Title pages will be prepared in manuscript.

WAR DIARY
or
INTELLIGENCE SUMMARY.
(Erase heading not required.)

Army Form C. 2118.

Place	Date	Hour	Summary of Events and Information	Remarks and references to Appendices
MARESQUEL	1/1/18		Batteries still training at LESPIGNOL, MARENLA and MARESQUEL	
			Roads still very bad.	
	2nd		— do —	
			Received orders to march to CREQUY.	
	3rd		Marched to CREQUY arriving at 1.15pm. Roads fairly	
			good for travelling. Orders to march to MERK St LEIVIN on 4th inst	
	4th		Marched to MERK St LIEVIN arriving at 1.30pm. Billets	
			bad. Roads were fairly good	
	5th		Cleaning up and training. Divisional Commander	
			to inspect the Divisional Artillery on or about the	
			11th inst.	
	6th		Batteries preparing for the Inspection	
	7th		Practice carried out on the inspection ground.	
			Began to thaw and roads were bad.	
	8th		Inspection Cancelled. Received orders to march	
			to	

D. D. & L., London, E.C.
(A7883) Wt. W807/M1672 350,000 4/17 Sch. 52a Forms/C/2118/14

Instructions regarding War Diaries and Intelligence Summaries are contained in F. S. Regs., Part II. and the Staff Manual respectively. Title pages will be prepared in manuscript.

WAR DIARY
or
INTELLIGENCE SUMMARY.
(Erase heading not required.)

Army Form C. 2118.

Place	Date	Hour	Summary of Events and Information	Remarks and references to Appendices
MECK.	9		Snowed hard in the afternoon and very cold. Wind suddenly went round to the West at 5pm when thaw set in	
	10.		Thawed hard all day. Preparations made for marching tomorrow.	
	11.		Marched to RENESCURE area. Billets in line ARQUES-CASSEL Road. G.O.C. Division inspected Brigade on the line of march just outside WIZERNES.	
	12.		Brigade marched to OUDEZEELE billeting in very bad and dirty farms just outside the village	
	13.		Brigade marched to POPERINGHE area marching into wagon lines taken over from 231st Brigade R.F.A. Ground very bad but plenty of accommodation for the men in Nissen huts & tents.	

D. D. & L., London, E.C.
(A7883) Wt. W809/M1672 350,000 4/17 Sch. 52a Forms/C/2118/14

Instructions regarding War Diaries and Intelligence Summaries are contained in F. S. Regs., Part II. and the Staff Manual respectively. Title pages will be prepared in manuscript.

WAR DIARY
or
~~INTELLIGENCE SUMMARY.~~
(Erase heading not required.)

Army Form C. 2118.

Place	Date	Hour	Summary of Events and Information	Remarks and references to Appendices
POPERINGHE	14		Remained in new wagon lines. Orders received that we are to carry on building reserve gun positions in the Army Reserve line in the neighbourhood of ST JEAN. 48 Remounts arrived.	
	15.		Digging party of one Officer and 20 men per Battery under Capt. MORRICE went up to St JEAN to work on gun positions mentioned above.	
	16.		Spent in trying to clean up. Lines getting into very bad condition. Very wet.	
	17		Quiet day. Nothing of interest. C.R.A. returned from a week's course with the R.F.C.	
	18		Very wet. One is up to ones knees in mud at the horse lines now.	
	19.		One Section per Battery went up to relieve one Section per Battery of the 33rd Bde R.F.A. 13th Battery to 32nd Battery 26 – 33 Battery. 92nd – 36th Battery & D/17 to 55th Battery.	

Instructions regarding War Diaries and Intelligence Summaries are contained in F. S. Regs., Part II. and the Staff Manual respectively. Title pages will be prepared in manuscript.

WAR DIARY
or
INTELLIGENCE SUMMARY.
(Erase heading not required.)

Army Form C. 2118.

Place	Date	Hour	Summary of Events and Information	Remarks and references to Appendices
POPERINGHE	19.		Parties proceeded by lorry to WIELTJE cross roads where guides from Batteries of 33rd Brigade met them. B.C. also went up on this day but returned in the evening.	
	20.		Remaining two sections per Battery of the Brigade took over from the remaining two sections per Battery of the 33rd Brigade R.F.A. H.Q. relieved H.Q. of 33rd Brigade. The relief was slightly impeded by heavy hostile shelling. Relief complete by 2pm.	
Field.	21.		Positions are some 4000 yards in front of WIELTJE. A very much quieter day which is a great relief after having had such an inauspicious entry yesterday. 92nd & D/17 are quite well off in their positions but 13 & 26 Batteries are in very bad positions. Brigade H.Q. is about 2300 yards from the nearest Battery which is D/17 and so it is a long walk round the Batteries taking about 3 hours.	

D. D. & L., London, E.C.
(A7883) Wt. W803/M1672 350,000 4/17 Sch. 52a Forms/C/2118/14

Instructions regarding War Diaries and Intelligence Summaries are contained in F. S. Regs., Part II. and the Staff Manual respectively. Title pages will be prepared in manuscript.

WAR DIARY
or
INTELLIGENCE SUMMARY.
(Erase heading not required.)

Army Form C. 2118.

Place	Date	Hour	Summary of Events and Information	Remarks and references to Appendices
Field	22.		A quiet day. The enemy shelled tracks & roads at night doing no damage apparently. Afterwards it was ascertained that a gun of 26th Battery which had been damaged by shell fire could not be repaired at the gun line so had to be taken to the I.O.M. It is no easy matter to get a gun out of position here. The ground is terribly cut up and very muddy and the only possible way of walking is by keeping to the duck boards which at times take you a long way round.	
	23.		Again a quiet day. It should have been mentioned in the previous paragraph that a Corporal of D/17 and one man of that Battery were hit by shell fire. The Cpl. was killed and the man wounded.	
	24		Very peaceful. We ~~[illegible]~~ hear that the enemy try to fraternize with our troops in the front line or what there is of it. This mud is very bad.	

D. D. & L., London, E.C.
(A7883) Wt. W803/M1672 350,000 4/17 Sch. 52a Forms/C/2118/14

Instructions regarding War Diaries and Intelligence Summaries are contained in F. S. Regs., Part II. and the Staff Manual respectively. Title pages will be prepared in manuscript.

WAR DIARY
or
INTELLIGENCE SUMMARY.
(Erase heading not required.)

Army Form C. 2118.

Place	Date	Hour	Summary of Events and Information	Remarks and references to Appendices
Field	25.		Very quiet, nothing of interest to report. Usual routine, we are very short of men and rather short of officers.	
"	26		Commenced doing Liaison Duty with the Left Battalion Headquarters. Still quiet. Padre living with us.	
"	27.		Quiet day. Enemy got excited about 9 pm. thus necessitating our firing a concentration, which in plain language is a burst of fire on a small or limited area. Lt Banks Williams returned	
"	28.		Scarcely any firing on our part although some registrations were carried out. 2/Lt GAYNER joined 26 Battery	
"	29.		16cm slightly more active. Another concentration fired at 11.15 am. Lt Fenwick returned from leave and went as A.P.M. to 1st Army H.Q.	
"	30.		Rather a noisy day in the neighbourhood of H.Q. The enemy fired 150 8" How. shell about 600 in front.	
"	31.		Very quiet again. T. C. Raley Capt. RFA for O.C. 17th Bde RFA	

D. D. & L., London, E.C. (A7883) Wt. W809/M1672 350,000 4/17 Sch. 52a Forms/C/2118/14

Instructions regarding War Diaries and Intelligence Summaries are contained in F. S. Regs., Part II, and the Staff Manual respectively. Title pages will be prepared in manuscript.

WAR DIARY
or
INTELLIGENCE SUMMARY.
(Erase heading not required.)

Army Form C. 2118.

Vol 24

Place	Date	Hour	Summary of Events and Information	Remarks and references to Appendices
			War Diary	
			of	
			17th Brigade R F A.	
			From 1 - 2 - 18 To 28 - 2 - 18	
			Vol No 35	

D. D. & L., London, E.C.
(A7883) Wt. W803/M1672 350,000 4/17 Sch. 52a Forms/C/2118/14

Instructions regarding War Diaries and Intelligence Summaries are contained in F. S. Regs., Part II. and the Staff Manual respectively. Title pages will be prepared in manuscript.

WAR DIARY
or
INTELLIGENCE SUMMARY.
(Erase heading not required.)

Army Form C. 2118.

Place	Date	Hour	Summary of Events and Information	Remarks and references to Appendices
Field	1/2/18		On the whole a quiet day. Very cold, mostly due to a wind but also some frost. Lt Colonel Murray D.S.O. granted one month's leave (special).	
	2/2/18.		Hun considerably more active. 13, 26, and D/17 Batteries all came in for some shelling with for the most part 15 cm. hows. Much warmer and clearer which latter circumstances perhaps accounts for increased hostile activity.	
	3/2/18		Some hostile activity but quieter. Weather still fine. Brigade fired 182 A. 6 Ax. Nothing of importance.	
	4/2/18		Considerably quieter. Still fine. Brigade fired 170 A. 3 Ax nothing of interest	
	5/2/18.		Very quiet and peaceful. Brigade fired 115 A 19 AX. Rat hunting is now the feature of interest. Barometer falling	
	6/2/18.		We are now taking over these guns for 13th Battery, with "Buffer Stops" fitted on which we are required to render a report on 21st of this month. We render reports nearly every	

D. D. & L., London, E.C.
(A7883) Wt. W803/M1672 350,000 4/17 Sch. 52a Forms/C/2118/14

H.Q.
17TH BRIGADE,
R.F.A.
No. ....
Date ....

Vol 25

War Diary

of

17th Brigade R.F.A.

From 1st March 1918 To 31st March 1918

Army Form C. 2118.

Instructions regarding War Diaries and Intelligence Summaries are contained in F. S. Regs., Part II. and the Staff Manual respectively. Title Pages will be prepared in manuscript.

WAR DIARY
or
INTELLIGENCE SUMMARY
(Erase heading not required.)

Place	Date	Hour	Summary of Events and Information	Remarks and references to Appendices
Reselhoek	1/3/18		Final between B and Warwick Blues replayed. Still no score at time. 10 minutes each way decided on and Warwicks score a goal by a scrimmage at five minutes to time, so Warwicks win 1 – 0. Sent for 26 remounts	
	2		Very cold. This is the day of the Rugger match between officers of 15th & 17th Brigades R.A. but 15th Brigade R.H.A. scratch at the last moment.	
	3.		Semi finals of the six-a-side inter Bty. Sections football match played off, not much interest shown in this although a 170 kilo. pig is the prize.	
	4.		D/17 win the pig much to the delight of everyone in the Brigade. Preparations being made for Ceremonial parade before the G.O.C. on 6/3/18. Batteries receive some very dirty guns.	

2449 Wt. W14957/M90 750,000 1/16 J.B.C. & A. Forms/C.2118/12.

Army Form

WAR DIARY
or
INTELLIGENCE SUMMARY
(Erase heading not required.)

Instructions regarding War Diaries and Intelligence Summaries are contained in F. S. Regs., Part II. and the Staff Manual respectively. Title Pages will be prepared in manuscript.

Place	Date	Hour	Summary of Events and Information	Remarks and references to Appendices
Peselhoek	to 5/3/18		Nothing to report. Preparations made for the Ceremonial Parade in PIPERINGHE Square tomorrow.	
"	6/3/18		Ceremonial parade in PIPERINGHE Square. Quite an event. The G.O.C. 29th Division inspected each Battery in turn and then each Battery marched past. The band played and as it was a very fine day things passed off quite pleasantly. Colonel Murray returned.	
"	7/3/18.		One Section per Battery relieved one Section per Bty of 33rd Brigade R.F.A. in action. The remainder relieve tomorrow.	
Field.	8/3/18.		Relief complete by 12.30 pm. a very quiet day. Major Daly went on course	
"	9/3/18		a quiet day in the line. No firing by order of Corps.	
"	10/3/18		Intermittent hurricane shoots fired at intervals throughout the day and night.	

2449 Wt. W14957/M90 750,000 1/16 J.B.C. & A. Forms/C.2118/12.

Army F

WAR DIARY
or
INTELLIGENCE SUMMARY
(Erase heading not required.)

Instructions regarding War Diaries and Intelligence Summaries are contained in F. S. Regs., Part II. and the Staff Manual respectively. Title Pages will be prepared in manuscript.

Place	Date	Hour	Summary of Events and Information	Remarks and references to Appendices
Field.	11th	6.10 am	Enemy attempted a raid on our Right Battalion but was repulsed with very heavy losses before he even reached our wire. Many German dead and wounded in NO MAN'S LAND. 3 Prisoners were Captured in the 29th Divisional front including a Sergt. Major who was captured on our front.	
"	12th		Exceptionally quiet.	
"	13		2.10 am. Enemy commenced heavy T.M. bombardment of our Right Btn. front and also on the Brigade on our right. S.O.S. Signal went up on our right. S.O.S. fire continued from 2.10 am – 3 am.	
	14		Quiet day nothing to report.	

2449 Wt. W14957/M90 750,000 1/16 J.B.C. & A. Forms/C.2118/12.

WAR DIARY
or
INTELLIGENCE SUMMARY
(Erase heading not required.)

Place	Date	Hour	Summary of Events and Information	Remarks and references to Appendices
Field.	17/3/18		H.Q. moving up nearer to the Batteries to a place Called KANSAS HOUSE.	
"	16/3/18		Nothing of interest. A very quiet day.	
"	17/3/18		" a few Shells in this neighbourhood. Rather a disturbed night owing to Hun restlessness.	
"	18/3/18		Quiet: weather still keeps perfect. Good visibility from KALLEMOLEN O.P. Some hostile movement observed.	
"	19/3/18		Weather has now broken up. H.Q. shelled at mid-day by 5.9 How. Battery. Enemy shelled with bursts of fire. Nothing of importance to report.	
"	20/3/18		Heavy gas bombardment during the night around our Batteries. No Casualties.	

2449 Wt. W14957/M90 750,000 1/16 J.B.C. & A. Forms/C.2118/12.

Army Form C. 2118.

Instructions regarding War Diaries and Intelligence Summaries are contained in F. S. Regs., Part II. and the Staff Manual respectively. Title Pages will be prepared in manuscript.

WAR DIARY
or
INTELLIGENCE SUMMARY

(Erase heading not required.)

Place	Date	Hour	Summary of Events and Information	Remarks and references to Appendices
Faidel	21/3/18.		Great battle opened down South. No definite news. Quiet up here	
"	22/3/18.		A certain amount of shelling from all calibres including gas shells. Still no definite news from South.	
"	23/3/18.		Our troops are retiring in the battle. Quiet here. German balloon reported in the news.	
	24/3/18		A certain amount of promiscuous shelling. German balloon again reported in the news from South.	
	25/3/18		Fine weather breaking up. Much colder. Very Quiet.	

2449 Wt. W14957/M90 750,000 1/16 J.B.C. & A. Forms/C.2118/12.

Instructions regarding War Diaries and Intelligence Summaries are contained in F. S. Regs., Part II. and the Staff Manual respectively. Title Pages will be prepared in manuscript.

WAR DIARY
or
INTELLIGENCE SUMMARY
(Erase heading not required.)

Army Form C. 2118.

Place	Date	Hour	Summary of Events and Information	Remarks and references to Appendices
Field	26.		Normal day. Slightly better news from South.	
"	27.		Heavy German bombardment from 3am - 7am. Shelling chiefly in back areas. All calibres including gas.	
	28.		Weather still dull. Glass falling. A quiet day.	
"	29		Germans held on "Armancourt - Brie" line down South. Still quiet up here.	
"	30.		Still quiet. Good news from the Battle. Enemy attack on VIMY and ARRAS broken.	
	31		Quiet. The winter has been very peaceful. The men have all had a good time considering the reputation of Flanders...	

2449 Wt. W14957/M90 750,000 1/16 J.B.C. & A. Forms/C.2118/12.

29th Divisional Artillery.

17th BRIGADE R.F.A. ::: APRIL 1918.

17 Bde R.F.A.
4/18

Vol. 37.

War Diary for 17th Brigade R.F.A.

From 1st April 1918 – 30th April 1918.

Instructions regarding War Diaries and Intelligence Summaries are contained in F. S. Regs., Part II. and the Staff Manual respectively. Title Pages will be prepared in manuscript.

WAR DIARY
or
INTELLIGENCE SUMMARY
(Erase heading not required.)

Army Form C. 2118.

26

Place	Date	Hour	Summary of Events and Information	Remarks and references to Appendices
Field	1		Quiet day. Weather dull. Good news from South where the Huns are held.	
	2		Orders to carry out a raid on TOKLE(?) Cotts issued. T.Ms. to cut wire. Notes 4.45 Hrs preparatory fire every evening	
	3		Very quiet. Hun very quiet. Pistol(?) blank(?) lights making walking across brooms(?) by night very hard. "Inspection" of Gun positions by [illegible]	
	4		Raid took place without success as there were no Huns at home and the information was secured by one Hun deserting to us later in the night.	

Instructions regarding War Diaries and Intelligence Summaries are contained in F. S. Regs., Part II. and the Staff Manual respectively. Title pages will be prepared in manuscript.

WAR DIARY
or
INTELLIGENCE SUMMARY.
(*Erase heading not required.*)

Army Form C. 2118.

Place	Date	Hour	Summary of Events and Information	Remarks and references to Appendices
Field.	5th		Very quiet day. If it were not for this "delightful" country nobody would know there was a war on. Drizzled all day.	
	6		Quiet day nothing to report. Rained in the afternoon.	
	7.		Quiet day in this sector some shelling of forward areas.	
	8.		Normal.	
	9.		Huns attacking south of us in the neighbourhood of MESSINES, ARMENTIERES.	
	10.		German attacks south going strong	
	11		13th Bde. returned to selected position in the Army Battle Line at St Jean during the evening	
	12.		Remainder of the Brigade including HQ returned to Army Battle Line positions. HQ at Hector House St Jean. One gun of 28, 92 and 2/17 left in forward	

D. D. & L., London, E.C.
(A7883) Wt. W803/M1672 350,000 4/17 Sch. 52a Forms/C/2118/14

Instructions regarding War Diaries and Intelligence Summaries are contained in F. S. Regs., Part II. and the Staff Manual respectively. Title pages will be prepared in manuscript.

WAR DIARY
or
INTELLIGENCE SUMMARY.
(Erase heading not required.)

Army Form C. 2118.

Place	Date	Hour	Summary of Events and Information	Remarks and references to Appendices
Field	12		positions under one officer per Bty. also 15 Pdr. Anti Tank Gun at Wallemolen.	
	14		Lt. Cameron proceeded to Kansas Cross to take over command of all forward guns including 3 belonging to 15 Brigade R.H.A. These forward guns carried out the normal firing of a Battery in order to deceive the enemy	
	13		92nd Bty. forward gun withdrawn. Batteries in action at St. Jean but out of range of the enemy. Very peaceful and quiet one would hardly think there was a war on in this sector and yet we have to retire.	
	15.		During the night the Batteries withdraw again to new Army Battle Line positions just North of YPRES. Bde. H.Q. moved to H.Q. close by. (Late 16 Cr. H.Q. and very comfortable until it rains 5.9s). Infantry withdrawn	

D. D. & L., London, E.C.
(A7883) Wt. W803/M1672 350,000 4/17 Sch. 52a Forms/C/2118/14

Instructions regarding War Diaries and Intelligence Summaries are contained in F. S. Regs., Part II, and the Staff Manual respectively. Title pages will be prepared in manuscript.

WAR DIARY
or
INTELLIGENCE SUMMARY.
(*Erase heading not required.*)

Army Form C. 2118.

Place	Date	Hour	Summary of Events and Information	Remarks and references to Appendices
Field	15		from Passchendaele front right back to behind WIELTJE leaving an outpost line on the STEENBEEK (Army Battle Zone line). Main line being WIELTJE line. Remaining Guns of 20" Battery R.G.A. were successfully withdrawn to main Bty. positions. The remaining 15 Pdrs. which could not be got out were destroyed. Wind dug-outs destroyed and everything made as uncomfortable for brother Boch as could be. The Canadian and party retired with the infantry.	
"	16		We are waiting for the enemy to come on. From statement of prisoner captured, it would appear that the enemy knew all about our retirement a week ago and they had orders to follow us up but not to fight.	
"	17		Enemy shelled YPRES heavily all night with all calibres, evidently hoping to catch us in retreat.	

Instructions regarding War Diaries and Intelligence Summaries are contained in F. S. Regs., Part II. and the Staff Manual respectively. Title pages will be prepared in manuscript.

WAR DIARY
or
INTELLIGENCE SUMMARY.
(Erase heading not required.)

Army Form C. 2118.

Place	Date	Hour	Summary of Events and Information	Remarks and references to Appendices
Field	18th		Nothing to report. Parties of the enemy seen approaching cautiously. YPRES shelled at night. Quiet in front.	
"	19th		Enemy seen advancing. Drove our outposts in from Hill 35, Counter attack at 10.30 re-established us there but enemy again took it at 11 in a snow blizzard. Hill 35 was bombarded at 12.15 for two hours.	
"	20th		Quiet day. Enemy appears to be endeavouring to get his guns up. Small parties seen and engaged. YPRES shelled as usual. Quite like 1915.	
"	21st		Quiet all day with the exception of intermittent shelling of the "Town". Enemy aeroplanes came over in strength last night dropping bombs from what we hear quite close to D.A.: so much so that they are borrowing our	

D. D. & L., London, E.C.
(A7883) Wt. W803/M1672 350,000 4/17 Sch. 52a Forms/C/2118/14

Instructions regarding War Diaries and Intelligence Summaries are contained in F. S. Regs., Part II, and the Staff Manual respectively. Title pages will be prepared in manuscript.

WAR DIARY
or
INTELLIGENCE SUMMARY.
(Erase heading not required.)

Army Form C. 2118.

Place	Date	Hour	Summary of Events and Information	Remarks and references to Appendices
YPRES Field	21		Lewis guns to night!!	
"	22		Heavy gas bombardment of YPRES at night	
	23		Heavy gas bombardment of YPRES at night.	
	24		Enemy attacked Eastward in strength. Position at Mount Kemmel obscure but the enemy are known to have advanced some distance.	
	25.		Situation South still obscure. YPRES is now shelled heavily day by day. Particular attention being paid to the "Dead End" close to which we are all unhappily situated.	
	26.		Enemy are too far round us on our right. We retired to "Army Line positions (Rear)" in the neighbourhood of GOLDFISH CHATEAU (half way between YPRES and VLAMERTINGHE). Infantry main line of resistance is withdrawn and only outposts are left at WIELTJE.	
	27.		Settling down in these new positions.	

Instructions regarding War Diaries and Intelligence Summaries are contained in F. S. Regs., Part II. and the Staff Manual respectively. Title pages will be prepared in manuscript.

Army Form C. 2118.

WAR DIARY
or
INTELLIGENCE SUMMARY.
(Erase heading not required.)

Place	Date	Hour	Summary of Events and Information	Remarks and references to Appendices
FIELD Goldfish Chateau.	28		Quiet day on our immediate front. Some enemy shelling of YPRES especially "Dead End". 1 man killed and wounded in wagon lines.	
	29.		We have fired approximately 250 rounds per gun per day, mostly expended in Counter Preparation to break up any of the enemy forming up for attack.	
	30.		One man killed in 9.2" Bty and one slightly wounded both by 77mm shell. Enemy has been shelling this area with 77mm. Bty. Shelling promiscuous	

[illegible] for
O.C. 11 Brigade R.G.A.

D. D. & L., London, E.C.
(A7883) Wt. W593/M1672 350,000 4/17 Sch. 52a Forms/C/2118/14

Vol 27

War Diary

17 Brigade RFA.

1-31 May 1918.

Vol. 38.

Instructions regarding War Diaries and Intelligence Summaries are contained in F. S. Regs., Part II. and the Staff Manual respectively. Title pages will be prepared in manuscript.

WAR DIARY
or
INTELLIGENCE SUMMARY.
(Erase heading not required.)

Army Form C. 2118.

Place	Date	Hour	Summary of Events and Information	Remarks and references to Appendices
Field	6		day in something or other line but "C'est la Guerre!" Fired 61a 10ax. Been very quiet. Major [illegible] returned from leave	
	7		Very quiet. Elaborate Schemes issued from 29 D.A. for testing the S.O.S. rocket signal. Let us hope it will be successful and that the Enemy Sends up the "Test" and not the proper S.O.S signal. News received that we may hope to be relieved on 12th & 13th of this month. Brigade fired 58 a 35 ax.	
	8.		Major Medley (?) went on leave also 4 Drivers (OR2). Leave is now running at about 10 months for the men and 4 months for the Officers. Brigade fired 41 rounds	
	9		The expected "TEST" S.O.S. Signals came at 1 am, 6.15 am, and 11.15 am. Rounds were fired in fairly good time, varying from ½ min. to 1 minute. H.V. Gun (5.9") active round these Headquarters all day. Very nasty weather, although there is no rain, as it is blowing hard and raw.	

D. D. & L., London, E.C.
(A7883) Wt. W803/M1672 350,000 4/17 Sch. 52a Forms/C/2118/14

Army Form C. 2118.

WAR DIARY
or
INTELLIGENCE SUMMARY
(Erase heading not required.)

Instructions regarding War Diaries and Intelligence Summaries are contained in F. S. Regs., Part II. and the Staff Manual respectively. Title Pages will be prepared in manuscript.

Place	Date	Hour	Summary of Events and Information	Remarks and references to Appendices
Field	10		Quiet day nothing to report	
"	11		Orders for relief issued.	
"	12		One section and half the Bty. Staff per Battery relieved by Batteries of 33rd Brigade R.F.A. Relief carried out under quiet conditions. Sections when relieved marched to wagon lines at VLAMERTINGHE.	
"	13		Remainder of Battery personnel and H.Q. relieved by 33rd Brigade. Relief completed by 12 noon when personnel marched to wagon lines.	
PESELHOEK	14		Took over from wagon lines of 33rd Brigade in PESELHOEK. Marched from VLAMERTINGHE at 9.30 am and arrived PESELHOEK 11.30 am.	
"	15		Settled down for our rest in new wagon lines. All ranks quite comfortable. 29 D.A. football tournament arranged	
	16		First matches of football tournament played off. D/17 beat 13 Bty 2 – 1 26 beat 92 Bty 3 – 2.	

2449 Wt. W14957/M90 750,000 1/16 J.B.C. & A. Forms/C.2118/12.

Army Form C. 2118.

WAR DIARY
or
INTELLIGENCE SUMMARY
(Erase heading not required.)

Instructions regarding War Diaries and Intelligence Summaries are contained in F. S. Regs., Part II. and the Staff Manual respectively. Title Pages will be prepared in manuscript.

Place	Date	Hour	Summary of Events and Information	Remarks and references to Appendices
PESELHOEK	17.		H.Q. 17th Brigade R.F.A. played No 3 Section 29 D.A.C. in the football tournament and beat them 4-1. A good game. Major ... previously Major commanding 92nd Battery R.F.A. has returned from England after having been away some 6 months. He is going to B Battery R.H.A. 15th Bde. R.H.A. as Captain.	
"	18.		M.G.R.A. 4th Army inspected all wagon lines etc. Expressed himself quite satisfied. Still very cold and hard frost at nights and fine during the day.	
	19.		Very cold but fine. D/17 beat 26 Battery 2-1.	
	20.		B Battery R.H.A. beat H.Q. 29 D.A. 7-2. Much warmer.	
	21.		H.Q. 17 Brigade R.F.A. played Headquarters 29 D.A.C. but were unfortunately beaten 2-1. Much warmer.	
	22.		Nothing to report. Lecture on reinforced concrete [illegible]	

2449 Wt. W14957/M90 750,000 1/16 J.B.C. & A. Forms/C.2118/12.

Instructions regarding War Diaries and Intelligence Summaries are contained in F. S. Regs., Part II. and the Staff Manual respectively. Title Pages will be prepared in manuscript.

WAR DIARY
or
INTELLIGENCE SUMMARY
(Erase heading not required.)

Army Form C. 2118.

Place	Date	Hour	Summary of Events and Information	Remarks and references to Appendices
Bussemaker	22.		ably in the evening. only trouble being that he told us how to make Concrete Pill Boxes in a totally different way we are at present making them.	
	23		Lecture by C.R.A. to B.Cs at 15' Bde. H.Q. at 10 am.	
			D/17 beaten by Alnwick 3-0.	
	24		17' Brigade Officers Rugby team had a very impromptu game Rather fun although as the R.S.M. said "It looked like murder".	
	25.		Lecture at 17' Brigade H.Q on the S.O.S rifle grenade and how to use it.	
	26.		G.O.C. lectured on "Deductions to be drawn from Central Pictures" at the Cinema Hall Steenvoorde. This was followed by a Special performance of the "Diamond Troupe". Both were greatly appreciated by the 20 Officers and N.C.Os. who were given places	
	27.		Final of the D.A. Inter Battery football Competition played	

2449 Wt. W14957/M90 750,000 1/16 J.B.C. & A. Forms/C.2118/12.

Instructions regarding War Diaries and Intelligence Summaries are contained in F. S. Regs., Part II. and the Staff Manual respectively. Title Pages will be prepared in manuscript.

WAR DIARY
or
INTELLIGENCE SUMMARY

(Erase heading not required.)

Army Form C. 2118.

Place	Date	Hour	Summary of Events and Information	Remarks and references to Appendices
PESELHOEK	27		The Warwick Battery R.H.A and 15th Brigade R.H.A. score one all, although an extra ten minutes each way was played. A very good match; nobody can tell who will win it when it is replayed. A great turn-out, fully 400 men watching including the Divisional Commander. The Divisional Band played.	
	28.		Officers Rugby practice. Weather very cold. Final between B R.H.A and Warwick Bty. R.H.A. will take place tomorrow. 1st [illegible].	
			T. C. [illegible] for Commanding 17 Bde R.H.A.	

29th S.O.S. fired for 20 minutes in the morning commencing at 3.15 am no enemy attack. Two B.Co. reconnoitred for O.P. but failed to find any as Grenne is very difficult.

30 S.O.S. fired again for 20 minutes at dawn no enemy attack followed. Colonel Murray has caught the influenza which has been prevalent in the brigade during the month. He has gone down to the wagon line and Major Duly has taken over command of the brigade. We were to have been relieved by 31st D.A. to-day but it has been cancelled.

T. C. Robinson
O.C. 17th Brigade R.F.A.

Vol

17th Brigade R.F.A.
June 1918.

[signature]
O.C. 17th Bde. R.F.A.

Instructions regarding War Diaries and Intelligence Summaries are contained in F. S. Regs., Part II. and the Staff Manual respectively. Title pages will be prepared in manuscript.

WAR DIARY
or
INTELLIGENCE SUMMARY.
(Erase heading not required.)

Army Form C. 2118.

28

Place	Date	Hour	Summary of Events and Information	Remarks and references to Appendices
Field.	1.		Preparations made for a minor attack to be	
			carried out tomorrow night to capture about 1000	
			yards of ground	
	2.		Preparations complete. 2/Lt Godwin detailed for	
			F.O.O.	
	3.		Zero hour 1 am 3/6/18. Attack a completely	
			successful. Captured 40 odd prisoners 4 M.Gs and	
			2 T.Ms. Casualties slight except for a clearing	
			party of the Brigade on the right which	
			suffered 37 casualties before the attack. General	
			Freyberg again wounded. Enemy made a bombing	attack
on these new			Positions at midnight to the Australians on	
			our left. The Australians had advanced	and
			captured 400 prisoners, 12 M.Gs. 4 T.Ms and	
			1 Field Gun on our left. This bombing	
			attack was completely repelled and left	6

D. D. & L., London, E.C. (A7883) Wt. W803/M1672 350,000 4/17 Sch. 52a Forms/C/2118/14

Army Form C. 2118.

Instructions regarding War Diaries and Intelligence Summaries are contained in F. S. Regs., Part II. and the Staff Manual respectively. Title pages will be prepared in manuscript.

WAR DIARY
or
INTELLIGENCE SUMMARY.
(Erase heading not required.)

Place	Date	Hour	Summary of Events and Information	Remarks and references to Appendices
Field.	3	-	Two prisoners in our hands.	
	4.		Colonels servant died of wounds received by shell which landed at ~~the~~ his feet in our garden. Balloon which was down a few days ago has been replaced but was again brought down this evening.	
	5.		Enemy is now confining most of his attention to shelling roads with bursts of fire. He is using a lot of this "Blue Cross" gas which makes you sneeze like hell.	
	6.		Quiet on the whole. Colonel went to see the Calibration School near St. OMER.	
	7th		Nothing to report.	
	8th		Hun exceptionally quiet. [May?] be brewing up for another attack.	
	9th		Raid planned for tonight postponed.	

D. D. & L., London, E.C.
(A7883) Wt. W803/M1672 350,000 4/17 Sch. 52a Forms/C/2118/14

Army Form C. 2118.

WAR DIARY
or
INTELLIGENCE SUMMARY.
(Erase heading not required.)

Instructions regarding War Diaries and Intelligence Summaries are contained in F. S. Regs., Part II. and the Staff Manual respectively. Title pages will be prepared in manuscript.

Place	Date	Hour	Summary of Events and Information	Remarks and references to Appendices
Field	10th.		Very quiet day. Weather perfect.	
"	11th		Nil. Brigade preparing to move forward 1000 yards.	
"	12th		Preparations continue. 30th D.A. are taking over our old positions. Heard rights up about gas projectors which are in the front line and are going to be blown off at the earliest possible moment. They contain N.C. which is the most deadly gas in existence. A German shell hit 3 projectors the other day which exploded, as our Box Respirators are no good (it is alleged) against this gas the troops near by did not put them on, but no one is any the worse. This promises well for its effect on the Hun.	
	13.		Quiet day.	
	14.		Last night the enemy gave us 4 hours continuous gas shelling with "mustard" gas. No casualties.	

D. D. & L., London, E.C. (A7883) Wt. W803/M1672 350,000 4/17 Sch. 52a Forms/C/2118/14

Instructions regarding War Diaries and Intelligence Summaries are contained in F. S. Regs., Part II, and the Staff Manual respectively. Title pages will be prepared in manuscript.

WAR DIARY
or
INTELLIGENCE SUMMARY.
(Erase heading not required.)

Army Form C. 2118.

Place	Date	Hour	Summary of Events and Information	Remarks and references to Appendices
Field.	15.		Slight hostile gas shelling at night. 3 am. Enemy attacked and recaptured LUG ~~[illegible]~~ and ANKLE FARMS and took FANTASY in addition. Everyone is sure the Hun will attack tomorrow.	
"	16		Our gas cylinders which have been the cause of so much annoyance to us lately were let off at 10 am.	
	17		Cloud went well. Enemy put down a slight ~~[illegible]~~ barrage but stopped after 10 minutes. Our men recaptured LUG, ANKLE and FANTASY farms shortly after at night.	
	#		Our Batteries moved forward to offensive positions at a range of 2000 yards from the front line (German). 148 Brigade R.F.A. 30th Div. took over our positions.	
	18.		Batteries busy registering from new positions. Counter attack on LUG FARM carried out with success at 12.45 am 19/6/18.	

D. D. & L., London, E.C.
(A7883) Wt. W803/M1672 350,000 4/17 Sch. 52a Forms/C/2118/14

Instructions regarding War Diaries and Intelligence Summaries are contained in F. S. Regs., Part II. and the Staff Manual respectively. Title pages will be prepared in manuscript.

WAR DIARY
or
INTELLIGENCE SUMMARY.
(Erase heading not required.)

Army Form C. 2118.

Place	Date	Hour	Summary of Events and Information	Remarks and references to Appendices
Field	19.		All our Batteries are now in forward positions ready to support attack in the line of the BECQUE, at mid-day we hear that it is all off	
	20.		29th Division infantry are being relieved by 31st Division. There are rumours that ~~that~~ the 29th D.A. may follow them but, when, nobody knows. H.Q. shelled during the morning with Phosgene Gas shells.	
	21.		An extraordinarily quiet day	
	22		A certain amount of shelling on our right during the night but quiet on the whole.	
	23.		Preparations made for an attack on [illegible] FARM (a farm 300 yards on our right)	
	24		Rained all day. Enemy shelled round at night but quiet on the whole.	
	25		Enemy shelled 92nd Bty. R.F.A. heavily all day	

A7092 Wt. W125 9/M1293 750,000. 1/17. D. D & L. Ltd. Forms/C2118/14.

Instructions regarding War Diaries and Intelligence Summaries are contained in F. S. Regs., Part II. and the Staff Manual respectively. Title Pages will be prepared in manuscript.

WAR DIARY
or
INTELLIGENCE SUMMARY
(Erase heading not required.)

Army Form C. 2118.

Place	Date	Hour	Summary of Events and Information	Remarks and references to Appendices
Field	25		with 5.9" hows. About 200 rounds in all were fired. During the evening 92nd and 86th Batteries went up in to forward positions by SWARTENBROUCH to join 13th and DA's Btie, already in forward positions. 92nd Battery R.F.A. just got out of their old position by the time this [illegible] 5.9" Battery started firing) about at 9 pm.	
	26		Preparations made for the ~~[illegible]~~ attack on ANKLE FARM. This attack was successfully carried out. We captured 16 prisoners. SWARTENBROUCH very heavily shelled by 4.2's during the night, some Phosgene Gas shells were mixed with the HE. PAPOTE was shelled throughout the day by 8 inch, several direct hits on the road were obtained, making the road impassable for some hours.	

2449 Wt. W14957/M90 750,000 1/16 J.B.C. & A. Forms/C.2118/12.

Instructions regarding War Diaries and Intelligence Summaries are contained in F. S. Regs., Part II. and the Staff Manual respectively. Title Pages will be prepared in manuscript.

WAR DIARY
or
INTELLIGENCE SUMMARY

(Erase heading not required.)

Army Form C. 2118.

Place	Date	Hour	Summary of Events and Information	Remarks and references to Appendices
Field	27th		Preparations were made for the attack to capture the line of the BECQUE, operation to take place on the morning of the 28th. Enemy shelled MORBECQUE ~~the~~ and PAPOTE Road throughout the day. X" Track running through the Forest received a certain amount of attention.	
	28th		Attack carried out successfully. Zero hour was 6 a.m. By 7.30 all objectives had been taken and Infantry consolidated their position. Captures were 242 Prisoners, 3 Field Guns and a number of Machine Guns. Prisoners stated that attack was a complete surprise to them. At about 11 am enemy started to shell GOMBERT FARM and GARS BRUGGE very heavily and continued throughout the day. Enemy barrage came down at 6.21 but was ~~very thin~~ at 7.15 it became very heavy.	

29 Div

8/29

C O N F I D E N T I A L

WAR DIARY

of

17th Brigade R.F.A.

From 1st July 1918
To 31st July 1918

Volume XXXIX.

July

1). 30th D.A. which came in to support our attack
went out to-day. Colonel Lewis who has been
staying with us has gone.

2). 13th and 26 Batteries relieved by A and B/165
Batteries. The 165 Brigade of 31st Div. is relieving us.
Colonel Murray and Major Holmes who are both
suffering from the after effects of the flu have
gone to WIMEREUX for a rest.

3) 92nd and D/17 relieved by C and D/165 Batteries.
H.Q. relieved by H.Q. 165 Brigade. Relief of Brigade is
now complete. Brigade marched into rest area at
WARDRECQUES.

4.) Cliés at WARDRECQUES. Batteries in tents.
H.Q. in very bad billet.

5) Preparations made for Sports. Everything is in a chaotic state.

6) Orders received that the Brigade will most probably go into action on the 8th in the left divisional sector of XV Corps

7) Major Daly and Adjutant went up to reconnoitre battery positions, these are quite good as Bty. positions but there is no accommodation for the personnel.

8) Brigade marched to LA BREARDE where they went into wagon lines. We were to have marched into action at 9 pm. but orders were received to remain in wagon lines (suppose the "Special Purpose" for which we are billeted in, after our "long"

8) "Rest" has been postponed. Rufach H.Q. were already in battle H.Q. when orders were received so stayed there. B. Co. who were already in their battery positions came back and stayed at there H.Q.

Much needed rain came at night.

9). Fine again and everything much fresher. No orders by 12 noon.

10) The weather has turned very stormy. Thunder storms every - hour.

11) Still no news of what we are waiting. "Hush" I cannot say what "yet". What we have heard is that the positions we have been working in are useless and we have got to start others.

Instructions regarding War Diaries and Intelligence Summaries are contained in F. S. Regs., Part II, and the Staff Manual respectively. Title pages will be prepared in manuscript.

WAR DIARY
or
INTELLIGENCE SUMMARY.
(Erase heading not required.)

Army Form C. 2118.

Place	Date	Hour	Summary of Events and Information	Remarks and references to Appendices
Tridel.	12.		Batteries busy digging in new positions. I suppose, when we have finished there, the Scheme will be altered again!	
"	13.		Nothing to report.	
"	14.		Batteries working on present positions sorting ammunition, building platforms etc.	
"	15		Raining hard. Still no news of our attack coming off.	
"	16		Fine and very hot, thunder storms in the evening.	
"	17.		Colonel Murray and Major Holmes returned from leave at Boulogne. Colonel Murray stayed at D.A.H.Q. at [illegible]. Major Holmes took over the work of Brigade Major during the absence of Capt: Thomson on a Staff Course. Batteries moved into action during the night. All in action	

Army Form C. 2118.

Instructions regarding War Diaries and Intelligence Summaries are contained in F. S. Regs., Par. II. and the Staff Manual respectively. Title pages will be prepared in manuscript.

WAR DIARY
or
INTELLIGENCE SUMMARY.
(Erase heading not required.)

Place	Date	Hour	Summary of Events and Information	Remarks and references to Appendices
			by 7am. Ammunition Wagons accompanied Blues to positions and dumped their ammunition	
Field	18		Brigade H.Q. moved forward to position N.E. of FLETRE. Colonel Murray returned to the Brigade in the afternoon. Operation was expected to take place during the afternoon but "oddly enough" it didn't	
	19.		At last, after long and extremely complicated orders the attack on "METEREN" took place at 7.55am. Barrage, which contained a large quantity of Smoke Shell, lasted for 57 minutes and was good. As far as could be ascertained at 12 noon all was successful. Hostile barrage was light but shelling afterwards was heavy. Complete success except on the 200 yards on the extreme left where the Black Watch were held	

A6945 Wt. W11422/M1160 35,000 12/16 D. D. & L. Forms/C./2118/14.

Instructions regarding War Diaries and Intelligence Summaries are contained in F. S. Regs., Part II. and the Staff Manual respectively. Title pages will be prepared in manuscript.

WAR DIARY
or
INTELLIGENCE SUMMARY.
(Erase heading not required.)

Army Form C. 2118.

Place	Date	Hour	Summary of Events and Information	Remarks and references to Appendices
Field	19		wire in a hedge 100 yards in front of their trenches. 240 prisoners taken. Our casualties rather heavy. Capt Williams 26 Battery R.F.A. slightly wounded in foot.	
"	20		Brigade withdrawn to wagon lines between 10 pm and midnight.	
"	21.		Brigade marched to join rest of the 29th Div in the WARDRECQUES area. That night we were informed that the whole of the 29th Division were marching North the next day to a destination unknown.	
"	22		Marched at 11.30 am to area of the Forest of Clairmarais. The whole brigade bivouaced as no shelter available. Tents subsequently were issued at the rate of 2 per Bty!!	
	23.		Rained all day. . a lorry brought 25 more tents	

Army Form C. 2118.

WAR DIARY
or
INTELLIGENCE SUMMARY.
(Erase heading not required.)

...tions regarding War Diaries and Intelligence Summaries are contained in F. S. Regs., Part II. and the Staff Manual respectively. Title pages will be prepared in manuscript.

Place	Date	Hour	Summary of Events and Information	Remarks and references to Appendices
Field	23		which arrived just in time as our Gun Covers, which were our only means of covering, leaked.	
	24		Nothing to report. Weather stormy. They are now taking away from us those few tents that we already have. Orders received for digging party of 1 officer and 20 men to go and dig positions in the forward area.	
	25.		Party for digging went forward. Weather bad.	
	26		Nothing to report.	
	27		Wind changed round from S.W. to N.W. Weather improving.	
	28.		Nothing new.	
	29.		Ceremonial parade and march past before the Divisional General has been arranged. Rumours that we are leaving South	
	20.		Ceremonial practiced. Quite a success.	

Army Form C. 2118.

Instructions regarding War Diaries and Intelligence Summaries are contained in F. S. Regs., Part II. and the Staff Manual respectively. Title pages will be prepared in manuscript.

WAR DIARY
or
INTELLIGENCE SUMMARY.
(Erase heading not required.)

Place	Date	Hour	Summary of Events and Information	Remarks and references to Appendices
Field	31		Ceremonial parade in the morning. Race ([illegible]) meeting in the afternoon. Both quite a success.	
"	1		~~On Station for the~~ 15th Bde. won most events	
			T. C. [illegible] for O.C. 17 Bde. R.F.A.	

(A9175) Wt W2358/P560 600,000 12/17 D. D. & L. Sch. 52a. Forms/C2118/15.

CONFIDENTIAL.

-oOo-

<u>WAR DIARY</u>.

of

17th Brigade Royal Field Artillery.
= = = = = = = = =

From 1st August 1918.
To 31st August 1918.

(Volume XXXXI).

Instructions regarding War Diaries and Intelligence Summaries are contained in F. S. Regs., Part II. and the Staff Manual respectively. Title pages will be prepared in manuscript.

WAR DIARY
or
INTELLIGENCE SUMMARY.
(Erase heading not required.)

Army Form C. 2118.

Place	Date	Hour	Summary of Events and Information	Remarks and references to Appendices
Goldfish Field	1		O/C Bty's guns are so worn that they are useless from present positions. Range for all Btys. is 6000 yards at the most and O/C cannot do this, the Section of O/7 Bty R.H.A. have therefore been moved back to position on Canal Bank YPRES.	
	2		During the evening the enemy fired about 100 rounds 8" in the neighbourhood of O/7 Btys. 4 guns. Very unpleasant!	
	3		Nothing to report. Goldfish shelled in the morning	
	4		attack expected tomorrow morning, evidence obtained from captured German airman. Double barraging fire and heavy counter preparations put down to catch his troops massing	
	5.		No attack. The past day was very quiet. Heavy rain and thunder storms.	

D. D. & L., London, E.C. (A7883) Wt. W803/M1672 350,000 4/17 Sch. 52a Forms/C/2118/14

Instructions regarding War Diaries and Intelligence Summaries are contained in F. S. Regs., Part II. and the Staff Manual respectively. Title pages will be prepared in manuscript.

WAR DIARY
or
INTELLIGENCE SUMMARY.
(Erase heading not required.)

Army Form C. 2118.

Place	Date	Hour	Summary of Events and Information	Remarks and references to Appendices
Field	6		Quite quiet.	
	7/8th		Very heavy German bombardment on our right commencing 3am and lasting until 11am 8th Aug. Goldfish Chateau heavily bombarded with H.E. and all sorts of gas, not more than 5 casualties in the Brigade and even very slight. Germans attacked the French on our right but only penetrated a very short distance. Intermittent shelling during the day. Colonel Murray has gone for 48 hours to D.A. H.Q.	
	9th		Very quiet again. Major Daly keeps him here until the Colonel returns. Orders received that the "Outpost" line will be the main line of resistance so that our Batteries will have to move forward to positions just north of YPRES. 92nd & 9/17 moved during the evening	
	10th		13th Bty moved forward in the evening to position just across the YSER Canal.	

D. D. & L., London, E.C. (A7883) Wt. W803/M1672 350,000 4/17 Sch. 52a Forms/C/2118/14

Instructions regarding War Diaries and Intelligence Summaries are contained in F. S. Regs., Part II. and the Staff Manual respectively. Title pages will be prepared in manuscript.

WAR DIARY
or
INTELLIGENCE SUMMARY.
(Erase heading not required.)

Army Form C. 2118.

Place	Date	Hour	Summary of Events and Information	Remarks and references to Appendices
Field	8th		17 Brigade H.Q. moved forward to new H.Q. (the same as we were in before we retired last time) at the RED HOUSE just north of YPRES. 26 Bty moved to position close to R.Q. during the evening.	
	~~11~~		Rumours that we will be relieved tomorrow	
	12		confirmed. Brigade relieved by 162nd Brigade. Relief complete by 9pm. All batteries rendezvoused at wagon lines. Lt Hindle killed by a chance shell during the relief. Heavy shelling of "Plumb Rd." but stopped when Brigade moved out.	
	13.		Brigade marched to BLARINGHEM to join 29th Division in 15th Corps. All under canvas.	
	14.		Remained at BLARINGHEM in rest. Very pleasant. Hostile aircraft active bombing at night.	
	15.		Guns and Hows went to the ranges at TILQUES for calibration.	

D. D. & L., London, E.C.
(A7883) Wt. W803/M1672 350,000 4/17 Sch. 52a Forms/C/2118/14

Instructions regarding War Diaries and Intelligence Summaries are contained in F. S. Regs., Part II. and the Staff Manual respectively. Title pages will be prepared in manuscript.

WAR DIARY
or
INTELLIGENCE SUMMARY.
(Erase heading not required.)

Army Form C. 2118.

Place	Date	Hour	Summary of Events and Information	Remarks and references to Appendices
Field	16.		Guns returned from TILQUES. Divisional band played for 1½ hrs. during the afternoon.	
	17.		Brigade went into action in the Forest of NIEPPE. Brigade H.Q. in the railway between MORBECQUES and HAZEBROUCK. Quite peaceful.	
	18.		Settling down in new area, finding O.Ps, building shelters etc. Very little firing.	
	19.		Quiet day.	
	20		Small attack carried out by the Division on our right successful. Heavy hostile shelling by 4.2" 5.9" 8" during the night on all roads.	
	21.		Enemy counter attacked at dawn. [illegible] did a raid at night at 11.26 pm and captured 2 men and 1 M.G. German garrison fought well and killed 1 officer and 2 O.R. of raiding party. Raiding party killed 20 Germans.	

D. D. & L., London, E.C.
(A7883) Wt. W803/M1672 350,000 4/17 Sch. 52a Forms/C/2118/14

Instructions regarding War Diaries and Intelligence Summaries are contained in F. S. Regs., Part II, and the Staff Manual respectively. Title pages will be prepared in manuscript.

WAR DIARY
or
INTELLIGENCE SUMMARY.
(Erase heading not required.)

Army Form C. 2118.

Place	Date	Hour	Summary of Events and Information	Remarks and references to Appendices
Field.	22nd		We are told that the enemy is certain to attack on morning of 25th May. He will, we are told, attack us both South of the forest. We are going to have a fearful time with Gas but the only thing that worries us is the fact that we may have to move our positions on the 24th.	
	23.		Lt Cunnison promoted Captain and posted to 15 Rgt. R.F.A. Capt Watson formerly of that Rgt posted to D.A.C. Lt ~~[illegible]~~ Martyn and Lt Webb posted from D.A.C. to ~~[illegible]~~ 26 & D/17 Btties respectively	
	24.		Nothing of importance to report.	
	25.		Reconnoitred reserve positions in the neighbourhood of MORBECQUES.	
	26.		C.R.A XV Corps (General Kirwin) inspected	

D. D. & L., London, E.C. (A7883) Wt. W803/M1672 350,000 4/17 Sch. 52a Forms/C/2118/14

Instructions regarding War Diaries and Intelligence Summaries are contained in F. S. Regs., Part II. and the Staff Manual respectively. Title pages will be prepared in manuscript.

WAR DIARY
or
INTELLIGENCE SUMMARY.
(Erase heading not required.)

Army Form C. 2118.

Place	Date	Hour	Summary of Events and Information	Remarks and references to Appendices
Field	26		Bty positions during the morning. Bde H.Q. moved forward 1½ miles in the afternoon so as to be near the Bties.	
			Carried out a raid in the evening - at least at 2.20 am. Capturing 1 Machine Gun and three prisoners.	
			Shelled in their H.Q. all night.	
Silent raid tried on BEAUCHE Farm a failure owing to M.G. fire	27.		2 am. two direct hits with 8" on our new H.Q. Luckily we were all in the cellars otherwise there would have been a lot of Casualties as the house was riddled with pieces. Lots of "Blue Cross" (Sneezing) gas.	
	28.		Colonel ill, and goes to 29 Div. H.Q. for a day. Adj. at [illegible].	
	29		New raid planned for tomorrow night. 13 Bties to take part to raid 2 shell holes.	
	30		Wire cutting in front of the aforesaid two	

Instructions regarding War Diaries and Intelligence Summaries are contained in F. S. Regs., Part II. and the Staff Manual respectively. Title pages will be prepared in manuscript.

WAR DIARY
or
INTELLIGENCE SUMMARY.
(Erase heading not required.)

Army Form C. 2118.

Place	Date	Hour	Summary of Events and Information	Remarks and references to Appendices
Field	30		Shell holes with the result that the enemy retaliated heavily on our part of the front.	
	31.		Raid carried out at 12.30 a.m. a failure. 12 casualties to raiding party. The enemy no doubt were aware of our intentions.	
			The month has passed quite uneventfully except for our retirements at Passchendaele and YPRES. We have not yet been in one of the big battles. We hear that the attack at SOISSONS is going well in the favour of the Huns, damn them.	

D. D. & L., London, E.C.
(A7883) Wt. W803/M1672 350,000 4/17 Sch. 52a Forms/C/2118/14

Instructions regarding War Diaries and Intelligence Summaries are contained in F. S. Regs., Part II. and the Staff Manual respectively. Title pages will be prepared in manuscript.

WAR DIARY
or
INTELLIGENCE SUMMARY.
(Erase heading not required.)

Army Form C. 2118.

Place	Date	Hour	Summary of Events and Information	Remarks and references to Appendices
Field	1.		One Section per Battery relieved one Section per Battery of the 12th Australian Army Field Artillery Brigade in the Nieppe Sector.	
	2.		Remainder of the 17th Bde. relieved the remainder of the 12th Australian Brigade in the Nieppe Sector. Battery positions good. Australians very pleasant.	
	3.		Batteries registered. Reconnoitred O. Ps. etc.	
	4.		Everything peaceful. ~~PRADELLES shelled from ... ... Nothing to report.~~	
	5.			
	6.		Weather wet. Hostile shelling of PRADELLES.	
	7.		Usual harassing fire carried out.	
	8.		Nothing to report.	
	9.		Wet day. Usual firing.	
	10.		Leave re-opened at a better rate. 4 Officers and 50 other ranks to go before the end of month.	
	11.		No news.	

(A9175) Wt W2353/P560 600,000 12/17 D. D. & L. Sch. 52a. Forms/C.2118/13.

Army Form C. 2118.

Instructions regarding War Diaries and Intelligence Summaries are contained in F. S. Regs., Part II. and the Staff Manual respectively. Title pages will be prepared in manuscript.

WAR DIARY
or
INTELLIGENCE SUMMARY.
(*Erase heading not required.*)

Place	Date	Hour	Summary of Events and Information	Remarks and references to Appendices
July	12		Fairly quiet day, during the evening STRAZEELE & back areas were harassed. Farm buildings at 92nd Battery position burnt down during the night, several 18 pr. Shrapnel were fire at this position.	
	13		Nothing to report	
	14		New Bde Headquarters were chosen North of PRADELLES in W.16 c 3 5. All Batteries moved forward into forward positions	
	15		preparatory to Operations on August 18th.	
	15		Very quiet day. Batteries were getting into new positions & registering. Very little hostile fire. a certain amount of harassing fire on roads & tracks in enemy.	
	16		Quiet day. Harassing fire was carried out during the night.	
	17		Usual harassing fire was carried out at night.	
	18		Zero hour for the attack was 11 am. There was no Artillery preparation, the forming up line for infantry was roughly along the line X26 b 70.80 to X22 a 60.50. The first objective was the	

(A9175) Wt W2355/P563 650,000 12/17 D. D. & L. Sch. 52a. Forms/C2118/15.

Instructions regarding War Diaries and Intelligence Summaries are contained in F. S. Regs., Part II. and the Staff Manual respectively. Title pages will be prepared in manuscript.

WAR DIARY
or
INTELLIGENCE SUMMARY.
(Erase heading not required.)

Army Form C. 2118.

Place	Date	Hour	Summary of Events and Information	Remarks and references to Appendices
Field	Contd		"Red line" a line roughly from X 26 d. 30.30 X 27 c 00.20 X 28 a 35.15 X 28 b 05.80 to X 22 a 50.20. This line was taken without opposition. The second objective was the "Blue line" a line roughly F 2 a 30.15 F 2 d 40.80 F 2 b 95.25 F 3 a 30.05 F 3 b 20.25 thence to X 28 a 30.15. This line was also taken, with little opposition. Our infantry went out beyond the second objective & took the hamlet of OUTTERSTEENE (SHEET 27) & several fortified farms. The German barrage put down was severe but irregular. This operation was carried out in conjunction with the 9th Division. About 800 prisoners were taken.	
	19		The Germans kept up a rather severe barrage in the early morning on the new front line. Back areas were left severely alone. At 5.0 p.m. we carried out a minor operation which was entirely successful, very little opposition was met with. The night was very quiet, no harassing fire was carried out as our patrols were out.	

Instructions regarding War Diaries and Intelligence Summaries are contained in F. S. Regs., Part II. and the Staff Manual respectively. Title pages will be prepared in manuscript.

WAR DIARY
or
INTELLIGENCE SUMMARY.
(Erase heading not required.)

Army Form C. 2118.

Place	Date	Hour	Summary of Events and Information	Remarks and references to Appendices
Field	20		Very quiet day. Our patrols were out the whole day & night getting in touch with the enemy, who was supposed to have withdrawn to a depth of 7 kilometres	
"	21		A very hot day.	
"	22.		Weather fine. Enemy fired concentrations of OUTTERSTEENE, MERRIS etc. [illegible] carried out the usual firing.	
"	23		Normal day. No action on our front.	
"	24.		Very little enemy activity. He seems to confine himself to bursts on OUTTERSTEENE and MERRIS.	
"	25.		Preparing forward section positions. Batteries firing from present positions at too long a range.	
"	26.		All very busy for the XV Corps Horse Show which is due to come off on 29th of this month. No fighting.	
"	27		Division on our right carried out an attack at 10 am [illegible].	
"	28.		Weather bad. XV Corps Horse Show postponed until	

c/1918

(A9475) Wt. W2358/P360 600,000 12/17 D. D. & L. Sch. 52a. Forms/C2118/15.

Army Form C. 2118.

WAR DIARY
or
INTELLIGENCE SUMMARY.
(Erase heading not required.)

Instructions regarding War Diaries and Intelligence Summaries are contained in F. S. Regs., Part II. and the Staff Manual respectively. Title pages will be prepared in manuscript.

Place	Date	Hour	Summary of Events and Information	Remarks and references to Appendices
Field	29		Fires burning everywhere behind the enemy's lines	
	30.		Learnt at 6am. that the enemy were retiring. Our patrols in and through BAILLEUL by 11am. Held up on MONT DE LILLE. Where our troops suffered casualties. Section of 92nd & D/17 Batteries ordered to move to positions close to old front line. Roads were badly blocked by night. MONT de LILLE in our hands by 10 pm, also RAVELSBERG.	
	31		No news at all. Brigade inactive.	

C. E. Bellamy Lieut R.F.A.
Adjt. 17th Brigade

Retain for Bde Major
[illegible]

17 Brigade R.F.A. 29 Div

WAR DIARY for September 1918.

[illegible] for
O.C. 17 Brigade R.F.A.

Instructions regarding War Diaries and Intelligence Summaries are contained in F. S. Regs., Part II. and the Staff Manual respectively. Title pages will be prepared in manuscript.

WAR DIARY
or
INTELLIGENCE SUMMARY.
(Erase heading not required.)

Army Form C. 2118.

Vol 31

Place	Date	Hour	Summary of Events and Information	Remarks and references to Appendices
September	1	-	Brigade inactive	
	2	-		
	3	-	Brigade moved forward to positions in T.26 (Sheet 28 S.W.) and registered on targets	
	4	-	8 am. was zero hour on Hill 63. in U.13d. The barrage lasted for 67 minutes and consisted of 23 lifts. Our troops entered PLOEGSTEERT but were driven out, concentrated fire was directed on the Village The Village was retaken during the night	

(A9475) Wt W2356/P360 600,000 12/17 D. D. & L. Sch. 52a. Forms/C2118/15.

Instructions regarding War Diaries and Intelligence Summaries are contained in F. S. Regs., Part II. and the Staff Manual respectively. Title pages will be prepared in manuscript.

Army Form C. 2118.

WAR DIARY
or
INTELLIGENCE SUMMARY.
(Erase heading not required.)

Place	Date	Hour	Summary of Events and Information	Remarks and references to Appendices
In the Field	September			
	5		PLOEGSTEERT was retaken by our Infantry, the right flank was left in the air. Several shoots were arranged, on demand by the Infantry.	
	6		~~On~~ A great deal of gas shelling in this area, shelling continued for three hours there were no casualties in the Brigade. The day was fairly quiet. A Creeping barrage was put down in order that the Infantry might straighten out the line	
	7		The area was again shelled during the night with gas shells & H.E. At 10 am we put down a barrage for the Infantry, to advance our line to the line of the LYS. on the right it was successful, but on the left heavy resistance was met with. Altogether the day was quiet.	
	8		Very little ~~at~~ activity.	
	9		Brigade moved up to more forward positions. Bde Headquarters also moved. The old H.Q. was shelled as we vacated them & the new H.Q. was shelled as we entered. Harassed the whole night	

Instructions regarding War Diaries and Intelligence Summaries are contained in F. S. Regs., Part II. and the Staff Manual respectively. Title pages will be prepared in manuscript.

WAR DIARY
or
INTELLIGENCE SUMMARY.
(Erase heading not required.)

Army Form C. 2118.

Place	Date	Hour	Summary of Events and Information	Remarks and references to Appendices
September	10		Harassing fire by 8" Hows round Bde H.Q. The Batteries moved back to old positions, leaving one section forward. Bde H.Q. remains in same position	
September	11		Harassing fire was carried out by our guns during the night on roads, tracks and Bridges across the LYS. Enemy artillery was quiet until about 11.30 am. Forward areas were shelled in the afternoon. A Barrage was put down on our front line at 1 pm. we retaliated by putting a Barrage down on our S.O.S. lines.	
September	12.		Fairly quiet day. The Brigade pulled out of action at 8 pm. & moved back into STRAZEELE AREA	
September	13		Brigade in Rest	
	14		Brigade in Rest.	
	15		Brigade moved by night march from BORRE-STRAZEELE area to DROGLANDT Area	
	16		Battery Commanders and Brigade Commander went to YPRES	

Instructions regarding War Diaries and Intelligence Summaries are contained in F. S. Regs., Part II. and the Staff Manual respectively. Title pages will be prepared in manuscript.

WAR DIARY
or
INTELLIGENCE SUMMARY.
(Erase heading not required.)

Army Form C. 2118.

Place	Date	Hour	Summary of Events and Information	Remarks and references to Appendices
September	16		to reconnoitre positions	
	~~7~~ 17		Batteries sent up working parties to YPRES to make positions.	
	18		Brigade in rest.	
	19		Brigade in rest.	
	20.		Capt. Robey returned from leave	
	21		Brigade marched at 7pm to new wagon lines in the Peselhoek area in front of POPERINGHE. Arrived in Camp 10pm.	
	22.		Ordinary Camp life. Ammunition Carrying to positions round the Square in YPRES.	
	23.		Do. Rumours in the air.	
	24.		So we are preparing for the Crowning victory of the war: but everything very Secret.	
	25.		Same as above. Everyone very excited.	
	26.		13th 26th 92nd Btts went into action at [illegible] and withdrew detachments	

(A9175) Wt. W2355/P565 650,000 12/17 D. D. & L. Sch. 52a. Forms/C2118/15

17 Bde RFA

~~WAR DIARY~~ or INTELLIGENCE SUMMARY.

(Erase heading not required.)

Army Form C. 2118.

VD 32

Instructions regarding War Diaries and Intelligence Summaries are contained in F. S. Regs., Part II. and the Staff Manual respectively. Title pages will be prepared in manuscript.

Place	Date	Hour	Summary of Events and Information	Remarks and references to Appendices
Field	Oct. 1.		Infantry still held up on the outskirts of GHELUWE. Weather conditions appalling. Roads, what there are, are very congested.	
"	Oct 2		Attack on GHELUWE at 6.7 a.m. Troops advanced half way through the village and were then again held up by machine guns. The infantry were very tired and wet which undoubtedly accounted for the advance being delayed.	
"	Oct 2nd		A captured ~~77~~ 10 cm. gun which has been turned round on the enemy by 17 Brigade R.F.A. H.Qrs. has been manned and quantities of ammunition have been fired into MENIN, no doubt causing considerable damage to the enemy. At night one section per Bty. of 187 Brigade R.F.A. relieved one section per Bty of 17 Brigade R.F.A. We are moving about 2 miles further north tomorrow night. Enemy shelled the MENIN Road heavily all night.	

(A9175) Wt W2352/P363 600,000 12/17 D. D. & L. Sch. 52a. Forms/C2118/15.

Instructions regarding War Diaries and Intelligence Summaries are contained in F. S. Regs., Part II. and the Staff Manual respectively. Title pages will be prepared in manuscript.

WAR DIARY
or
INTELLIGENCE SUMMARY.
(Erase heading not required.)

Army Form C. 2118.

Place	Date	Hour	Summary of Events and Information	Remarks and references to Appendices
Field.	4.		Batteries moved North at 8 pm. to positions in the neighbourhood of TERHAND.	
"	5.		Remained in this area. Shelling heavy by night.	
"	6		" . " . Ordinary firing carried out. Hostile shelling heavy at night.	
"	7		[illegible] moved back from 13", 92nd and D/[illegible] Batteries to positions behind DADIZEELE. Much quieter in this area. Enemy still shelling old positions forward.	
"	8		Normal day. Reconnoitred good O.P. in front of DADIZEELE and [illegible] LEDEGHEM Church being [illegible]	
"	9		Nothing to report.	
"	10		Normal day. We are preparing to carry on	
"	[illegible]		the advance.	
"	11		Weather continues bad. Ground in bad condition.	
"	12.		Nothing to report.	

Instructions regarding War Diaries and Intelligence Summaries are contained in F. S. Regs., Part II. and the Staff Manual respectively. Title pages will be prepared in manuscript.

WAR DIARY
or
INTELLIGENCE SUMMARY.
(Erase heading not required.)

Army Form C. 2118.

Place	Date	Hour	Summary of Events and Information	Remarks and references to Appendices
Field	13.		Colonel Murray posted to 15 Brigade RHA.	
			Colonel Macalpine, late Commanding "J" Bty. RHA	
			Came to command 17 Brigade R.F.A. Btys moved	
			to their forward positions in the afternoon. The day	
			is tomorrow.	
"	14		Zero hour 5.35 am. Operations successful. By	
			10 am. infantry were in front of MOORSEELE (a	
			4 mile advance). Btys advanced at 7 am and	
			Came into action behind that village. 13 Bty. R.F.A.	
			took 3 prisoners. Enemy retired in fairly good	
			order and left comparatively few prisoners and	
			guns in our possession.	
"	13		Attack continued at 9 am. under barrage and	
			by 12 noon HEULE had been captured. 9 Division	
			on our left in CUERNE. Hundreds of civilians	
			liberated. Hostile shelling negligible.	

(A9475) Wt W2351/P560 600,000 12/17 D. D. & L. Sch. 52a. Forms/C2118/15.

Instructions regarding War Diaries and Intelligence Summaries are contained in F. S. Regs., Part II. and the Staff Manual respectively. Title pages will be prepared in manuscript.

WAR DIARY
or
INTELLIGENCE SUMMARY.
(*Erase heading not required.*)

Army Form C. 2118.

Place	Date	Hour	Summary of Events and Information	Remarks and references to Appendices
Field	15.		Casualties to horses and men in the brigade heavy but all due to chance shells and bombs. We were compelled to leave behind guns and wagons in order to enable us to move batteries with any speed.	
"	16.		Crossings over LYS just North of COURTRAI taken by night. Enemy machine guns were holding us up	
"	17.		Orders are that the 29th Division will hold the line we are now on. French Cavalry operating North of us in neighbourhood of THOROUT. 36th and 41st Divisions on our right bringing left up into line. During the night our troops withdrew to the Eastern bank of the LYS as they were in no strength across the river.	
Irrelevant (initialled)	18.		We hear that OSTEND and BRUGES have been taken	

Instructions regarding War Diaries and Intelligence Summaries are contained in F. S. Regs., Part II. and the Staff Manual respectively. Title pages will be prepared in manuscript.

WAR DIARY
or
INTELLIGENCE SUMMARY.
(Erase heading not required.)

Army Form C. 2118.

Place	Date	Hour	Summary of Events and Information	Remarks and references to Appendices
Field (COURTRAI)	18 (Contd)		also LILLE. Everyone is very cheered by the news. During the past 14 days we have had 16 % casualties in the brigade. The following officers 2/Lt GOODWIN (26) killed, 2/Lt KELLOCK (13) killed. 2/Lt WHITLEY (92), 2/Lt BEAVER (92), 2/Lt MOLSON (13) 2/Lt BROOKER (92) all wounded.	
"	19		Holding on in front of CUERNE, N.E. of COURTRAI.	
"	20		attacked at 9 am. Advanced 6 miles, occupying COURTRAI, STASEGHEM, St LOUIS.	
"	21		Brigade remained in mobile reserve in the neighbourhood of COURTRAI	
	22		Moved into action during the night close up to the front line in the neighbourhood of BANHOUT BOSCH East of St LOUIS.	
	23		Fired a barrage 9 am in support of attack which should have taken us to the ESCAUT River. Attack completely failed.	

Incorrect the line was advanced considerably RM

(A9573) Wt W2353/P560 600,000 12/17 D. D. & L. Sch. 52a. Forms/C2118/15

Instructions regarding War Diaries and Intelligence Summaries are contained in F. S. Regs., Part II. and the Staff Manual respectively. Title pages will be prepared in manuscript.

WAR DIARY
or
INTELLIGENCE SUMMARY.
(Erase heading not required.)

Army Form C. 2118.

Place	Date	Hour	Summary of Events and Information	Remarks and references to Appendices
Field.	23.		Division including artillery moved out to billets at CUERNE (N. of COURTRAI). Billets bad and brigade not in until 3 am.	
	24.		Moved into action again by night and attached to 9th Div.	
	25.		Supported attack by 9th Division in front of OOTEGHEM. Attack again held up 1000x from our starting point by machine guns. 9th Division suffered heavy casualties. The enemy is decidedly stiffening his resistance. Moved out of action again by night to the old billets at CUERNE. Bde. H.Q. at HEULE.	
	26		Cleaning up and trying to square up generally. We are very short of personnel and equipment.	
	27.		Marched to billets two miles East of TOURCOING.	

(A9175) Wt W2358/P360 600,000 12/17 D. D. & L. Sch. 52a. Forms/C2118/15.

WAR DIARY
or
INTELLIGENCE SUMMARY.
(Erase heading not required.)

Army Form C. 2118.

Instructions regarding War Diaries and Intelligence Summaries are contained in F. S. Regs., Part II. and the Staff Manual respectively. Title pages will be prepared in manuscript.

Place	Date	Hour	Summary of Events and Information	Remarks and references to Appendices
Peselhoek	27.		D/17 and H.Q. moved up by night. H.Q. took up its abode in the "Hole in the Wall" in the S.E. Corner of the YPRES Ramparts. Battery detachments came into action, who can tell what tomorrow will bring forth?	
YPRES	28		The great attack. Zero hour 5.30 am. Great success GHELUVELT captured, Belgians doing well on our left. As was expected the state of the roads was appalling and considerable difficulty was experienced in advancing the batteries in support of the infantry but in spite of all difficulties 92nd Bty. pushed on three miles and came into action 1500 yards behind GHELUVELT 13 Bty. R.F.A. followed them and came into action close beside 92nd Bty. R.F.A.	
	29.		Infantry held up in front of GHELUVELT by machine guns. 13th and 92nd Btys. advanced to positions a little in front of GHELUVELT. Rel. H.Qrs. advanced to	

Instructions regarding War Diaries and Intelligence Summaries are contained in F. S. Regs., Part II. and the Staff Manual respectively. Title pages will be prepared in manuscript.

WAR DIARY
or
INTELLIGENCE SUMMARY.
(Erase heading not required.)

Army Form C. 2118.

Place	Date	Hour	Summary of Events and Information	Remarks and references to Appendices
	29.		the same area. Btries. heavily shelled all day and were forced to move back behind GHELU-VELT.	
	30.		Enemy reported retiring. 13th and 92nd Btries. advanced again, this time to positions 2 miles E of GHELUVELT on the YPRES - MENIN Road. 92nd Bty. advanced a section to the outskirts of GHELUWE but owing to the intense machine gun fire that they were subjected to the guns had to be left. (These were subsequently recovered by night)	
			Casualties during the above operations were:-	
			2/Lt GODWIN (26) Killed. Lt BEAVER (92), 2/Lt BROOKER (92), 2/Lt WHITLEY (92), Lt KELLOCK (13) wounded. Two other ranks killed and 20 wounded.	
			[signature] for O.C. 17 Brigade R.F.A.	

(A9175) Wt W2338/P560 600,000 12/17 D. D. & L. Sch. 52a. Forms/C2118/13.

Instructions regarding War Diaries and Intelligence Summaries are contained in F. S. Regs., Part II. and the Staff Manual respectively. Title pages will be prepared in manuscript.

WAR DIARY
or
INTELLIGENCE SUMMARY.
(Erase heading not required.)

Army Form C. 2118.

Place	Date	Hour	Summary of Events and Information	Remarks and references to Appendices
Field	27 (cont.)		Billets good. Arrived in by 1pm.	
"	28		Generally cleaning up. We hear that we may hope for a week's rest but we all "wonder"!	
"	29		Preparing for a ceremonial parade for G.O.C. XV Corps (General Sir B. de Lisle). Ceremonials are not popular especially now when the men and horses are very tired indeed and in addition very dirty and no fresh clothes are procurable.	
"	30.		Practise Ceremonial 11 am. Not good. Colonel Maitland and Colonel Murray again changed over brigades so we have Colonel Murray once more.	
"	31.		General cleaning up and endeavouring (without result) to obtain new clothing for the men. The new "Rationing" scheme is in progress whereby a totally inadequate supply of clothing is only available.	

[illegible]
LIEUT.-COLONEL, R.F.A.
COMDG., 17TH BDE., R.F.A.

33

9182

C O N F I D E N T I A L.

W A R   D I A R Y.

O F

17th BRIGADE ROYAL FIELD ARTILLERY.

From 1st November 1918.
To 30th November 1918.

****
Volume XLIV.
****

Army Form C. 2118.

WAR DIARY, 17th Brigade R.F.A.
or
INTELLIGENCE SUMMARY.
(*Erase heading not required.*)

Instructions regarding War Diaries and Intelligence Summaries are contained in F. S. Regs., Part II. and the Staff Manual respectively. Title pages will be prepared in manuscript.

Place	Date	Hour	Summary of Events and Information	Remarks and references to Appendices
FIELD	Nov.1,1918		Brigade at rest at BLANC-FOUR.Forty-four reinforcements,mainly drivers,arrived from the base.	
	2,		At rest at BLANC-FOUR.	
	3,		Brigade marched to TOURCOING area.Accomodation fair.	
	4,		Cleaning up for ceremonial parade for G.O.C.,XVth Corps.	
	5,		Ceremonial parade cancelled owing to wet.	
	6,		Brigade holiday. Y/29 T.M.B.(2 mobile 6"Newton Trench-mortars)attached to the Brigade.	
	7,		On transfer of the 29th Division to Xth Corps,the 17th Brigade marched to TOMBROEK area. 29/T14 and 15. Hostile artillery appeared very active.	
	8,		In conjunction with the Divisions on right and left,the 29th Division received orders to attempt the crossing of the SCHELDT to the north-east of HELCHIN,the attack being timed to take place on the morning of Nov.10th.With this in view,Battery Commanders reconnoitred battery positions in the vicinity of POELDRISCH?,29/U17 b,18 a and12 c.Hostile artillery showed little activity compared with the previous day,and it appeared likely that the enemy was about to withdraw.During the night 250rounds per gun were taken up to battle positions.	
	9th,		During the night the enemy ~~retrea-~~ retreated from the line of the SCHELDT.In conjunction with the 88th Infantry Brigade,the 17th Brigade was ordered tomove up at once with a view to pursuit. THe Brigade reached DRIES and ST.GENOIS by 1500 hours,but ~~wre-~~ was unable to cross the SCHELDT that night as no pontoon had been completed.	
	10th		At 0700hours the Brigade crossed the SCHELDT(being the first artillery of three Corps across theriver) by the pontoon bridge at HELCHIN and proceeded to ARC-AINIERES37/E 22 and 23.No contact was established with the enemy and we were held up by a small stream at 37/F19 c 0.8.A Sergeant of the 9th Bavarian Field Artillery Regiment,who had remained in the village when the enemy retreated, gave himself up to the Brigade.	
	11,		At 0700 hours a start was made on bridging the stream which had held us up the night before, nails,lashing,etc.,being dropped by aeroplane.THe material was cut from a small copse near by. The bridge,about 24 feet across,was completed by 0930 hours and the 13th Battery moved across it. As hostilities ceased at 1100 hours,the 13th Battery moved back and the Brigade remained in the same area.Thebridge made by the 17th Brigade appeared to be the only one within miles for limbers and wagons. The inhabitants were very enthusiastic.	
	12,		Rested at ARC-AINIERES.We heard that the 29th Division was to be transferred to the IInd Corps, one of the Corps of the IInd Army,~~that whicwh-~~ which is to be one of the two British Armies selected to form part of the ARMY of OCCUPATION in GERMANY.Themarch is to commence at once.	
	13,		Brigade marched from ARC-AINIERES to WODECQ area.The civilians were very poverty-stricken and rather sullen.	

(A9173) Wt W2351/P360 600,000 12/17 D. D. & L. Sch. 52a. Forms/C2118/15

Instructions regarding War Diaries and Intelligence Summaries are contained in F. S. Regs., Part II. and the Staff Manual respectively. Title pages will be prepared in manuscript.

Army Form C. 2118.

WAR DIARY
or
INTELLIGENCE SUMMARY.
(Erase heading not required.)

Place	Date	Hour	Summary of Events and Information	Remarks and references to Appendices
	Nov. 14th - 17th.		The Brigade rested at WODECQ.During this period the Batteries were reorganised on a four gun battery basis.Surplus personnel,horses and vehicles were detached under the orders of the XIXth Corps on Nov.17th.The march proper into GERMANY starts to-morrow.	
	18th,		The Brigade marched from WODECQ to ROMONT and MANHAAG.The 13th.Battery was detached for duty with the Advance-guard under the orders of G.O.C.88th Infantry Brigade.	
	19th,		The Brigade rested at MANHAAG.The area was very poor.	
	20th,		Rested.	
	21st,		The Brigade marched to a very good area just west of SAINTES.THEcivilians were very enthusiastic and received us very well.	
	22nd,		The Brigade rested at SAINTES.Most of th e officers went to BRUSSELS,to see the formal entry of King Albert.British troops were received with open arms everywhere.	
	23rd,		The Brigade marched to MONT ST.PONT area.	
	24th,		Rested.A large number visited the field of WATERLOO.	
	25th,		The Brigade marched to HEVILLERS and BLANMONT.the march was rather a long one,and the batteries did not arrive till after dark,but they had an excellent welcome from the population.	
	26th,		Rested.	
	27th,		The Brigade did a very short march to LES CINQ ETOILES.Billeting was rather close.	
	28th,		The Brigade marched to FORVILLE and SERON.The inhabitants are not quite so pleased to see us as they were at first, and most of the big farmers seem tobe almost hostile.	
	29th,		The Brigade marched to LES COMMUNES and OUTRELOUXTE.	
	30th,		The Brigade marched to COMBLAIN-AU-PONT.As the orders to march were cancelled early in the morning and were not given again till 0900 hours the Brigade did not get in till 1730 hours.Billeting was very close,horses being tied up along the roads,and matters were not improved by the attitude of the inhabitants,which is now becoming more hostile every day.	
			--	
			The following officers,N.COs,and Men were granted immediate awards as specified below,during the operations from Sept.28th. to Oct.25th,1918.	
			THE MILITARY CROSS.	
			Lieut.R.H.BEAVER, 92nd Battery,R.F.A.	
			2/Lieut.J.H.BROOKER, 92nd Battery,R.F.A.	

			THE DISTINGUISHED CONDUCT MEDAL.	
			745204 Sgt.A.G.SPRAY, 92nd Battery,R.F.A.	
			44290 Sgt.R.W.HILL, 92nd Battery,R.F.A.	

(A9175) Wt W5355/P560 650,000

Army Form C. 2118.

WAR DIARY
or
INTELLIGENCE SUMMARY.
(Erase heading not required.)

Instructions regarding War Diaries and Intelligence Summaries are contained in F. S. Regs., Part II. and the Staff Manual respectively. Title pages will be prepared in manuscript.

Place	Date	Hour	Summary of Events and Information	Remarks and references to Appendices
			THE MILITARY MEDAL.	
			69688 Cpl.C.V.NEWMAN, 26th Battery,R.F.A.	
			1625 Dvr.W. FELLS, 26th Battery,R.F.A.	
			80139 Dvr. G.BADDELEY, 26th Battery,R.F.A.	
			74527 Dvr.D.L.HUGHES, 26th Battery,R.F.A.	
			25287 Cpl.F.J.JONES, 92nd Battery,R.F.A.	
			210611 Dvr.J.W.BENDON, 92nd Battery,R.F.A.	
			88138 Gnr.H.KEARNEY, 92nd Battery,R.F.A.	
			92nd Battery,R.F.A.	
			82549 Dvr.J.BRODIE, 9 2nd Battery,R.F.A.	
			2	

(A9175) Wt W2353/P560 600,000 12/17 D. D. & L. Sch. 52a. Forms/C2118/15.

WAR DIARY.

17th Brigade R.F.A.

Volume 46

December 1918.

Army Form C. 2118.

Instructions regarding War Diaries and Intelligence Summaries are contained in F. S. Regs., Part II. and the Staff Manual respectively. Title pages will be prepared in manuscript.

WAR DIARY
or
INTELLIGENCE SUMMARY.
(Erase heading not required.)

Place	Date	Hour	Summary of Events and Information	Remarks and references to Appendices
			Reference Map - Marche 1/100,000	
GERMANY	Dec.	1-2-3	Brigade resting at Comblain-au-Pont. Rifle practice was carried out. Billets rather poor.	
	Dec.	4th.	Brigade Marched to AYWAILLE. Billets good.	
	Dec.	5th.	Marched to NIVEZE via SPA. All the large houses were occupied by the Armistice Commission and consequently Brigade Billets were very poor.	
	Dec.	6th.	Marched to MALMEDY, crossing the German frontier at about 0930 hours. (Reference Map Germany 1-L) The inhabitants were quite friendly and certainly more French than German was spoken in the town.	
	Dec.	7th.	Marched to MONTJOIE. Billets poor. The inhabitants were not at all inclined to put themselves out until ordered to. The Brigade Lorry broke down miles away from anywhere and could not be traced for 24 hours.	
	Dec.	8th.	Marched to ROLLESBROICH. Billets very bad.	
	Dec.	9th.	Marched to ZULPICH, one of the old German walled towns. Billets good and the inhabitants friendly	
	Dec	10th.	Marched to HURTH. The 29th Division concentrated round this area to rest and clean up before the formal entry into COLOGNE. The inhabitants round this area were more hostile in their attitude, especially the factory hands. This left only one march to be carried out before arrival in final area. Since the Brigade left WODECQ we had covered 230 miles in three weeks. In spite of this the horses were in good condition, but owing to a break-down of transport arrangements, the men did not get a single change of clothing all through.	
	Dec.	11th.	Cleaning up. Fortunately a certain amount of cleaning material arrived.	
	Dec.	13th.	II Corps crossed the RHINE and the 29th Division marched through COLOGNE and crossed over by the HOHENZOLLERNBRUCKE, the salute of the Brigade being taken by the Corps Commander. The attitude of the population was one of curiosity and in spite of the pouring wet day, turned out in very large numbers to see the passing of the Division. The Brigade marched on to rather poor billets in and around PLATZ, 2½ kilometres east of BENSBERG.	
	Dec.	17th.	Field Marshall Sir Douglas Haig, Commander in Chief of the British Armies in the Field inspected a detachment of the 29th Division at the CADET ESCHULE at 1000 hours. A detachment of 12 Officers and 200 other ranks from the 17th Brigade represented the Divisional Artillery. The weather was very bad.	
	Dec.	20th.	The final billetting area of the Brigade was decided upon and reconnoitred.	
	Dec.	21st.	Brigade marched to their winter quarters IN BERG GLADBACH. The area was very good. All horses were under cover although the 26th Battery require side cover before they will be really comfortable. Men's billets were everywhere excellent.	

Instructions regarding War Diaries and Intelligence Summaries are contained in F. S. Regs., Part II. and the Staff Manual respectively. Title pages will be prepared in manuscript.

WAR DIARY
or
INTELLIGENCE SUMMARY.
(Erase heading not required.)

Army Form C. 2118.

Place	Date	Hour	Summary of Events and Information	Remarks and references to Appendices
	Dec.	22nd.	VICTORIA SALLE was settled on as a suitable place for the Brigade Canteen.	
	Dec.	25th.	As a result of a complete break-down of transport arrangements, the Christmas rations failed to turn up. As, however, the likelohood of this had been forseen, the Batteries had provided themselves with pigs, etc, on the march, consequently they managed to carry on.	
	Dec.	26th.	Brigade Canteen opened.	
	Dec.	27th.	The Brigade Educational school started its classes.	
	Dec.	29th) 30th) 31st)	Demobilization of Coal Miners and Pivotal and Demobilization men commenced. In three days the following were despatched: Coal miners 37; Pivotal 1; Long Service men 4	
		31st.	Cafe Chantant was held in the Brigade Canteen from 2100 hours to midnight to see the New Year in	
			MENTIONED IN DISPATCHES	
			Major D. Daly, M. C. — December 21st, 1918	
			No. 144571 Gr. Brooks, L.C.D. — December 21st, 1918	

J. M. Banks-Williams
Capt.
Adj. 17 Bde R.F.A.

(A9175) Wt W2335/P360 600,000 12/17 D. D. & L. Sch. 52a. Forms/C2118/15.

Confidential.

W A R D I A R Y

of

17th Brigade Royal Field Artillery

January 1919

VOLUME XLVI

Instructions regarding War Diaries and Intelligence Summaries are contained in F. S. Regs., Part II. and the Staff Manual respectively. Title pages will be prepared in manuscript.

WAR DIARY
or
INTELLIGENCE SUMMARY.
(Erase heading not required.)

Army Form C. 2118.

Place	Date	Hour	Summary of Events and Information	Remarks and references to Appendices

BERG GLADBACH -
For month ending January 31st, 1919.

The Brigade occupied the same billets and quarters for the month of January as outlined in the war diary for the month of December, 1919.
The following items of interest occurred during the month:

1. The educational scheme for the Brigade was well attended. Classes were held in English Arithmetic, Geography, History, shorthand, Book-keeping, French, German, English Composition.

2. A general review was held by the G.O.C. 29th Division on January 26th at which the following medals were presented ;
   Lieut-Col. W. A. Murray, DSO - Croix de Guerre a l'Ordre Armee
   Major A. W. Standford, M.C. - Croix de Guerre a l'Ordre Brigade
   18757 Farr.Sgt. Baker, W.J. - Croix de Guerre a l'Ordre Regiment.
   Major D. Daly, M.C. - The D.S.O.
   69688 Cpl. Newman, C.V. - The M.M.
   ~~1025 Dvr. Falls, W. - The M.M.~~
   11582 Sgt. [redacted], A - The M.M.
   BUMER. M.

3. During the month of January 37 Other Ranks proceeded for demobilization. Demobilization was suspended January 12th owing to the lack of re-inforcements.

4. The health of the men in general was very good.

Captain, RFA
Adjutant, 17th Brigade, R. F. A.

(A9175) Wt W2355/P360 600,000 12/17 D. D. & L. Sch. 53a. Forms/C2118/15.

36

Confidential.

W A R   D I A R Y

of

17th Brigade Royal Field Artillery

February 1919.

VOLUME XLVII.

Army Form C. 2118.

Instructions regarding War Diaries and Intelligence Summaries are contained in F. S. Regs., Part II. and the Staff Manual respectively. Title pages will be prepared in manuscript.

WAR DIARY
or
INTELLIGENCE SUMMARY.
(Erase heading not required.)

Place	Date	Hour	Summary of Events and Information	Remarks and references to Appendices

Berg Gladbach, Germany.

For the month ending February 28th, 1919.

The Brigade still continued to occupy the same billets and quarters.

1. The Educational Scheme for the Brigade continued to be well attended and much interest taken.

2. A General Parade was held by the C. R. A. at which the following were presented with medals.

B. S. M. Redican, J. L. - The Belgian Croix de Guerre.
Sergeant Dyers, H - The Belgian Croix de Guerre.

3. A General Inspection of the Brigade was conducted by ~~xxxxxxxxxxx~~ C. R. A. who found the Brigade in excellent condition. All Batteries, stables, dining rooms, billets, recreational rooms, etc were inspected.

4. Much interest was evidenced in the Army scheme for bonus and a large number of re-enlistments were made for two and three three years with the colours.

[signature]
Captain, RFA
Adjutant, 17th Brigade, RFA

www.ingramcontent.com/pod-product-compliance
Lightning Source LLC
Chambersburg PA
CBHW080805010526
44113CB00013B/2331